Creative Web Design

Springer
*Berlin
Heidelberg
New York
Barcelona
Budapest
Hong Kong
London
Milan
Paris
Santa Clara
Singapore
Tokyo*

Michael Baumgardt

CREATIVE
TIPS AND TRICKS STEP BY STEP
WEB DESIGN

With CD-ROM

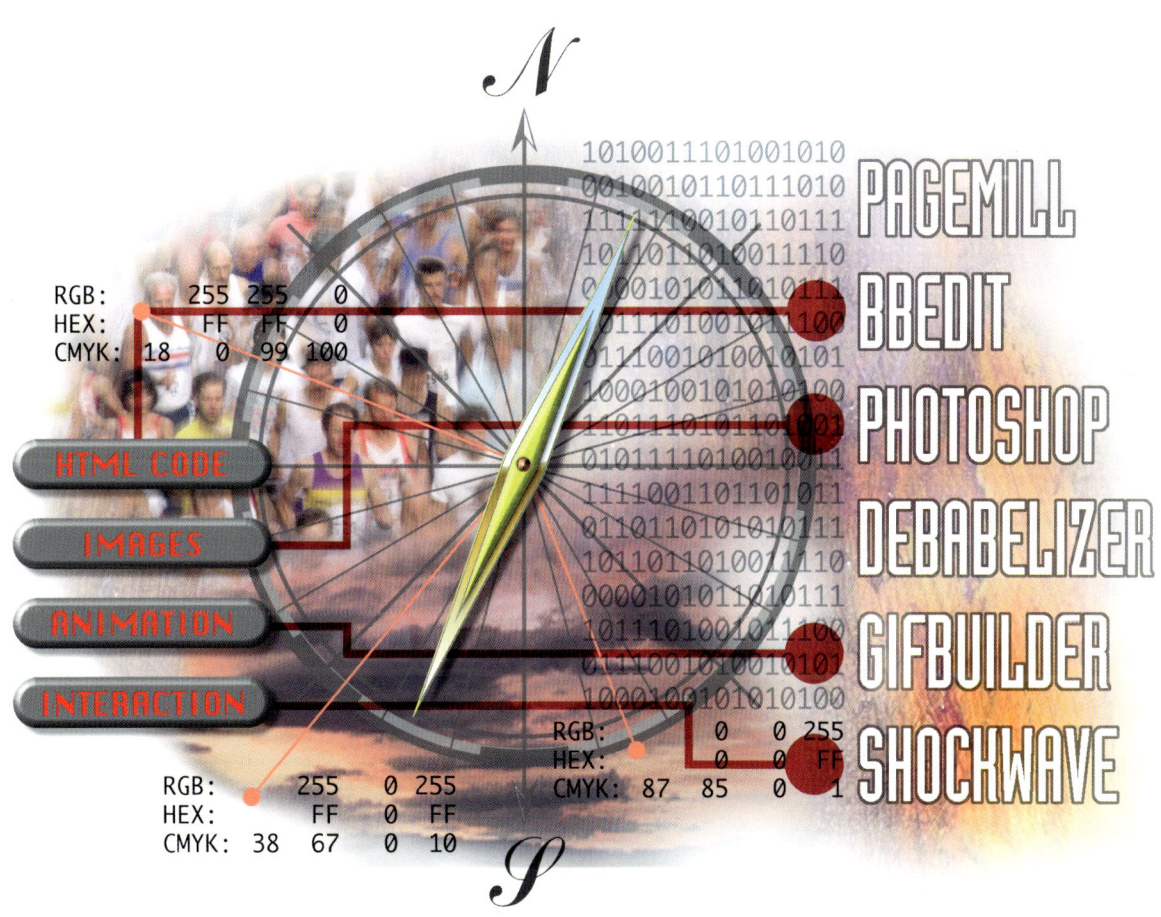

Springer

Michael Baumgardt
e-mail: MBaumgardt@compuserve.com

Cataloging – in – Publication Data applied for
Die Deutsche Bibliothek – CIP-Einheitsaufnahme

Creative Web Design: tips and tricks step by step / Michael Baumgardt. –
Berlin; Heidelberg; New York; Barcelona; Budapest; Hong Kong; London;
Milan; Paris; Santa Clara; Singapore; Tokyo: Springer.
Dt. Ausg. u.d.T.: Web Design kreativ!
ISBN 3-540-62662-X
Buch. – 1998   CD-ROM. – 1998

ISBN 3-540-62662-X Springer-Verlag Berlin Heidelberg New York

This work consists of a printed book and a CD-ROM packaged with the book, and is subject to copyright. All rights are reserved, whether the whole or part of the material is concerned, specifically the rights of translation, reprinting, reuse of illustrations, recitation, broadcasting, reproduction on microfilms or in any other way, and storage in data banks. Duplication of this publication or parts thereof is permitted only under the provisions of the German Copyright Law of September 9, 1965, in its current version, and permission for use must always be obtained from Springer-Verlag. Violations are liable for prosecution under the German Copyright Law.

Springer-Verlag or the authors make no warranty for representation, either express or implied with respect to this CD-ROM or book, including their quality, merchantibility, or fitness for a particular purpose. In no event will Springer or the authors be liable for direct, indirect, special, incidental, or consequential damages arising out of the use or inability to use the CD-ROM or book, even if Springer-Verlag or the authors have been advised of the possibility of such damages.

© Springer-Verlag Berlin Heidelberg 1998
Printed in Germany

The use of general descriptive names, registered names, trademarks, etc. in this publication does not imply, even in the absence of a specific statement, that such names are exempt from the relevant protective laws and regulations and therefore free for general use.

Layout, design, typesetting: Michael Baumgardt
Cover illustration: Michael Baumgardt
Cover design: Künkel + Lopka, Heidelberg
Printing: Schneider Druck, Rothenburg ob der Tauber
Binding: Schäffer, Grünstadt
SPIN 10569056   Printed on acid-free paper   33/3142 – 5 4 3 2 1 0

For Steve Zierer and Vera Waldmann
You both define the true meaning of friendship.
Thanks for being in my life.

The Web ist the best thing that could have happened to designers: it creates a huge demand for design and if you have been working in the desktop publishing or multimedia field, you can easily make the leap to the Web. But Web design is more than writing HTML code and designing nice images, it is the design of communication and information, and in this book you will often see the term Information Architecture. What this means and how some of the

Photo: Paul Ehrenreich

leading Web designers approach this challenge can be read in the interviews and seen in the many examples that I gathered for this book. These interviews offer insights into the design trends on the Internet, and I hope you have as much fun reading them as I had writing them. Because all these people I interviewed have one thing in common: they are very enthusiastic about the possibilities that arise through the World Wide Web and they have a deep passion for global communication – something that I share with them. The Information Highway brings us closer together, no question about it. When we are able to visit the homepage of a buddhist monk in Kyushu, Japan, or read the online diary of a 21 year old boy, who lives with his grandfather on a farm in Arizona, we will be much more in touch with the global community than by zapping through the news channels. We can't foresee the effect the Web will have on society, but one thing is clear: the architect of the future will be an information architect.

CHAPTERS

13 CONCEPT
13 Getting an Internet Service Provider
14 Basic Information from Your ISP
15 The Basics About HTML Code
15 Browsers and the Limitations of HTML
16 Web Design Programs
17 What You Should Know to Come Up with a Concept
19 Setting Up the Folders of a Mirror Site
20 Filenames
20 Checking Your Web Site in a Browser
20 The World Wide Web Consortium [W$_3$C]

25 LAYOUT
25 NetObjects Fusion
27 Adobe PageMill
28 Some Tips on Creating Your Web Layout
31 Basic HTML
32 Defining Colors in HTML
33 Positioning with the SPACER Tag or Invisible GIFs
34 Adobe Acrobat
34 Positioning with Frames
34 The Layout Solution
34 Changing the Font
35 Hypertext Links
35 The BLINK Tag
37 Horizontal Rule
37 How to Work with Paths

45 IMAGES
45 The Difference Between JPEG and GIF
47 PNG: The Cool New Graphic Format
48 Raster and Vector Images
48 The Resolution
48 Color Depth
49 Color Table
50 Pantone Internet Color System Guide
50 Optimizing Your Images
50 Working with the WWW Color Palette
51 Placing an Image
52 Step-by-Step:
    Preparing a GIF Image in Photoshop
53 Equilibrium DeBabelizer
54 Step-by-Step: Using Transparency in GIF Images

Contents

- 54 Step-by-Step: The 50% Transparency Trick
- 55 Imagemaps
- 55 MetaCreation Painter
- 56 How to Set Up Client Side Image Maps
- 57 Step-by-Step: How to Create Background Tiles in Photoshop
- 59 How to Set up Server Side Image Maps
- 59 Background Tiles
- 59 Special Effects with the Background
- 60 The Problem of the Browser Offset
- 60 Preloading Images

65 TABLES
- 66 The Table Tags and Attributes
- 68 Background Color and Images
- 68 Imagetable
- 72 The Imagetable Pitfall
- 72 The NOBR Alternative

83 FRAMES
- 83 Frame Document
- 84 Defining Frame Sizes
- 84 The Three Ways to Define Frame Sizes
- 84 Defining the Margins of a Frame
- 85 Scrollbars in a Frame
- 85 Disabling Resizing
- 85 Invisible Frame Borders
- 85 Common Mistakes
- 86 Nesting Frames
- 86 Naming and Targeting Frames
- 87 Special Target Names
- 89 Controlling Two Frames with One Anchor

93 GIF ANIMATION
- 93 The GIF 89a History
- 93 What Programs Can You Use?
- 94 How to Use GIFBuilder for Macintosh
- 95 Optimizing the Animation
- 95 Transparency and Disposal Methods
- 96 Looping
- 96 Creating Animations with Director
- 96 A Simple Animation Using the META Tag
- 98 Step-by-Step: How the Rotating KATV Logo Was Created

109 CASCADING STYLE SHEETS
110 Combining Style Sheets
110 A Condensed Guide to the CSS1 Syntax
112 Step-by-Step: Installing CSS with BBEdit
114 Backward Compatibility: Blending Two Worlds

117 SHOCKWAVE
117 How to Prepare a Streaming Shockwave Movie
118 Using Audio in Your Shockwave Movie
120 Embedding a Shockwave Application in Your HTML Page

125 JAVASCRIPT
125 Java and JavaScript
125 How to Implement Java and JavaScript
126 Interactive Buttons and Pop-Up Menus
127 Rotating Banner
128 Scrolling Status Bar
129 Opening a New Window
130 Loading Several Images with One Mouse Click
130 Changing the Color of a Page
131 Step-by-Step: Creating Buttons with Eye Candy

133 MUSIC & AUDIO
133 Installing a Sound File
134 Some Tips on How to Record Audio
135 Optimizing Audio for the Internet
135 Audio Formats for the Web: MPEG Layer 3
138 Using RealAudio
138 Audio Formats for the Web: RealAudio
139 Steinberg Cubase VST
140 Bias Peak
141 Step-by-Step: Optimizing CD Tracks for the Web

151 UPLOADING & REGISTERING
151 How to Be Top in the Search List
152 Using Many Images on Your Web Site
154 Use a Strong Title
154 The Intro Page
154 Submit-It
154 Updating Your Web Page
155 Step-by-Step:
     Uploading Your Pages to the Server via Fetch
156 Uploading via Netscape
156 Excite
156 Infoseek

156 Lycos
157 WebCrawler
157 Yahoo
157 Famous Last Words

INTERVIEWS/SITES

21 Rocket Science, Robert Gagnon
38 Pixelpark, Rikus Hillmann
58 Persistence of the Spirit
62 Oaklawn
70 KATV
74 Studio Archetype, Clement Mok and Mark Crumpacker
90 Aristotle, Christopher Stashuk and Elton Pruitt
97 B-98.5
100 Avalanche, Peter Seidler
122 Blender, Greg Knoll
136 Warner Music Latin
144 David Bowie Site • N2K, Inc. Marlene Stoffers and Ben Clemens
153 FAO
158 Michael Simross, Internet-Artist

161 Thanks and Acknowledgement
162 URLs
164 Index
168 About the Author
170 The CD-ROM

CHAPTER 01

Concept

How to get started is a difficult question. In a book about journalism that I once read, the author emphasized how important it is to have a strong beginning to capture the interest of the reader. In his opinion, the key to a good opening was to find something that would surprise the reader and keep his or her attention. How about this: All you need to know to create award winning Web sites can be taught in a week or less. Surprised? Do you think it is unrealistic? Well, it is, depending on your background. If you have never designed before and have no basic knowledge of computers and how program languages work it might take you a little bit longer. But if you have worked before as a print media or multimedia designer you can make the leap into the world of Web design fairly easily, simply because you already have design skills, something that even a good book couldn't teach you in a week. Understanding the limitations of the Web and learning how to solve them is the smaller part of the challenge. As a designer it is more important to understand the information architecture on the Internet and its logic and the possibilities, because that is the real challenge. In this book you will find many interviews with designers and HTML authors that will give you an idea of how to create the information architecture for a site, and along with that, you will also see solutions that people have come up with. If you are a designer who wants to use this book to create a homepage for yourself or your company, you will still find all the information that you need. But because this book cannot be a complete guide to HTML, JavaScript, or Shockwave, I have reduced the information to that which is most significant. I will explain how you can create interactive buttons with JavaScript, because they are an important element of interface design. If you want to find out more about how to program in JavaScript I would suggest getting a book that is dedicated to that subject. This book is geared towards designers who are already familiar with design software and now want to start creating Web sites.

Getting an Internet Service Provider

The first step in putting out your own Web site is getting on the Internet and booking some server space. Many books overlook this basic step and assume you have, somehow, inherited this knowledge when you bought your modem. So let me take this quick excursion to explain how you get on the information highway. To access the Internet, you sign up with an Internet Service Provider (ISP) in your city. They are listed in the yellow pages and you should call a couple of them to compare their rates and ask them if there is any Web server space included. Accessing the Internet

Lee Jeans wanted a Web site to attract a younger audience. Avalanche designed an interface that looks very fashionable and unconventional. It uses a large photocomposition as a background image and the navigational elements are placed in the middle and to the left.

and putting a Web site on the Internet are two different things. Some of the ISPs who offer unlimited Internet access will charge for every MByte of server space while some offer 10 MByte or more. More and more ISPs offer unlimited Internet access including 10 to 20 MByte of Web server space, but before you sign up, be sure to ask how much they charge for the installation of a domain name. A domain name is the address of your site, like "www.my-name.com", and if you don't get your own domain name, you will reside under their Web server domain name, which could look like this: "www.cherry.com/~your_name". Even though this might be okay for a personal Web site, it certainly isn't for a corporate site. And the clock is ticking: every day hundreds of domain names are registered, and you should get your domain name registered as soon as possible. You can let the ISP do the registration or you can do it yourself through companies like Internic (rs.internic.net). Before you sign up with any specific ISP, compare the monthly charges and setup fees because some of the ISPs have really unrealistic rates. Once you are signed up, you will get a username, a password, the servername that hosts the Web sites, and the name of the folder where you have to put your Web site from the ISP. Together with the dial up number of the server, you are ready to put your site on the World Wide Web: I will explain later in this book how you upload the Web site. If you are a member of CompuServe or America Online, you can access the Internet through them and even put your own homepage on their server. Signing up with them might be interesting, not for the server space, but because they are so widely available in the US and (or in particular in the case of CompuServe) around the globe. This allows you to maintain your Web site from all over the world without any long distance charges. So for example, you might buy server space in New York, but maintain it from Munich in Germany.

BASIC INFORMATION FROM YOUR ISP

Before you start creating your Web site you should contact your ISP and ask if the Web server runs on Windows NT, UNIX, or a Macintosh and ask for the path to the root directory of your Web site. Your ISP will give you all the information on how to upload your Web site to the server. The information that you get will look like this: 1. The access telephone number, 2. Username, 3. Password, 4. Directory (could be named: public_html), 5. Domain name of the Web server (like ppp.cherry.com).

This is also a good way to shop for the best price, because some Internet Service Providers don't require you to sign up with their Internet Access program, you can just buy the Web site hosting.

THE BASICS ABOUT HTML CODE

In order to make Web pages displayable on any computer platform, HTML code consists of ASCII characters only. All the formatting of the text is done by placing tags in the stream of ASCII characters which the browser then interprets (the browser hides the tags from the viewer, but you can view them by using "Document Source" in the "View" menu of Netscape or "Source" in the "View" menu of Microsoft Explorer). Such a tag always consists of a '<' and '>' character and the tag name. Most of the tags have an ending tag that starts with a '/' character before the tag name. Some tags also have attributes that give the designer more control over the display:

<tagname attribute="value">
This is some text </tagname>.

Tag name and tag attributes are case-insensitive, but the tag names should come directly after the '<' character (with no white space). The closing tags for some elements are optional, but some tags do not have a corresponding closing tag (for example <BR>, <INPUT>, <HR>, <IMG>, and <!-- ... -->, which is used to place comments into the HTML syntax). HTML code is very simple to learn and understand. If you are using a program like Adobe PageMill or NetObjects Fusion, you won't have to deal with the code too much, but as long as the features of HTML continue to be so far ahead of the HTML authoring programs, you will always run into the need to go into the HTML code, make changes, add some features, or fix some bugs.

BROWSERS AND THE LIMITATIONS OF HTML

The good news is – now that the browser war is almost over – you only need to design your Web site for Netscape and Microsoft Explorer to reach over 80% of the viewers. This can still be challenging, because HTML was not intended to create WYSIWYG (What You

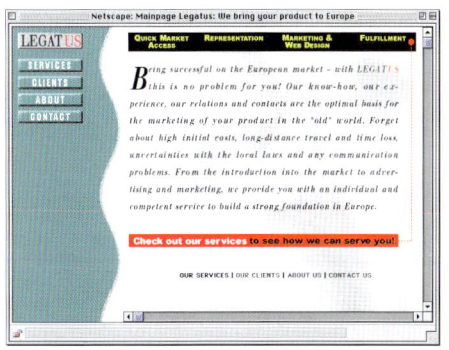

This is a page from the Legatus website. Because of the limitations of HTML to format text, I did two versions of the site: one for slow connections that uses regular text, and one for fast connections, where the text was converted into images.

See Is What You Get) design. The tags were designed to simply give the browser some information about the structural content of the document, by telling the browser "this is the headline", but not which font or which size (those are then set by the browser). For example <H1>, <P>, and <BLOCKQUOTE> define a headline, a paragraph, and a quote, but when you use them, the results can vary. Most browsers render <P> with a blank line, but it could appear with an indent and no blank line instead. <BLOCKQUOTE> means only that the marked element is a block quotation: in Netscape it would produce right and left margins, but in Internet Explorer blockquoted text appears in italics. Because the structural tags are so unreliable in their appearance, many Web designers avoid them altogether and use procedural tags instead. Procedural tags, like <B> or <I> (which stands for bold and italic), provide only information about the style, but say nothing about a docu-

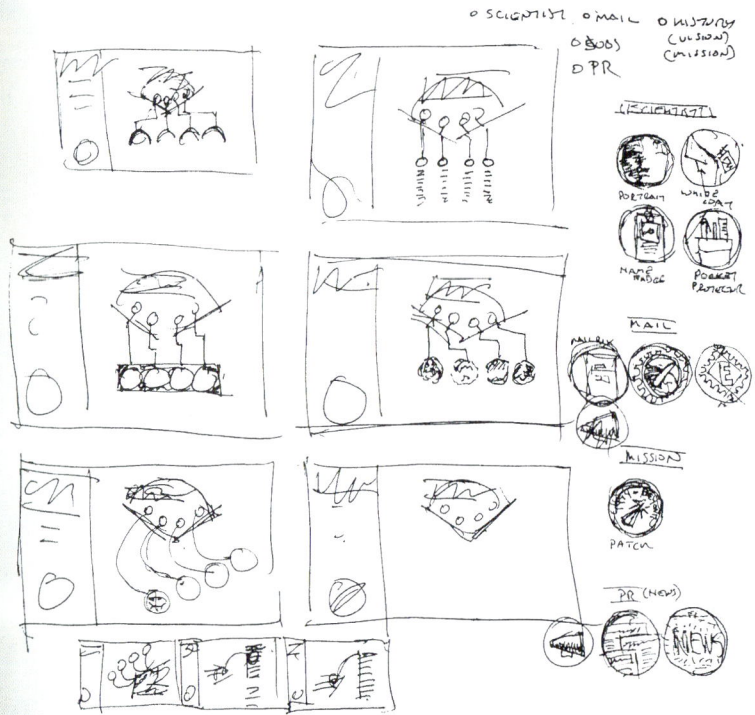

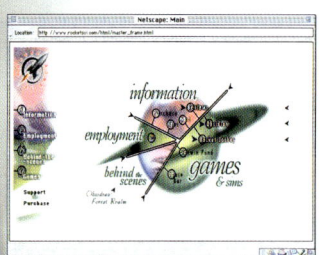

Robert Gagnon, designer at Rocket Science, the game company that developed Obsidian, scribbled his ideas for the interface first and then started composing the elements in Photoshop.

ment's structure. Using only procedural tags, however, undermines the idea of Hypertext Markup Language (HTML) a little. The solution to all the formatting problems in HTML is CSS (Cascading Style Sheet), an extension to the HTML 3.2 specification. Style sheets, as defined by the W3C CSS1 specification, allows you to control margins, line spacing, the placement of text and graphics, colors, font faces, and font sizes. The great thing about the CSS concept is that you can put all formatting information into a separate file, which then changes the complete appearance of a Web site, very much like styles in a layout program such as QuarkXPress or Pagemaker. Browsers that don't recognize CSS just ignore the formatting information and use the structural and procedural tags. This means that your design might look very different in older browser versions like Netscape Navigator 3.0. So if you intend to use CSS, you should check how your site looks in Navigator 3.0 and on different platforms. To do this you don't need to upload the data onto the Web server: you can check out the appearance of your site by loading it directly from the hard drive into the browser using the "File: Open" command of the browser.

WEB DESIGN PROGRAMS

Now the question is, how to create the HTML code? You can create Web pages in any text editor that allows you to save the text as "text only". But this is not a very pleasing way to design a Web site. You should get yourself an HTML author program such as Adobe PageMill for the Macintosh or NetObjects Fusion, which is available for Windows and Macintosh. The problem with authoring programs is that they can't keep up with the rapidly evolving HTML standard and so you need to do some manual HTML editing if you want to add special features. Some authoring programs, like PageMill, allow you to switch to the HTML display mode where you can type the code directly into the text. Although this is a great feature, you then have the problem that they can't display the

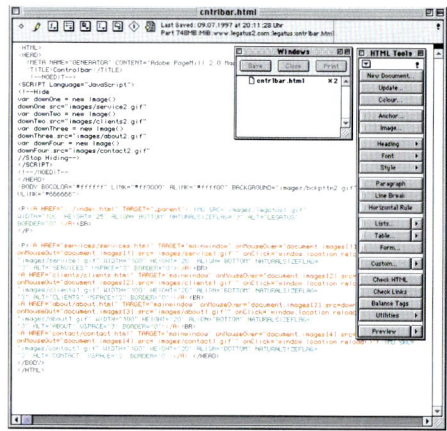

BBEdit is a text editor for the Macintosh, with specialized features for HTML programming.

effect. There are other ways of creating HTML: one is by using a filter or converters that translate a QuarkXPress, Pagemaker, FrameMaker, or Word-file into HTML. Another way is to get an HTML editor, like "BBEdit HTML Tools", and load the result into your browser for display. BBEdit is a high performance text editor for the Macintosh. The difference between a text editor and a word processor is that the focus of a text editor is on the transformation and manipulation of text as data, rather than on manipulation of visual attributes. A text editor is optimized for the editing, searching, transformation, and manipulation of text. BBEdit includes some features that are specifically tuned to the needs of HTML authors, such as an HTML tool palette where you drag-and-drop HTML tags, image files, and links. Besides this it checks the HTML syntax, provides tools to manage large and complicated Web sites (multi-file search and replace capability). BBEdit is a great tool to utilize in making the final edits of a site, even if you work with an authoring program, because you can define your own tags. Then, you always have the latest HTML tags right at your fingertips. No matter what program you use to create the HTML source code, you still have to load your web site in as many browsers as possible to check it looks the way you intended (check also backward compatibility with older versions of the browsers and cross-platform compatibility).

What You Should Know to Come Up with a Concept

Many Web designers call the process of structuring the information for a Web site information architecture. If you come from the world of print media, it will probably be the most difficult part at first. Brochures or Books are straightforward concepts with an established interface design that the user is familiar with and that most designers know how to design. That isn't quite the same with Web design and it takes some experience to create good interfaces. Mark Crumpacker from Studio Archetype distinguishes between global, parallel, and local navigation:

• **Global Navigation** uses navigational elements that appear on every page of the site and represent the main sections of the web site.

• **Parallel Navigation** is used to move across different subcategories and subsections. For example, you have a section called "Services": when your visitor clicks on this link, he or she jumps to a page that contains all the links to several services that you offer – he or she moves parallel within the category "Services".

• **Local Navigation** is used when you get to the end of a line and want to go to local sections within that part, like a table of contents that helps the viewer to quickly jump to the information on the same page. Let's say, for example, that one of your services is "logo de-

INTERFACE DESIGN

The home page of Studio Archetype was created by Mark Crumpacker, who wanted to use it as an example of his idea of good information architecture and interface design (see also the interview in this book).

The main page has at the top the navigational buttons (global navigation) for the main sections and in the middle some of the content (content surfacing). Once you enter a section you have parallel navigational buttons.

sign". Once a visitor clicks this link he finds himself on a page with all the various offerings. You provide a table of contents at the beginning of the text so that the visitor can quickly jump to the information on the page that most interests him.

Another big question on your mind should be, "How do I pull people into my site?". Visitors decide in seconds if they think your site is worth their time. So it is important to build their curiosity. One way of doing this is a technique called content surfacing. An analogy to this would be the first page of a newspaper that has all the main feature stories on it which you can already start reading, but those stories are only teasers – they all continue on other pages inside the publication. Studio Archetype, for example, uses several images on the first page of their site which lead you to new stories within their Web site.

Using an intro page is another technique that designer have come up with. Instead of accessing the main page directly, the visitor sees first a page with an illustration or animation that establishes the theme of the site. Look at it like designing a cover for a brochure: in a brochure you wouldn't put content on the first page. Your intro page in your web site is like a cover. Some designers use also an exit page, which gives the site the feeling of a story with a beginning, middle, and end.

Another question you should ask yourself is, Is it clear to the visitor what the site is all about and what contents can be expected? I have seen web sites of designer and design companies that were beautiful, but didn't offer any hint that this was actually a design company and not something else. This is certainly a mistake you should avoid. To solve this problem, you could create an intro page for your site that explains, in a few sentences, what the site or the company provides. This has the practical advantage that this page is loaded very quickly, and while the visitor is reading that text, you could use the idle time to pre-load some images. When she then enters the site, most of the images are already in the cache of the browser and the pages open very quickly (the technique of pre-loading images is explained in the chapter on images, but basically what you do is to place several images on the page and scale them down to one pixel, so that they are almost invisible).

Another advantage of an intro page is that many search engines use the first 200 words to create a searchable index and/or use this text to display the content of the site in their listings. This has a big impact on how many hits you get and is particularly important if you design a frame based Web site.

A frame based page always consists of at least three HTML files: one that stores all the layout information of the frames and then two, or more, HTML files that contain the actual information that is then loaded into the frames. By default the file with the frame layout doesn't contain any information about the content of a site and search engines cannot create any indexes for those sites. You can read more on that in the chapter on frames, but for now just keep in mind that for any frame based Web site you should use an intro page. Also important for search engines, as well as users, is that you give your site a clear and strong title. The title of the site is displayed in the browser window and is also used when somebody bookmarks your site. It wouldn't help much, to call the first page "Intro" (something I have actually seen in the Web site of a big online content provider). Last but not least, you should take bandwidth into consideration when you design your site. There is a certain limit to how much data each page should contain, because if your visitor has to wait longer than a minute, you risk that he hits the stop button in the browser or switches to "text only display". It should be your goal to have between 30–70 KByte as the maximum per page. The good news is that all elements that had been downloaded in previous pages can always be reused, without being retransmitted, as they are already in the cache of the browser. So create a concept for your site where many elements can be reused on other pages.

Setting Up
the Folders of a Mirror Site

Once you have created the concept for your site, you need to set up folders on your hard drive the same way that you want them to appear on the server. This mirror site helps you to test and maintain your site before you put it on the server. When you create a structure for the folders, take into account that you might want to use some of the images on different pages and thus you might want to keep them in a general folder called "images". All the other images that are only used locally could be placed directly in the folder of the page or in a subfolder. This structure is not a must, but I found it very helpful in updating parts of a site.

It is important to name the first page "index.html" in the topmost folder be-

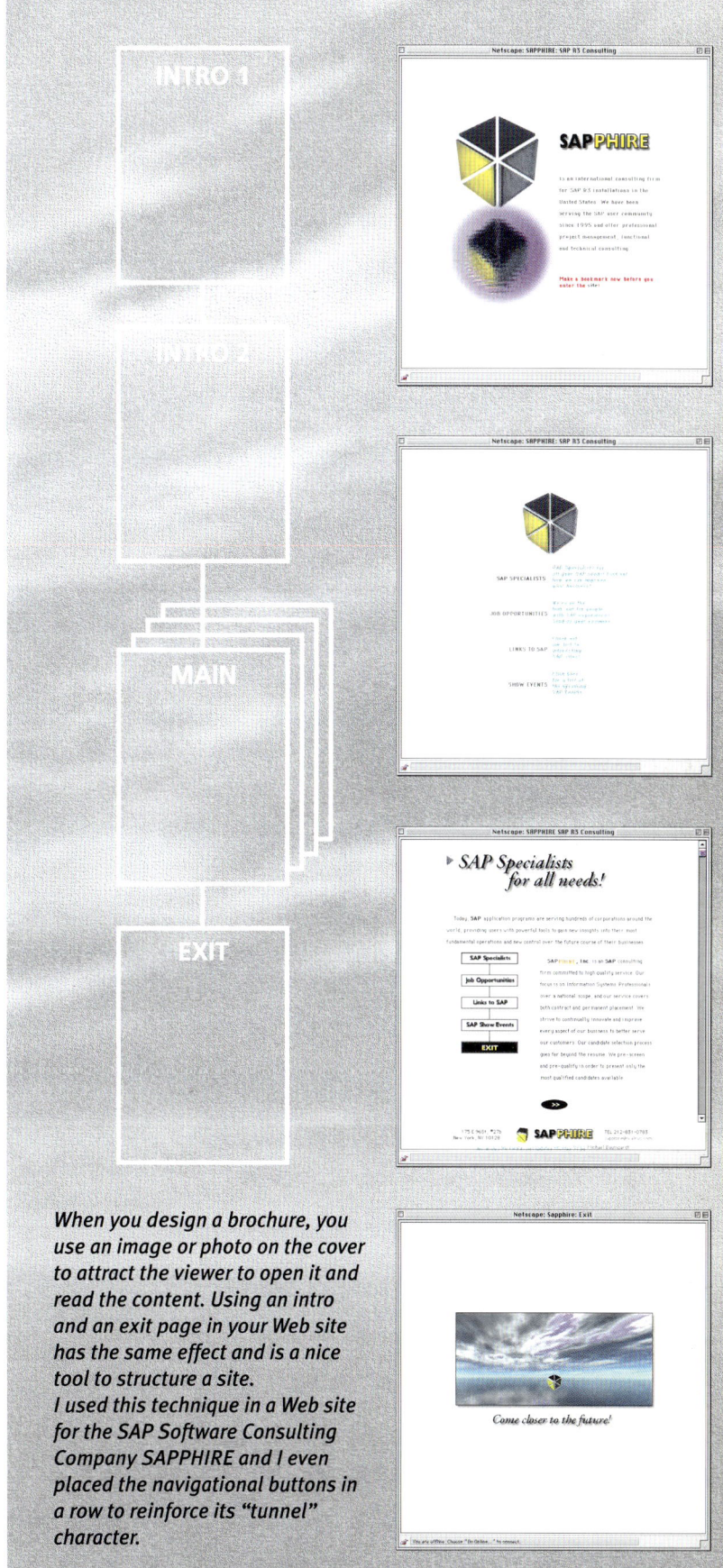

When you design a brochure, you use an image or photo on the cover to attract the viewer to open it and read the content. Using an intro and an exit page in your Web site has the same effect and is a nice tool to structure a site.
I used this technique in a Web site for the SAP Software Consulting Company SAPPHIRE and I even placed the navigational buttons in a row to reinforce its "tunnel" character.

[Mirror Folder]
index.html
  [images]
    ...
  [about_us]
    about_us.html
    abusicon.gif
    ...
  [services]
    service1.html
    service2.html
    service2.html
    service2.html
    servicon.gif
    ...
  [feedback]
    feedback.html
    ...

[ ] = Folder
... = more documents

This is an example of how you could set up the folders on your hard drive. All the images that are identical on all pages (like buttons) could be placed in the general image folder. The other images would be placed together with the HTML document in the sections folder. If it is a larger Web site, then put the images of each section in a subfolder, but this is just my recommendation. You are free to use any folder structure you want.

cause it will then, by default, be loaded automatically when people access your Web address.

FILENAMES

All files need a filename extension: forgetting the appropriate extension for a file or graphic will turn up some cryptic information in the Web browser window, because it will display the data of the file, rather than interpreting it. Use only alphanumeric characters, and, instead of a blank, use an underscore ("_") or hyphen ("-"). The space would otherwise become ASCII-encoded (as %20) and all the links to the file would be broken. Also keep in mind that servers are case-sensitive, for example, "home.html" or "Home.html" are two different files.

CHECKING YOUR WEB SITE IN A BROWSER

You can work on your HTML document and also have it loaded simultaneously into the Netscape and Explorer browser. After editing the page, when you save it and hit "Reload" in the browser window it loads the new page into memory and shows the changes. Sometimes it doesn't, and the reason for this is very simple: browsers cache the information once it is downloaded either in their memory or on the hard drive. This might be a problem if you are developing a site because the browser might display the cached version instead of the actual one. To avoid this, you need to check out the preferences of the browser for the cache settings (in Netscape you find them under "Network Preferences: Cache") and set it from "Once per Session" to "Every Time". This option now checks the creation date of a file and loads the most current one every time. You should also lower the disk cache (which is usually set to 5 Mbyte) of the browser to gain some speed because the larger the disk cache is, the more files the browser has to check before it can display the page.

THE WORLD WIDE WEB CONSORTIUM [W3C]

The W3C is the organization that develops the HTML protocol and is an industry consortium jointly run by the MIT Laboratory for Computer Science (LCS) in the USA, the National Institute for Research in Computer Science and Control (INRIA) in France and Keio University in Japan. For more information about the World Wide Web Consortium and the actual HTML protocol, see http://www.w3.org

Rocket Science

Interview with Robert Gagnon

Rocket Science is the company behind a couple of CD-ROM games. Their last game "Obsidian" has already gotten great reviews and many people see this game as the "Myst" of the next generation. It is indeed a very impressive game that comes on several CD-ROMs with amazing animations. Even though the game is sold through SegaSoft, Rocket Science wanted to have their own Web site to promote the game and to give the fans a behind-the-scenes look. Robert Gagnon, who was hired to work on Obsidian and who did a lot of design for the PDA that plays a major role in the game, ended up also designing their Web site. Even though it was the first Web site he designed, it became so well known and popular that Rocket Science's site became linked to many other sites.

"They were looking for a graphic designer at Rocket Science and they would bring in freelance help. When they brought me in here I knew nothing about multimedia, I had no idea what to expect and I didn't know anything about compression. So the only reason why they hired me was that they really liked my portfolio and thought, I could add something to the game," he remembers. Originally Clement Mok from Studio Archetype did the first design of the site. In some of the books that he has written he highlights the sites that he has worked on and he mentions the Rocket Science site in a few of them. "But that was back then when HTML was pretty basic and so the site was pretty straightforward" explains Robert why Rocket Science decided to do a redesign. Part of the reason is also that "after SegaSoft became our main publisher, they took over our site, but we felt that we needed a separate presence from SegaSoft." This was to the advantage of the site, because "we didn't need to follow the direction of where they were going with their site" and instead of a selling tool, their site became more a marketing tool,

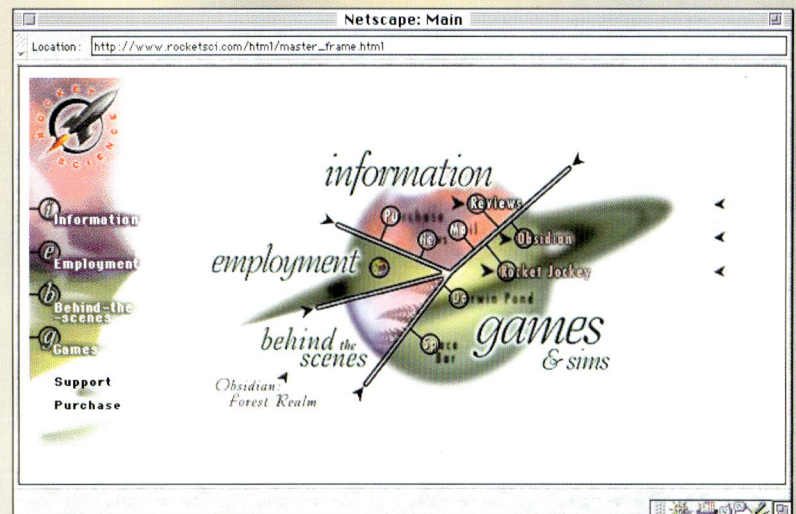

where the main focus was on creating an engaging Web site that was fun to explore. Another contributing factor to the site was that "as we developed the site, we would move every time a little bit deeper into it and make it more flavoured." Originally the design was very straightforward with a colored side bar, but "the side bar wasn't quite matching what was going on in the site. We are a game company and we are allowed to

Top: When you enter the site, you are given the choice between two connection speeds.
Bottom: The navigational elements on the left are placed in an invisible frame. Originally this navigational bar had a solid colored orange background, but Robert Gagnon gave it a more organic and artistic feel.

On the main page is an image of a planet, that features all sections and subsections. Robert Gagnon used for all the sections only the according part of the main illustration. The user is able to move parallel between those sections via the control bar to the left.

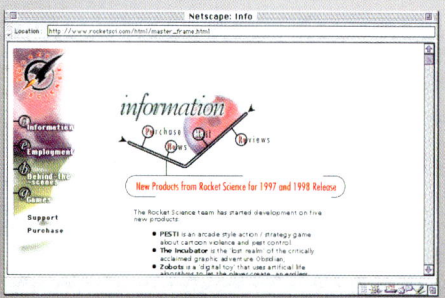

be subsections. It takes some time to find a good solution for the information structure on a web site."

Designing this information structure can be very time consuming. It might take up more time than the actual creation and is very often a team effort. "We don't have marketing people here, but I was discussing with Susanne Richards which information we wanted to have put on the site. Then we created the flowchart and had some sketches done. I passed out those sketches and made sure that everybody was in tune with the design."

be creative and try out different things," and so Robert designed a more organic looking side bar, with an irregular shape instead of just a solid background. "The great thing for me was that, because there is no client to answer to, I could take advantage of it and make changes and experiment almost as much as I wanted." Learning by doing, Robert Gagnon discovered the challenges of Information Architecture for the Web: "As a designer I was also in charge of creating the flowchart of the site. I was playing around with different pages and formats and in that process we all learned that we didn't need certain segments, and other segments didn't need to be fleshed out that much so that they could

Our site wasn't about selling the game, but rather selling an image of who we are at Rocket Science Games.

Interestingly enough, one of the main challenges for Robert Gagnon in designing a Web site for Rocket Science wasn't the creation, it was the quality of work that was done for Obsidian. "My first sense was to just take the images of Obsidian and pop them up on the screen," but that wasn't really the vision that Rocket Science had for their site. "Our site wasn't about selling the game, but rather selling an image of

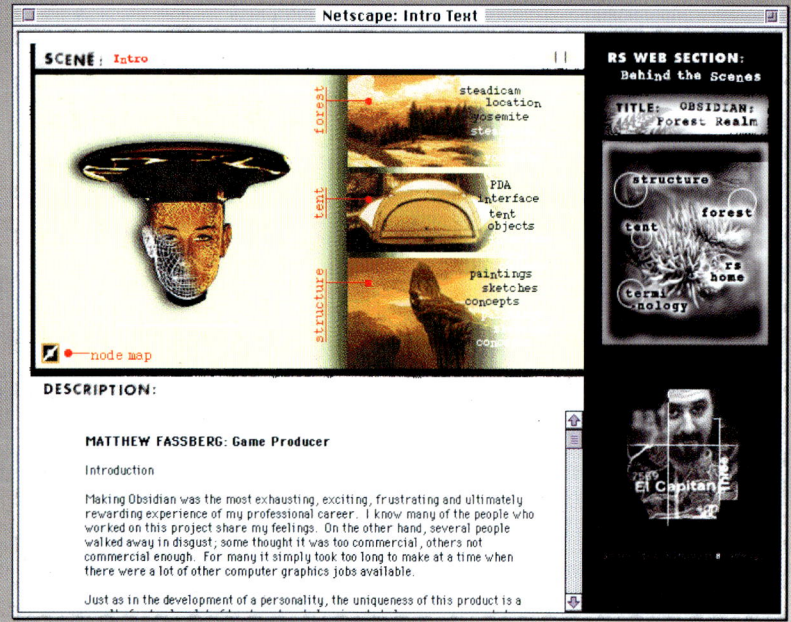

One of the main sections is "Behind the Scene", which features information on the creation of Obsidian. It has its own navigational concept and many downloadable Quicktime Movies.

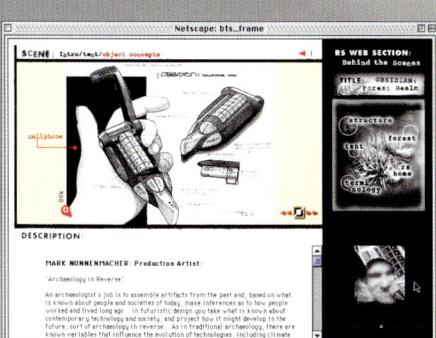

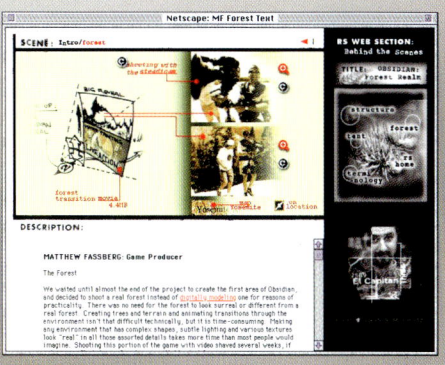

This page: Each section of the "Behind the Scenes" features interviews with the designers and producers of the game Obsidian.

who we are at Rocket Science Games. The one direction that I got was that we wanted to say, we are a really cool company and we do very good work."

Robert Gagnon eventually created a unique style for the Rocket Science site that got many fans and received a couple of awards. His main tools were Adobe Illustrator and Photoshop. For the animations he created on the "Behind the scenes" page for Obsidian he used Photoshop to prepare the images before importing them into GifBuilder. Those animations have a unique style which he created by putting elements on different layers in Photoshop and moving them around.

> *I'm not handling design with gloves. To me it's meant to be replaced.*

Robert Gagnon wants to stay in the Web and multimedia area, because he "likes to tell a story." Another thing that fascinates him about the Web is its flexibility and dynamics: "I remember in college I had a professor and he didn't care how we presented our projects. He said, it wasn't important that these pieces would last forever and for some reason that stuck in my mind and so I have a throwaway or crash mentality. I'm not handling design with gloves. To me it's meant to be replaced and that's why I constantly redesign our Web site."

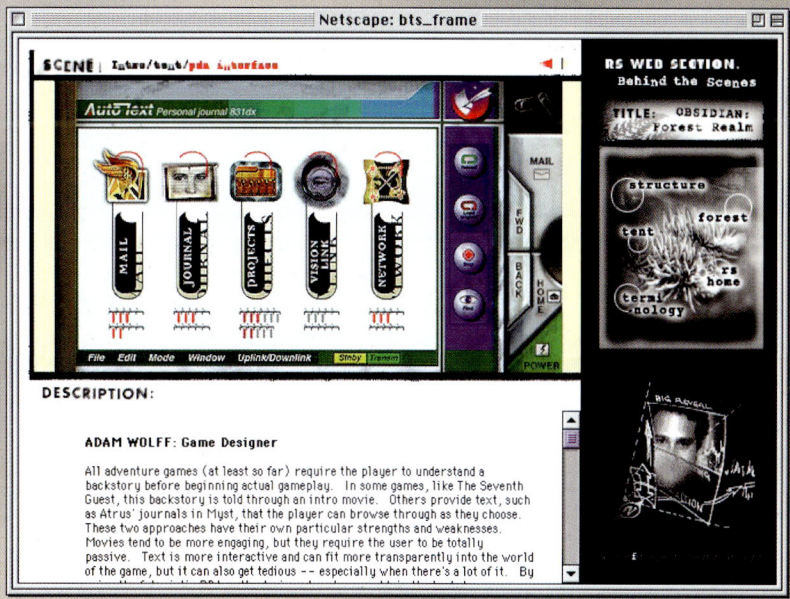

CHAPTER 02

Layout

Imagine this: you are designing the layout of a magazine and everything looks great. While you are away from your computer to get yourself a cup of coffee, the editor walks in and changes the width of the text column and also the font type. You are shocked to find, when you return, that everything looks different and your carefully arranged text and pictures are not where they are supposed to be. Designing for the Web is pretty much like this, because you have no control over the size of the browser's window and neither can you anticipate in which font the user might view your site. And that was pretty much the intention of the inventors of the HTML code. The code was designed primarily to provide structural information to the browser. It is only because of the pressure of designers, who weren't really pleased about this, that HTML has increasingly accommodated itself to the world of desktop publishing. From the viewpoint of a designer, this is very important, because in a medium where the elements can be moved freely, you can't really do advanced design.

To design Web pages you don't necessarily need an HTML authoring program. You could work with any text editor, but typing in HTML code and always double-checking the result in a browser doesn't appeal to everyone. I want to introduce you quickly to two authoring programs, NetObjects Fusion and Adobe PageMill. Fusion has a very interesting approach and PageMill is very popular.

NETOBJECTS FUSION

Many companies are competing for the Web and HTML authoring program market, among them NetObjects Fusion. What makes this software so special is that it works almost like a layout program with absolute positioning of elements, something that it achieves by putting everything in tables and using invisible GIFs. It's stunning how well this program works. While other authoring programs, such as Adobe PageMill, hardly produce WYSIWYG (What you see is what you get), pages created with Fusion will almost look the same in the browser.

Clement Mok, founder of Studio Archetype and also the founder of NetObjects, has an approach to Web design that can be seen clearly in this software. His philosophy, that a designer shouldn't have to deal with HTML programming, is reflected in Fusion where you will hardly see the underlying code. That doesn't mean that it is inflexible and attributes can't be added to tags, but these are done only via dialog boxes. For good reason, because the source code of the pages is very difficult to read due to the extended use of tables. This might be the only drawback of the program.

Nevertheless, the advantages outweigh this disadvantage because Fusion

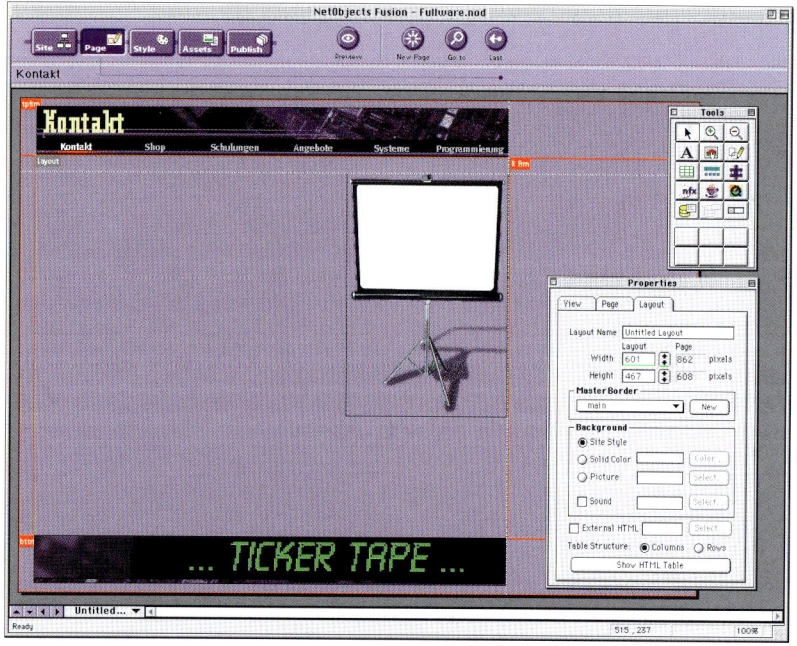

Clement Mok is the founder of NetObjects as well as the chief creative officer. He had the idea of Fusion, while he was working on 24 hours in Cyberspace. "Rick is an old friend of mine and we had looked for a project to work on together for years. I like things that had never been done before and when he came up with the idea for 24hours in Cyberspace, I said "Okay" without realizing that there was a big publishing problem. We had to publish hundreds of pictures and stories from around the world within 24 hours and none of the editors or designers really knew HTML. So I developed a tool that would allow us to produce those pages without knowing the HTML code. This was the first version of NetObjects Fusion".

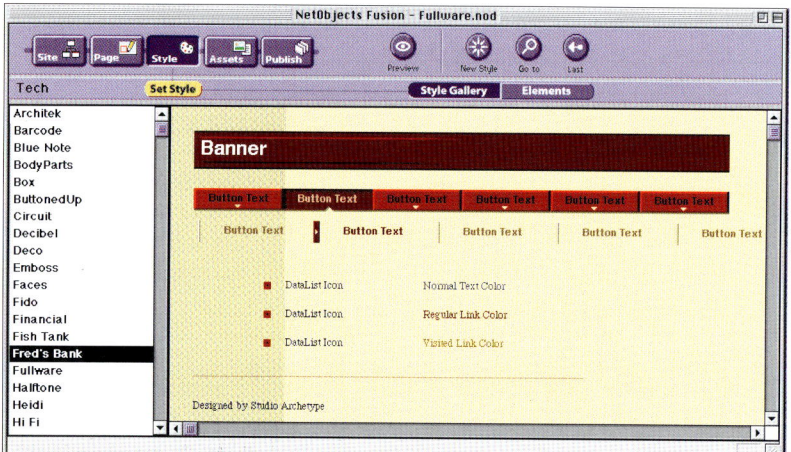

The Page View and the Style View. In the Style View you select one style for your site or define your own. This style is then used for all the pages in the Page View.

automates so many things that it is very easy to create advanced Web sites with it. Java applets can be embedded in your Web page and customized without knowledge of Java. To create, for example, a Ticker Tape with scrolling text, you place the applet on your page and enter the parameters in a dialog box and that's it. NetObjects Fusion even automates the creation of CGI scripts for forms.

More important, Fusion makes it easy to create a consistent design for your whole Web site. It does this the same way layout programs work: by defining templates. In those templates you specify buttons and banners or color of backgrounds and links. Fusion will then apply those settings to your whole site or to individual pages and automatically create the links for the navigational elements. A Web site with several sections and navigation will take only minutes to define. For example, if you want to create a site with four sections (Service, Products, Contact, Clients) simply drag page icons into the site structure window, where you then arrange the hierarchical layout of the site. After selecting the template, switch over to the page view mode and all the buttons and links to navigate between the sections will have been laid out and named! Changes to the navigational elements, such as rearranging them or changing their appearance, will change other pages accordingly, which saves a tremendous amount on time. All that is needed now is to place the content. One of the advantages in designing with a layout program like QuarkXpress is that text and images can be easily combined. But placing text on an image with other HTML authoring programs usually requires switching to Adobe Photoshop to add the text there. Fusion allows you

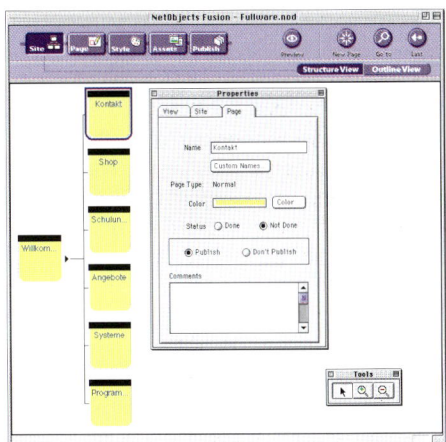

The Structure view lets you arrange the hierarchical structure of your site.

to add text to an image directly in the program by placing text on a picture and choose the font, size and alignment. The text now becomes part of a new image file when you publish the site. Changing the text later is no problem, because Fusion keeps the original files. When you publish the site you even have the choice of automatically creating alternative sites. For example, you can create a text based site for all the people who have browsers that can't display images, or low bandwidth sites, where all the images are half of their original resolution. Those alternative sites can then be uploaded together with the other version directly to the Web server via FTP.

From the designer point of view, NetObjects Fusion is the most convenient way to create Web design: with little or mediocre knowledge of HTML, you can create advanced websites. My favorite feature of the program is that it can download complete websites from the Internet and save a full functional mirror site on your hard drive. This is particularly helpful for documentations that are online: choose the URL – and the level to which Fusion should follow the links – and download the elements and pages. Later you can read the documentation, conveniently offline, as you enjoy a cup of coffee.

ADOBE PAGEMILL

That PageMill is so well known and used by so many is certainly due to the good reputation of Adobe as well as the fact that PageMill is affordable. Like many other HTML authoring programs, PageMill has problems keeping up with the very fast evolving HTML standard. This, as well as the pressures of the market, forced Adobe to release this product too early. The 2.0 version has many annoying handicaps, chief among them being that even though it is supposedly a WYSIWYG editor, it hardly lives up to this label. Images can be dragged and drop-

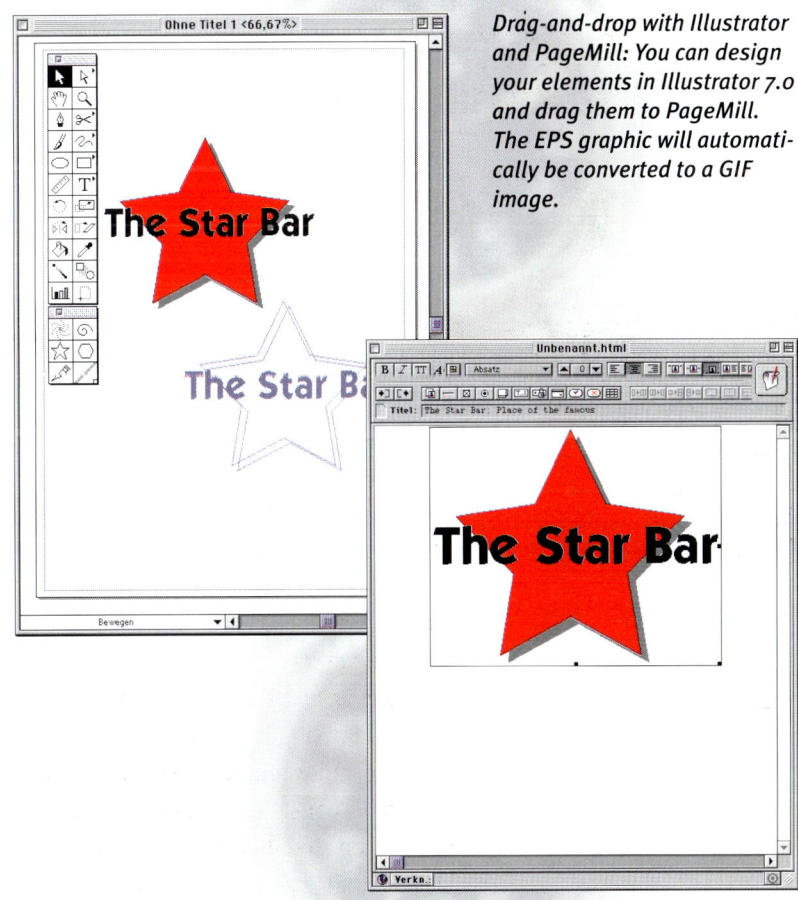

Drag-and-drop with Illustrator and PageMill: You can design your elements in Illustrator 7.0 and drag them to PageMill. The EPS graphic will automatically be converted to a GIF image.

ped conveniently onto the page, but as soon as you work with images in tables, you have to double-check the result simultaneously in a browser. Unfortunately, using tables is a must to create advanced Web design, and fixing HTML code isn't much fun.

The new version will certainly correct many weaknesses of this program. If you already have PageMill you should consider getting BBEdit, because these programs work well in conjunction. I usually create the basic visual appearance with PageMill and do then the fine edit with BBEdit. This is particularly important if you want to use JavaScript on your Web page. PageMill radically erases or modifies your JavaScript code when you save your page, even if you use a special PageMill placeholder tag which should, supposedly, prevent PageMill from doing this. There is nothing more frustrating than to program several lines of JavaScript and then, suddenly they are gone, nothing, njet, back to nirvana.

But there are also great features, for example, if you work with Adobe Illustrator 7.0 and PageMill 2.0 on the Mac, you can drag-and-drop graphical elements from Illustrator to an open PageMill document. The EPS graphics will be automatically converted to a GIF file with its own optimized color palette.

Nevertheless, Adobe PageMill is a very helpful program and it makes the creation of a Web site much more fun than doing the HTML coding by hand.

SOME TIPS ON CREATING YOUR WEB LAYOUT

How do you now actually start creating your layout? If you are working with an authoring program like PageMill or Fusion, you can import your text and images and start designing.

If you are not working with NetObjects Fusion, use at least one invisible table (with only one cell) as a main container on each page because it is the most helpful tool to prevent surprises (see the chapter on tables). You can determine the width of a table in pixels, something you can't with the width of the browser window (though there is a way to do this with JavaScript).

Some designers use markers on an intro page, encouraging the visitors to resize their window according to the markers. I personally don't think this a very cool thing to do and prefer using a table.

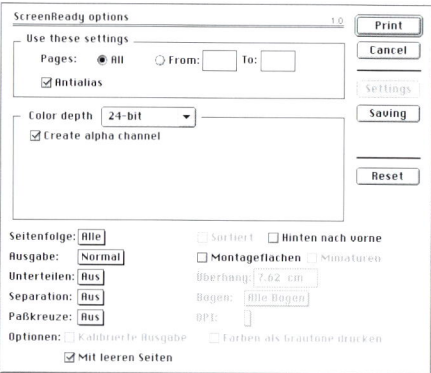

With Adobe ScreenReady, you can design the Web site in a layout program and convert the screens to a PICT file.

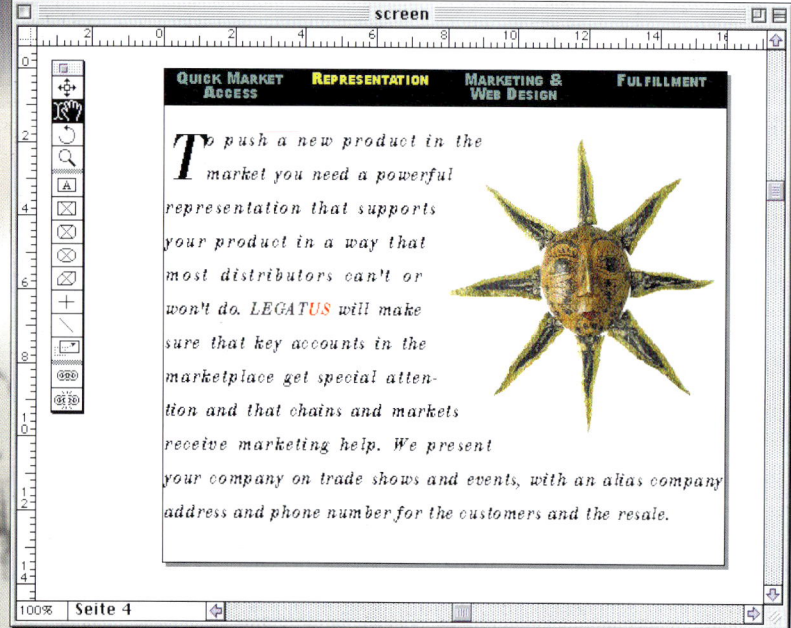

The width of the browser has no influence on a table and its contents, with the effect that users will automatically resize their browser.

Because of the boundaries set by the table, you are now only dealing with the reformatting caused by the different fonts and font sizes. And even that is predictable if you set the fonts with the FONT tag and the FACE attribute or use Cascading Style Sheets.

Nevertheless, you will soon discover that designing Web pages is not as spontaneous and flexible as you are accustomed to from traditional layout or design programs. You can find yourself constantly adding or deleting cells to tables, especially if you are still experimenting and have no scribbled concept. Some designers therefore go through the first design phase completely in Adobe Photoshop. This gives them the flexibility to move the elements around freely and, because the resolution is 72 dpi, the file size remains very reasonable. Once they are happy with the result, they export the individual images and try to rebuild the layout with an HTML authoring program.

Alternatively, you can work with your favorite layout or design program, place images and text with all the flexibility that you are used to and then render it with Adobe ScreenReady. Adobe ScreenReady, which is only available for Macintosh, is a great tool to transform EPS graphics to a PICT file. It renders the page in 24-bit, with antialiased text and alpha channel, if you wish. You can then import the file into Photoshop and customized cut and paste various elements, like images or headlines, into a new document and then save it as JPEG or GIF. In particular, using rendered text

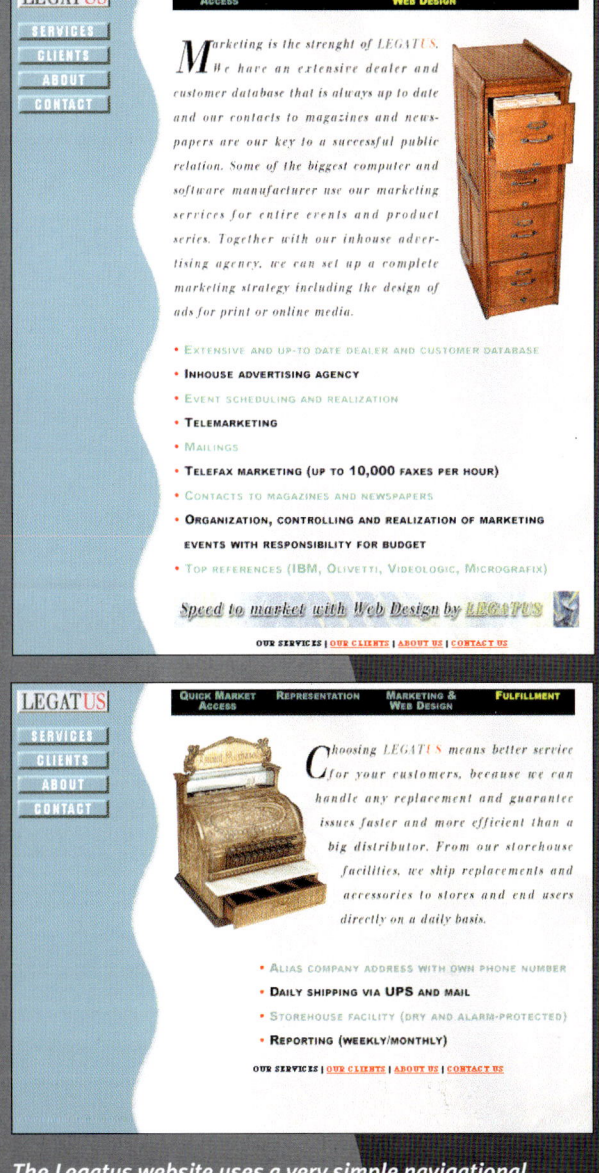

The Legatus website uses a very simple navigational structure: the main sections are placed on the left in an invisible frames, to keep them present all the time. Parallel navigation for each section is done via buttons on the top of the page.
Designing a website for a company you are very often faced with the challenge that the website has to reflect the corporate identity. If this even includes special fonts, you have a problem. For the Legatus website I had to use a customized font and also needed precise control over the text. That's why I designed the layout in QuarkXPress and converted it with Adobe ScreenReady to a PICT file. In Photoshop I reduced the color palette and saved the screens as GIF.
The final "images" were only about 15 KByte.

An example for an HTML document: The DOCTYPE declaration at the beginning followed by the HTML tag.

With BASEFONT and the attribute FACE you specify a font size and the font face of the page. In the BODY tag you can set the colors of the links and the background.

To avoid the reformatting of the text if the user resizes the browser window, the whole text is put in an invisible TABLE with a width of 400 pixels. To make the table invisible set the BORDER attribute to "0". The TR and TD tags are necessary to define a table row with one cell (TD). The H1 tag is used for headlines and you can color text by adding a FONT tag with the COLOR attribute.

This document also shows how to work with anchors and links (they are colored red). The "Table of Contents" at the beginning of the document allows the user to jump to a section of the text. This is done by placing anchors in the text and linking to them (HREF="#Anchor1"). For a link to an external document, just enter the URL of the document (see the word "background", which is embedded in an A tag). The last link on this page links to an email document (mailto:).

With the SPACER tag used by Navigator, you can create an indent. Indentation can now be controlled via Cascading Style Sheets, but you can use this tag if you want to create a document that is backward compatible.

The image of a pen was simply placed by adding the IMG tag.

You can see the result on the facing page.

```html
<!DOCTYPE HTML PUBLIC "-//IETF//DTD HTML 3.0//EN">
<HTML>

   <HEAD>
       <TITLE>This is a HTML Page</TITLE>
   </HEAD>

<BASEFONT SIZE="3" FACE="Helvetica,Arial">
<BODY TEXT="#000000" LINK="#FF0000" VLINK="#AA1177" ALINK="#FFFF00"
  BGCOLOR="#66CCCC">

   <TABLE WIDTH="400" BORDER="0">
   <TR><TD>
      <CENTER>
      <H1><FONT COLOR="#FF0000">More on PNG Compression</FONT></H1>
      </CENTER>
        <H3>TABLE OF CONTENTS</H3>
      <OL TYPE="1" START="1">
         <LI><A HREF="#Anchor1">Alpha Channel</A>
         <LI><A HREF="#Anchor2">Gamma Correction</A>
         <LI><A HREF="#Anchor3">Interlacing</A>
      </OL>
      <P>PNG basically combines the image types of JPEG and GIF: it supports
      truecolor, grayscale and palette (8-bit). It also has... compressable. </P>
      <P><A NAME="Anchor1"></A><B>Alpha Channels:</B> This is a way to  ...
      good against every <A HREF="http://www.background.com"> background.
      </A><BR>
      <SPACER TYPE="horizontal" SIZE="14">The great thing is that the alpha
      ... <BLINK>six levels of transparency</BLINK>. That will ... halos.<BR> </P>
      <P> <A NAME="Anchor2"></A><B>Gamma Correction:</B> Macintosh-genera-
      ted images ... value is sufficient. <BR>
      File Integrity Checks: Transmitting images ... corrupted files.<BR></P>
      <P> <A NAME="Anchor3"></A><B>Interlacing:</B> PNG also has seven-pass
      interlacing, a feature that allows the browser to display a low resolution
      version of the image while it is downloading. </P>
   <HR><BR>
      <CENTER><IMG SRC="../../images/pen.gif" WIDTH="235" HEIGHT="28">
      <BR>
      Contact the <A HREF="mailto:MBaumgardt@Compuserve.com"> Webma-
      ster</A></CENTER>
   </TD></TR>
   </TABLE>

</BODY>
</HTML>
```

An example for a typical HTML document 02-01

for headlines is a nice way of enhancing your Web site because it doesn't require much space and can be compressed very nicely by limiting its color table to 3-bit (read more about this in the chapter on images).

Whatever approach you take, keep in mind that you have visitors with only a 13" monitor and 640 x 480 pixels. Even though they have a scrolling bar in their browser, if they have to scroll too much and never actually enjoy a full look at the site, they will lose interest. Limit the amount of text that you put on a page and that the user has to scroll through. Split the information up and spread it out on several pages that you can then connect with "Previous" and "Next" buttons.

Basic HTML

Because this is not an HTML book, I will not go through all the possible tags you could use to design your site. There is much HTML documentation on the Web that you can get for free by just checking out Netscape's home page for developers (http://developer.netscape.com/library/documentation/communicator) or Microsoft's home page (http://www.microsoft.com/workshop/author/). You can also find more HTML documentation on the web by typing in "HTML Documentation" in one of the search engines. But Microsoft's and Netscape's home pages are the best resources because they also list special features that they themselves add to the HTML syntax. In this book I will focus on a few HTML tags that I think are either important to understand or that are new to HTML specification, such as the Cascading Style Sheet.

Throughout this book, all tags and attributes are capitalized to make them

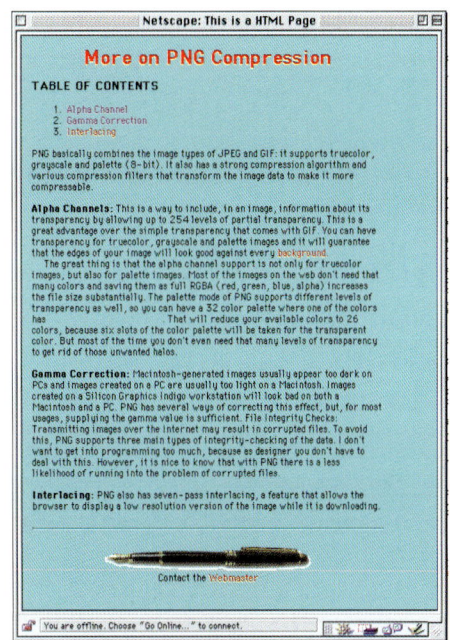

This is the result of the HTML code on the facing page.

easier to spot in the text. How you write them doesn't really matter, because HTML is case-insensitive.

If you are already familiar with HTML syntax [02-01] you can skip this part, but, if not, here is a crash course on the basics of HTML.

As explained in the previous chapter, all HTML tags are placed between the characters '<' and '>'. Each HTML document has some required tags such as HTML, HEAD, and BODY tags [02-02].

<HTML> ... </HTML> encloses the entire document and identifies it as HTML (the only exception is the <!DOCTYPE> tag which is a SGML declaration and is placed before the HTML tag. According to the HTML 3.2 specification, every con-

```
<HTML>
    <HEAD>
        <TITLE>...</TITLE>
    </HEAD>
        <BODY>
        </BODY>
</HTML>
```

HTML Main Containers 02-02

forming HTML 3.2 document must start with the !DOCTYPE declaration ‹!DOCTYPE HTML PUBLIC "-//W3C//DTD HTML 3.2 Final//EN"›).

The ‹HEAD› ... ‹/HEAD› tags encloses the header tags with the TITLE tag. The TITLE tag is obligatory and defines what is going to be displayed in the head of the window of the browser. It is also used by search engines to list your document, so you should use a title that describes the contents of the document. Another important tag that might be used within the HEAD tag is the META tag. How to use this tag is explained in detail in the chapter "Registering your URL". The META tag can be used to put further information and keywords in your document which will be very helpful in ensuring that your site turns up in searches with Infoseek or other search engines.

The ‹BODY› ... ‹/BODY› tags enclose the body of the document. Any text or graphic you place on your Web page will

DEFINING COLORS IN HTML

To color elements in HTML, you can use one of 16 color names (aqua, black, blue, fuchsia, grey, green, lime, maroon, navy, olive, purple, red, silver, teal, white, and yellow) or, if you want to create your own colors, type in the RGB values in hexadecimal (e.g.BGCOLOR="#C0FFC0"). Understanding hexadecimal encoding isn't that difficult: you use the numbers 0–9 and the letters A–F, which allows you to count up to 16 (ten numeric and six alphanumeric values).

Because each color channel is represented by two digits, you have a total of 256 values for each channel (16 x 16) and if you multiply all three channels, you get a total of 65 536 possible colors. This means that on a monitor with 65 536 colors, you can choose any HTML color and have it display without dithering.

Translating colors into hexadecimal is usually done automatically by the Web authoring program and you won't have to deal with it. More important to know is that many users still have only monitors with 256 colors, so if you don't want your colors to be dithered, you have to stay with the Web save color cube.

When the creators of HTML came up with this color cube, they used a very straightforward method: they used increments of 20% for each color channel, because from a programmer's point of view they are easy to program. Use only the hexadecimal values 00, 33, 66, 99, CC, FF in your HTML source code and you can be sure that your color won't get dithered. This, by the way also tells you why the Web save color cube has only 216 colors: you have six possible values (0, 20, 40, 60, 80 and 100%) for three channels, which means that you have to multiply 6x6x6, which equals 216 (the remaining 40 colors on a Windows computer are reserved for the system and the desktop).

This knowledge can also be useful, if you are working with Photoshop and you want to have a Web save color. In Photoshop's color picker, you can choose a color and then look at the RGB values. All the web save colors have the factor 51, so to find the closest web save color you only need to type in the closest value that is divisible by 51. For example if Photoshop's color picker shows that your chosen color has the value R: 105, G: 170, and B: 218, you then type in R: 102, G: 153, and B: 204, to get a color that comes closest to your original choice.

occur inside these tags. You have several attributes for setting the color of text, links, and background:

ALINK="color"
BACKGROUND="bgURL"
BGCOLOR="color"
LINK="color"
TEXT="color"
VLINK="color"

The TEXT, LINK, ALINK, and VLINK attributes are important in designing the look of the text on your page. TEXT changes the color of normal text and can be represented either by a hexadecimal red-green-blue triplet or by a color name.

To make all the links in your document distinguishable, you should use a color that attracts attention and will only be used for your links (set that color with the LINK attribute). Avoid a color that might be too close to another text color you are planning to use.

ALINK, which stands for active link, is the color setting for a link while the user has the mouse button pressed. More important is the VLINK attribute because that defines how the link is going to look after the viewer has visited that link. A good choice would be to use a color for the VLINK (visited or followed link) that is close to the main body text color. For example, use grey if your body text is black.

When you set the colors of your links to override the preferences set by the user, you should also set the background color of the document with BGCOLOR.

Now that you know the three main HTML containers and how you set the text colors, you could already start creating your pages.

The SPACER tag has five attributes:
ALIGN="left, right, top, absmiddle, absbottom, texttop, middle, baseline, bottom"
HEIGHT="pixel_size"
SIZE="pixel_size"
TYPE="horizontal, vertical, block"
WIDTH="pixel_size"

The SPACER tag 02-03

POSITIONING WITH THE SPACER TAG OR INVISIBLE GIFS

There are many differences to be adjusted to if you are coming from the desktop publishing world. For example, when working with layout software or a text editor like Word, indenting the first line of a paragraph is common practice. But within the realm of HTML you are not able to control this. The indent is controlled by the browser and you, the designer, have no influence over line spacing or indentation. Up to Internet Explorer 3.0 and Navigator 4.0, designers had to create a workaround and use an invisible image or a spacer tag (a Netscape extension) to create indentation.

Luckily, Cascading Style Sheet solves this problem (see also chapter on CSS in this book) and the Invisible GIF or Spacer trick is only important if you want to create a Web site that is backward compatible.

Only Netscape 3.0 offers an alternative to the "Invisible Image" trick with the SPACER tag. You can basically achieve the same result with this tag as with the invisible image: specify the TYPE attribute and then set the size for the vertical or horizontal space with the SIZE attribute [02-02]. So a typical use to create horizontal space might look like this: ‹SPACER TYPE="horizontal" SIZE="14"›.

The invisible GIF trick: All that is needed for the invisible GIF trick is a 1 pixel image, saved as transparent GIF image and placed at the beginning of your text. The same image could be used over and over again in the same site to control the positioning of elements or the indent of text by scaling the image with the WIDTH and HEIGHT attributes.
You can use the HSPACE and VSPACE attributes in the IMG tag instead of scaling the picture. Those attributes define the space around a picture. Using them has the further advantage that your page still looks good even if the user has turned images off in the browser.
The invisible image trick is becoming more and more redundant as people upgrade to the new versions of Navigator and Explorer, which allow more precise control over the positioning of elements. But never underestimate the number of people who are still working with older versions.

Adobe Acrobat

Years ago Adobe created software to solve the problem of cross-platform distribution of documents. This software is called Acrobat and it allows the designer to layout pages in any program and then embed all the fonts and images in a so-called PDF document. With the boom of the Internet, Adobe adapted this technology for the Web, making it possible to view PDF files with a special plug-in. The only drawback with earlier version was that the document needed to be downloaded entirely before it could be displayed. With the 3.0 version of Acrobat, Adobe solved this problem and now documents can be viewed and downloaded page by page, if you have the free Acrobat Reader 3.0 plug-in. Another big improvement is that Acrobat reduces redundancies within PDF files, so if several pages use the same image, the image will be included only once. This decreases the file´s size tremendously and a complete page with text and graphics might need as little as 10 KByte. Chances are that you will see more and more Web sites with PDF-files, not so much as an replacement for HTML, but more as a means of distributing manuals or documents, because they usually exist already as Postscript files. If you want to create a PDF file from your QuarkXPress or Pagemaker document, you need the program PDF Writer which works like a virtual printer. To place a PDF file on your HTML page is easy: simply use the EMBED tag. <EMBED SRC="document.pdf"> will display a PDF file in the entire space of the browser window.

If you wanted to use the SPACER tag like an invisible image, you would define the type as a block and specify the relationship to text with the ALIGN attribute:
<SPACER TYPE="block" HEIGHT="40" WIDTH="65" ALIGN="absmiddle">

The HEIGHT and ALIGN attributes apply only when the spacer is of type "block". If you don't specify a value for ALIGN, Navigator uses "bottom" as the default. For more information on the ALIGN attribute, see the chapter Images.

Positioning with Frames

Another typical feature of the Web is the use of frames. You might have seen some sites that use frames to display navigation elements. The basic idea behind frames is to divide the main frame of the window browser into separate frames that can contain different HTML documents. Those frames can have their own scrolling bar and most designers use this to keep the company logo and navigation buttons always visible. For more on frames turn to the chapter Frames.

The Layout Solution

Tables and transparent GIFs have been the only way to gain some control over the absolute positioning of elements so far. But with Netscape's Navigator 4.0 (Communicator) and Microsoft's Internet Explorer 4.0, designers finally got what they want. The approach of these competitors is slightly different. Netscape uses a new LAYER tag while Microsoft uses an extension, called "Regions", to the World Wide Web Consortium's Cascading Style Sheets (CSS, level 1).

With Layers and Regions you are able to position text, applets, or images with absolute x-y coordinates and even add a third dimension by stacking images through a z coordinate. This last feature allows, for example, more interactive elements like buttons that change their appearance if the user moves over them. Unfortunately, Microsoft and Netscape use different approaches. Only the future will tell which approach will succeed, so until then you might have to design two versions of your site.

Changing the Font

You can define a set of fonts that the browser should look for on the user's hard drive. When they are found, the browser is instructed to use fonts in the order of your preference (with the Cascading Style Sheet you actually gain even more control and the FONT tag will eventually become redundant, but it is helpful to have your site backward compatible).

You also have some control over the font size, but not as much as you might hope. With the BASEFONT tag and the SIZE attribute, you can specify a default font size for the document that overrides the preferences set by the user (you can choose from 1 to 7. If the basefont is not defined, the default is 3).

The BASEFONT tag needs no end tag and you can use the FONT tag to change the font size relatively. For example: ‹FONT SIZE="+3"› would display the text in size 5 if the basefont is set to 2.

Relative changes with the FONT tag are not cumulative, so putting two ‹FONT SIZE="+2"› elements in a row doesn't change the font size from 3 to 7.

The FONT tag has two more attributes that allow you to control the appearance of the font. One is for the preferred font, where you simply add the attribute FACE with a list of font names, separated by commas, and Navigator or Explorer will search for those fonts in order of appearance on the hard drive.

Another attribute for the FONT tag allows you to change the color of the font. A typical example might look like this: ‹FONT FACE="Ariel, Helvetica, Geneva" COLOR="purple"› ... ‹/FONT›. The COLOR attribute is a hexadecimal red-green-blue triplet or a color name. A very common setting for the face attribute is either "Arial, Helvetica" or "Times, Palatino". Those are the fonts that come with the Windows and/or Mac Operating Systems.

Hypertext Links

Even though this is not really a layout feature, it is important to quickly address this function, because it is one of the main differences from designing for print media and will affect the way you design your page.

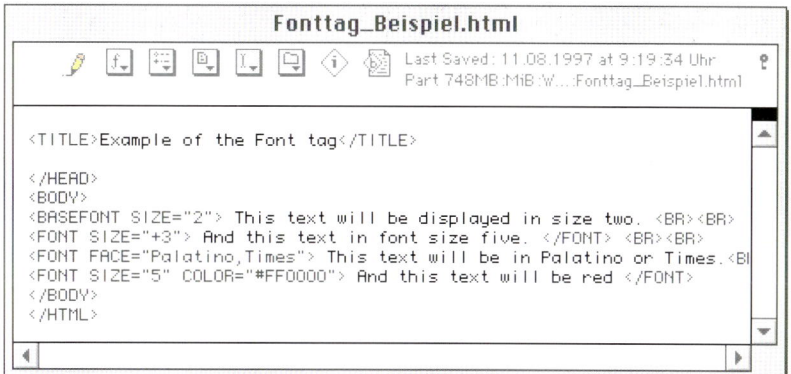
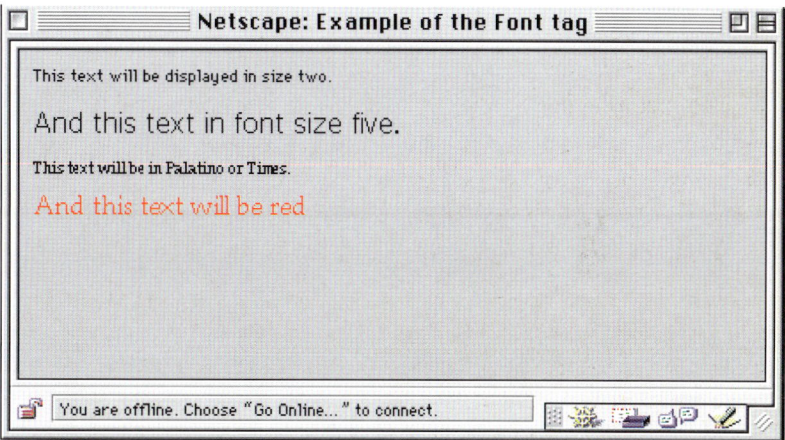

This is an example of the FONT tag and how it will display in the browser window.

The BLINK Tag

Would you like to attract some attention to a word or a sentence? The BLINK tag highlights the text that is between the start and end tag flash: ‹BLINK› **This text will flash** ‹/BLINK›. There are no further attributes and I only mention this tag because many HTML authoring programs do not have a function for it and you need to insert the tag manually.

```
<A HREF="#chapter01"><H2>Arrival in
New York</H2></A>

...

<A NAME="chapter01"></A>
```
Linking with the A tag to an Anchor 02-04

An example of how your HTML script might look for a table of contents: The first A tag links to an anchor named "#chapter 01" and clicking on the text "Arrival in New York" will bring the user to the part of the document where the anchor (the second A tag) is placed.

In an HTML document you can define images or text to be a link to a different location or document. When the user clicks on text or an image with a link they will be transported there instantly.

Linking to a place in your document is great for the Table of Contents and is done by placing an anchor at the location you want to jump to on your page. Linking to a different document is very useful if you mention something in your text and you want to provide more information. That information can be a different document on your site, but could also be any document on the Internet.

To create an anchor or link, use the <A> tag. Everything you put between the start and end tag will then become "hot" and the cursor will change to signal that this is a link.

If you want to place an anchor somewhere in your document, you do this by writing <A NAME="anchorName"></A>.

You do not need to place text between the start and end tag; all that is required is to name your anchor. This anchor can now be referred to from within the same document by using HREF="#anchorName" in an A tag or – if it is in another document – by using the document name (HREF="document.html#anchorName") before the anchor name.

The first A tag in example [02-04] marks the phrase "Arrival in New York" as a hyperlink to an anchor (because of the "#"). Clicking on it would scroll the window browser to the location in your document where you have placed the anchor <A NAME="chapter01"></A>.

If you wanted to address a particular anchor in another document, you would just add the document name (including the path or the absolute URL, if it is not in the same folder), but that is very uncommon. Usually you link only to another document without addressing an anchor.

More likely you are going to use a TARGET attribute with a link. This attribute is particularly important if you are using frames in your layout or want to open the document in a new browser window. Using a TARGET attribute is something that I would always recommend, particularly if you are linking to other web sites. This allows you to ensure that your visitors still have a window with your Web site on the screen while they are surfing in a different site. To read more about the TARGET attribute, go to the "Frames" chapter.

More importantly, you can specify in a link an email address or an FTP site. Sometimes you see at the bottom of a page a phrase such as: "Please send comments to the Webmaster", where

Creating a link to an email address with Adobe PageMill is very easy. Just select the text you want to become an email link and type mailto:name @server.com into the text field at the bottom of the window where it says "Link To:".

the word Webmaster is a link that opens an email window with the email address already in place. That is done simply by using "mailto" in the HREF attribute. So our example would look like this: ‹A HREF="mailto:webmaster@server.com"› WEBMASTER‹/A›.

To give you also an example for a standard link: ‹A HREF="http://www.spiderman.com/ index.html"›click‹/A› would link you to that domain address. That's all you need to know about hypertext links.

If you are working with an authoring program you don't usually need to deal with the HTML syntax, but now you have at least an idea how it works.

Horizontal Rule

This is the last layout feature I want to mention and for good reason: don't use it too often. The HR tag draws a horizontal line across the document frame or window and because this has a certain fascination to everyone who starts designing web pages it usually gets overused at first [02-05].

ALIGN is set by default to centered, if it is not specified, and only makes sense for lines that do not span the entire width of the page. Usually the line has a sort of 3D touch to it and you can remove the shading of the line by setting the NOSHADE attribute (has no value). With SIZE you indicate the thickness of the line in pixels and WIDTH sets the width of the line in either number of pixels or a percentage. The HR tag doesn't require a closing tag.

```
ALIGN="center, left, right"
NOSHADE
SIZE="pixThick"
WIDTH="value"
```

The HR attributes 02-05

How to Work with Paths

To be able to locate a file on a server, you need to type in the path to this file. This path looks like the path that you see as address in the browser. For example if you create a link to a file on a different server, you would type in ‹A HREF="http:// www.server.com/folder/file›. Each '/' character represents a subfolder and this form is called an "absolute address". You guessed it, if there is a absolute address, than there is also a relative address. This sort of address is used If the file is on the same server or site. To signal the browser that it is a relative address you use two dots at the beginning. For example: if the file "service1.html" is in the folder "services" and has a link to a file called "contact.html" in the folder "contact_us", the link would be ‹A HREF="../contact_us/contact.html"›.

This was easy because the files and the folder were in the same level in the hierarchy. But how would you link to a file that is in a different level? You add for every level another "../" to the relative address. For example: imagine you have an image of a pen stored in an image folder (topfolder/image-folder/pen.gif) but the HTML page is in the fourth level (topfolder/level1/level2/level3/document.html). The address in the HTML document would be: "../../../image-folder/pen.gif".

Interview Rikus Hillmann from Pixelpark

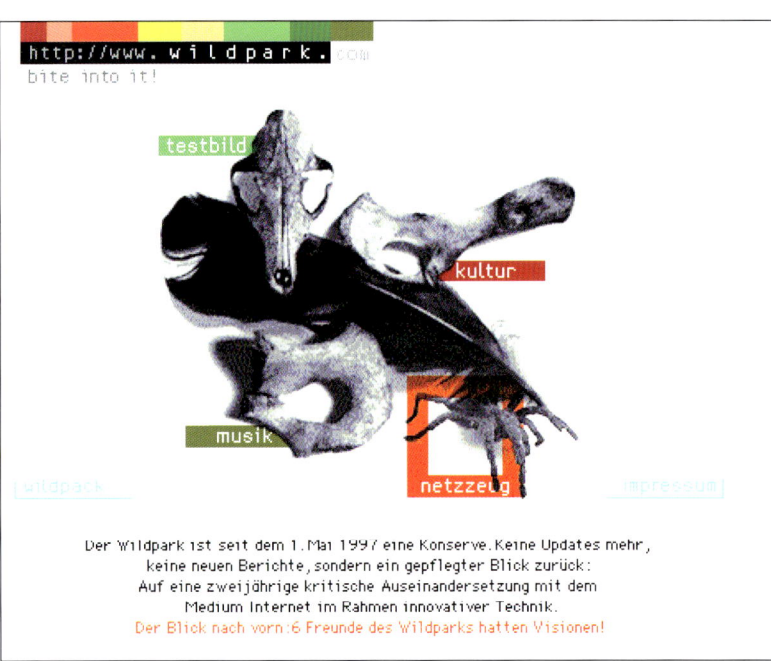

The main page of the Wildpark Web site.

Pixelpark, one of the most established and well known German Multimedia- and Web-Agencies, has many big German corporations such as Adidas, Langnese, Rotring, and Barmer as clients. For the sportswear company Adidas, for example, Pixelpark developed a strategy for the complete integration of digital communication. Their Web site contains information on the company and its products, tips on games, and, in the section "adidas events", a list of streetball challenges or training with top atheltes in the Adidas basketball-Ccamps (URL: http://www.adidas.de). But Pixelpark does not only create Web sites for corporations. Songwriters such as Herbert Grönemeyer, a very well known German songwriter and singer, have also used Pixelpark to create their Web presence. "It is important for me, that people have continuous access to information and that they can communicate with me in a way that wouldn't be possible otherwise," said Herbert Grönemeyer in March of 1996 in a live chat with his fans. Many of the Web sites were designed by Rikus Hillmann, Art Director at Pixelpark, who is the mind behind not only the Grönemeyer homepage (URL: http://www.groenemeyer.de) but also the e-zine "Wildpark".

Wildpark is an e-zine with a vision, a magazine in the Internet, about the Internet, and for the Internet. Techno, Pop, People, Science, Art, Movies, and Stars are the topics of this interactive and audiovisual magazine. It was brought to life in the summer of 1995, and has since been available for access but is no longer being updated. Designed by Rikus Hillmann and edited by Sabine Fischer, communication was important for Wildpark: questions, answers, and comments on each story could be placed by its visitors. I talked to Rikus Hillmann, Art Director at Pixelpark, mostly about his experience in designing an online magazine.

Pixelpark has brought with Wildpark a very ambitious project to life. Can you tell me more about the intentions that you had in respect to the content and the design?

Rikus Hillmann: The idea with Wildpark was to create an online magazine that could exist by itself. True online magazines without a pendant in the print media are rare, and when we started with Wildpark, the Web was still in its infancy. We wanted to capture the online culture in all its facets, from music to movies. The design plays with the tension of organic objects, such as bones, and the geometric elements like the color code logos. But our main focus was to create a visual and functional framework to reduce the production costs and to make sure that the magazine would have a visual identity in which we could embed the individual design of each story. Since the original concept for Wildpark, created by Mike Meire and Peter Saville back in 1995, the visual concept has seen three major changes that adapt the magazine to the functional and visual evolution of the Web, such as the use of frames and JavaScript.

What was the most appealing aspect of working for Wildpark for you?

Rikus Hillmann: The great thing about Wildpark was the opportunity to experiment with content and to adapt functionality and structure to content. With an online magazine you have the great advantage of being able to update it gradually because the content is not as static as in print.

Where were the main difficulties in designing an Online magazine?

Rikus Hillmann: The problem with Wildpark was to create a structure in which you could update the magazine as easily as possible. We had to do this simply for economic reasons because we had to publish between three or four stories a day. To solve this problem we designed many templates that would already have the needed function where we would only have to change the text and the images.

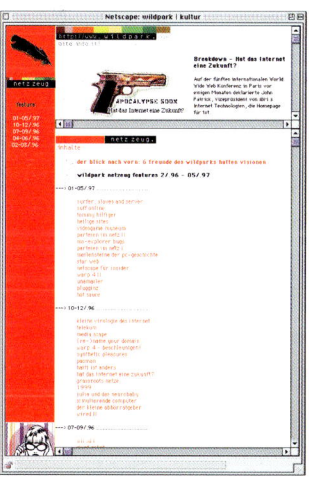

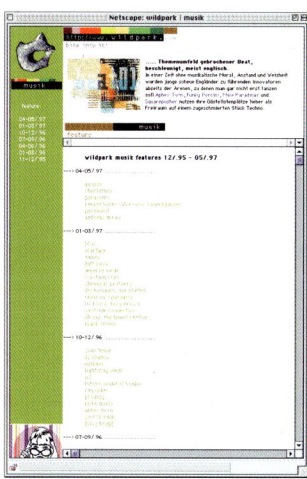

http://www.wildpark.com
bite into it!

The Internet is a pretty new medium and while print magazines have certain established standards, you didn't have any such standards when you started with Wildpark. What has been your experience?

Rikus Hillmann: Wildpark started out as a very complex site and we realized pretty soon that we need to simplify the structure. We reduced the sections from ten to four to make it easier for the reader to navigate and to find new stories. For each of these four sections we created its own mainpage that would present a special every day. The next logical step was to present on the main pages parts of the content. Visitors could then start to read the story on this main page and decide if it was of interest to them. I think that this concentration of information is very important and I would personally like to take it even a step further and present content on the homepage.

Similar to the cover of a newspaper, where you read the beginning of a story that continues then on the following pages?

Rikus Hillmann: Yes, but making it more advanced with search engines or homepages that work with artificial intelligence. So far this is seldom done because it is a huge technical challenge.

Why was Wildpark discontinued?
Rikus Hillmann: Even though Wildpark was quite successful, so far it has been hard to make any money with an e-zine in Germany. But as an innovation and information platform, Wildpark had been very valuable for Pixelpark.

I guess you could bring it together in the sentence, a lot to learn, nothing to earn. For a very long time Wildpark had been the image project and I can imagine that at least the public relation spin off has helped the agency quite a lot?

Rikus Hillmann: I think that the experience and the know-how that we gained in this project have pushed Pixelpark a lot in the online market to make it into one of the leading agencies. But the heads of the company decided that Pixelpark want to focus more on being a Multimedia agency and stay out of the publishing business.

How do you see the future for an online magazine in general, because right now there is a big trend in providing free content on the Internet and to make revenues with advertising?

Rikus Hillmann: I definitely see a future for online magazines, but it is hard for me to see how you can make money with it and how you can market it. In my opinion the online magazines are very important, on one hand as a complement to a print magazine because they extend the

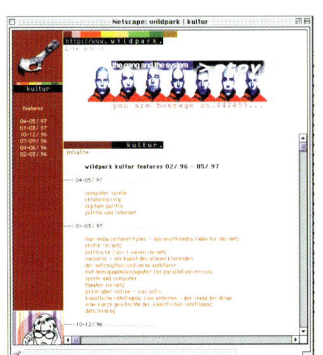

possibilities of it and supersede the disadvantages of it, but also as an independent medium because you can do totally different things with it than with a print magazine. I am currently working on a project to create an online version for the magazine Buzz. We use the online version to publish the interviews in full length or simply to aid the stories with audio.

What do you think needs to be improved with the online magazines so that they succeed?

Rikus Hillmann: The text in most of the online magazines is too long and, I think, that is also due to the fact that most online editors had worked prior to that in the print media. But in the near future we will have more and more online editors who have developed their own style that is more suitable for this medium. Just to put images and text into the Internet doesn't work. This has been a big problem right from the beginning and we now need to find solutions, but I think that the Internet will create its own art form with its own visuality and functionality.

If I get you right, you think it is now time to create a new visual language that is a combination of audio, animation, text, and images?

Rikus Hillmann: Exactly, but this will always depend on how economical the solution has to be. Wildpark was pretty static: we got the text and two images and had to bring it as quickly as possible on the net. We had only a little budget and had to keep it simple, just with text and images, but this has, to me, always been too static. I wish we had done more advanced things, but this is the same problem that other online magazines have also: you can see that the stories were done very simply, sometimes with a nice visuality, but usually without any media-specific functionality. Most of the time you can just jump from one page to another. What I would like to do is to create a functionality that is part of the story. This is very difficult to accomplish because it requires that the designer and the writer develop the story in advance, something that isn't done very often.

This is very interesting, because it seems to me that there are many parallels to the CD-ROM magazines. Jason Pearson, Art Director and cofounder of the New Yorker CD-ROM magazine Blender has told me in an interview that they had to learn how much text can be presented on screen. Today they limit themself to a maximum of 2500 characters in the main story plus an

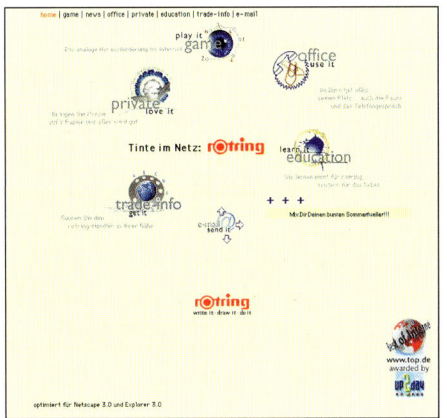

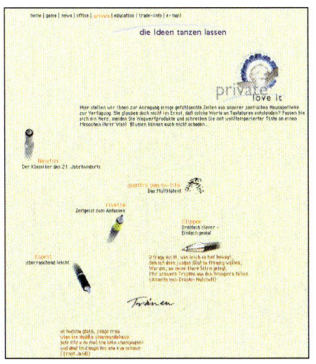

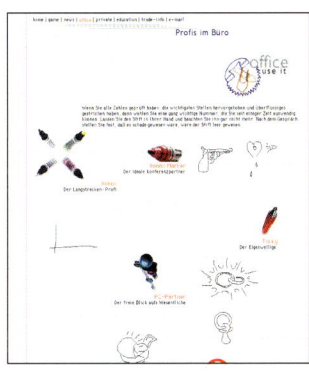

Distributor, designers and editors don't have to use a pencil to get in touch with this company – an email is enough. With the goal of optimizing communication with the distributors and establishing in the long run an order system on the net, the company Rotring released its Web site in 1996. The product world of this fabricator of pens and pencils is presented here in the three sections "office", "private" and "education". Project management: Anja Berendes; Creative Direction: Claudius Lazzeroni/Michael Kutschinski

Left: You find the mainpage at http://www.rotring.de

http://www.wildpark.com
bite into it!

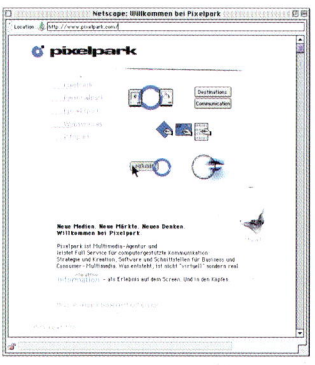

"Pixelpark Online is our own Web site, where we present the agency and its services, and the idea was to create a contrast to the relatively static content of this site," says Rikus Hillmann, Art Director at Pixelpark. For this reason the visual elements on the page are changed dynamically via a CGI script, to always give the visitor a new visual appearance and to use the advantage "of a dynamical design, because this is the difference in comparison with the print media."

additional 1500 characters in the hyperlinks. He also said that features get much better if designers and editors have worked out a concept before the interview.

Rikus Hillmann: Such a situation is really desirable, but it is rarely possible. Unfortunately there are not many projects were you can do this. At Pixelpark we work for many clients where such an innovative way of content design isn't desired. Most of the big corporations want a very linear presentation of the content for their Web site. As you work longer with the Internet medium, like I do, you begin to wish you would see more progress in this area.

If you had all possibilities at hand to create your own online magazine, how would it look then?

Rikus Hillmann: The optimal online magazine should have only one page, everything short and condensed without a complicated navigation and with only one story that changes daily. In a way like an informative soap opera, without an archive or a long history. It is too time consuming for me to check out a complete site. Instead I prefer to have one good story and on the next day something new. The complexity of information is too much for me and the shorter and tighter everything is, the more I like it.

Besides Wildpark you have created many other Web sites for Pixelpark and in the short history of the World Wide Web you are a veteran. I would like to know which programs you used to create your sites.

Rikus Hillmann: I design all the graphic elements in Photoshop 4.0 and FreeHand 7.0, and the animations are all done in GifBuilder. For the HTML code we use the program BBEdit and World WideWeb-Weaver, the latter in particular because of the very clean HTML code that it generates and the good and precise design functionality.

Designing for the Web has many restrictions, but also many possibilities. What appeals to you and what bothers you about it?

Rikus Hillmann: The World Wide Web is, in its core, not a design medium. It was created to allow communication, transmit information or make transactions, which is why the design for the Internet must be functional. In my view this has a very strong impact on the design itself, therefore it is important to find a balance between the amount of data, navigation with common sense, and a logical structure. What appeals most to me is the challenge to make communication and information accessible through design. The rapid development of the medium and the technology is also a stimulus for me, because this always gives me something new to learn. Because of this I don't see the restrictions with the color palettes or with the different browsers and operating systems as a burden, they are part of what makes it appealing to me. Today you can be confronted with a problem that won't exist in a year, but by then you will be faced with new ones.

For many designers the switch to Web design is a problem due to the technical limitations. What did you find to be the most challenging for you when you started Web design?

Rikus Hillmann: Mainly to design for different browsers and platforms. You constantly run into compatibility problems, in particular in designing for different browsers, like, for example, with JavaScript on Netscape Navigator and Microsoft Explorer.

Another important factor seems to be that the user interface has a much higher significance than in print. Interface design is an important aspect in the design for the Internet and for most designers, who come from the print media, it is the biggest challenge. What is, in your opinion, a good interface design, what are examples of bad interface design, and how do you think interface design for the Web will evolve?

Rikus Hillmann: Interface design in the future should have a stronger relationship between content and interface, because it makes the information more experiential.

Do you mean the use of metaphors, like you did on the DJH website?

Rikus Hillmann: Exactly, because in the trend of commercialization of the Internet the emphasis is more and more on the corporate design aspect and the technical functionality rather than the information. The interface design of the future should be logical and support the information that it tries to transport. For the service and information page of the Deutsche Jugendherberge (German Youth Hostel) we used for example the metaphor of a backpack with all its paraphernalia, that represent each section of the website.

Since April '97 travellers and globetrotters can get online information about special offers, information, and services of the German Youth Hostel (DJH). DJH members have a broad service spectrum to plan their trip: the possibility of making reservations for railway tickets and overnight stays, ordering of inexpensive travel and vacation utilities, to online booking of interesting travel offers. A special service is the online youth hostel directory where the user can find all the necessary information about the 600 youth hostels in Germany. In addition a bulletin board helps to get in touch with other travelers where they can search and find everything from scuba diving equipment to travel companions.

You can check out the DJH site at http://www.djh.de

CHAPTER 03

Images

The pictures in your site are like the spices in soup. If they are great, visitors will be enthusiastic even though what was served was mainly water. You are not convinced? If you're not convinced try surfing the Web and you'll discover that there are just a few recipes used to create a Web site, with the only difference between a mediocre and fantastic Web site being the images that are used.

The Difference Between JPEG and GIF

The two dominant image formats for the Web are GIF and JPEG, because both formats allow compression of data, which results in much smaller file sizes than any TIFF image. Therefore, an understanding of the basic principle of both formats is needed to determine which one fits your particular purpose.

The rule of thumb is that you use JPEG for all larger images or any photographic images that require the best color display and GIF for all little images that don't require that many colors, like control buttons. The reason for this becomes clear once you look at the way both formats work. GIF, short for Graphical Interchange Format, uses a compression algorithm that works with pattern recognition to compress the image. It does this in two ways: one is to index every color that occurs in the image and then looks for runs of the same-colored pixel. Picture this: if you have a piece of paper with the word "Color" written on it 200 times you could compress the text by writing "200 times Color" and you would still have the same amount of information. The GIF algorithm also looks for patterns within every horizontal pixel line and indexes those as well. To continue with the example of a text, it would be like looking for how often a complete phrase or sentence occurs in a novel. The good thing about this compression technique (called Lempel-Ziv-Welch after the inventors) is that you get compression ratios of up to 4:1 without loss of quality and the decompressed image looks like the original.

Other nice features of GIF89a (which builds on the 87a standard) are that one color can be assigned to be transparent and you can also make animations (covered in the chapter Animation).

The JPEG format, short for Joint Photographic Experts Group and pronounced Jay-PEG, has a compression ratio from 10:1 to 100:1. That means you can store a 1 MByte image in 10 KByte. This can't be done without sacrificing some of the quality of the image, but even with such a high compression ratio, it produces amazingly good results. JPEG compression reduces file size by keeping the brightness information in a picture and eliminating subtle color changes that our eye can't distinguish. It doesn't do this line by line, but, rather, in blocks, something that can easily be detected

JPEG

Here are two examples of a JPEG image, saved with two different settings. The expanded Image is 670 kByte, but the top one was saved with the least amount of compression in Photoshop (quality setting 10) and the second one with the higgest compression (setting 0). The top image still has a file size of 48 816 bytes, while the second one is only 21 542 bytes. As you can see in the second image, the text gets a little bit blurred, due to the way the JPEG compression works: it does it blockwise. In the bottom picture you can see this effect in 600% magnification – at the screen you hardly see the difference.

when you zoom in a JPEG image. The lower the quality setting, the more easy you can detect those blocks, because some of them look a little blurred (blurring an image before compressing with JPEG allows a better compression rate). The more contrast an image has, the larger the resulting file size. If you are using text in your image, JPEG may not be a good choice, because its compression algorithm blurs the text.

Keep in mind that even though the file size might be very low, the image will decode to the full size that it had previously. This is especially important to remember with large JPEG files, which might cause the visitor's browser to crash, because of memory overflow: JPEG always uses the color depth of the monitor setting, so if the monitor is set to 16 million colors (24-bit) the memory requirement of the image will be three times as big as when viewed with 256 colors (8-bit).

The decompressed image size can be seen in Photoshop in the bottom left

This image shows how an interlaced image might appear to a viewer: he will first see an image in low resolution (left), that stepwise will show more details (middle) until it is displayed in its full resolution (right)

corner of the window. Keep file size inflation in mind while creating your site.

GIF and JPEG allow you to interlace the image in the Web browser. This means that the viewer will first see a low resolution version of the image with a progressively more detailed preview until the final image is loaded. The number of passes for JPEG (3–5), can be defined – for GIF it is set to four passes. If you are using transparency with your GIF, avoid using interlacing because it can cause problems.

PNG: The Cool New Graphic Format

Ping, as the Portable Network Graphic format is called, will most likely be the successor of the GIF format because it offers some great features, such as completely lossless compression with a better compression than GIF, a cross-platform gamma correction (!), and an alpha channel for transparency.

What does that mean for the designer? First of all it means that you can use transparency in an image without any halos because the alpha channel provides you with several levels of transparency.

The image will display perfectly in the browser because you are not limited by a color palette of 256 colors and the brightness of the image is adjusted, depending on the platform on which you are viewing it. A viewer on an IBM-compatible will see the image exactly the same way as someone on a Macintosh.

Does that mean that GIF will become redundant? Not as long as PNG can only be viewed with a plug-in, which is still the case with most browsers. Besides this, PNG doesn't support animations like GIF does (by the way, Photoshop can save images in the PNG format).

GIF

How well the GIF compression algorithm works depends on the source. Here for example are some 45 x 45 pixel GIF images and their different file size. All images were saved with a 256 color palette. Reducing the color palette can save you up to 800 bytes.

Left: The white image has 870 bytes. Saved with an optimized color palette would decrease it to 78 bytes.
Right: This image has almost no regularity and needs 2391 bytes.

Left: There is almost no difference between horizontal and vertical stripes. The left image has 933 bytes, the right one 932 bytes. Saving this image with an optimized palette would decrease it by 800 bytes.

When you convert in Photoshop to Indexed, you can choose "Diffusion Dither" to make up for colors that are not in the color palette. But dithering increases the file size, because you have fewer reruns of the same color in the image.

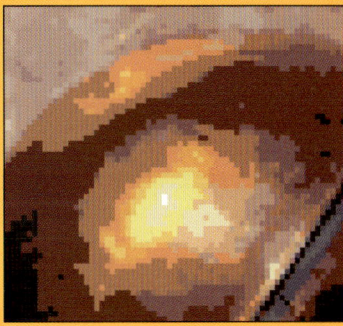
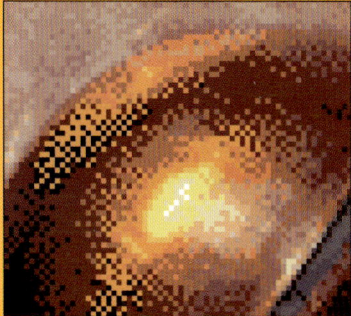

13 443 bytes
no dither

16 837 bytes
with dither

With Shockwave Flash 2 you can display and view vector-based graphics in a browser. The required plug-in is very small and can be downloaded freely from the Macromedia Web site. But Shockwave Flash can even more: create animations with the vector elements and link sounds, such as a button click or a voice-over, to objects.
Right: an example of a Shockwave Flash Animation. Because all the elements are vector-based, they are downloaded very quickly and appear almost immediately in the Web browser.

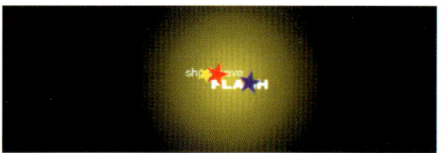

Raster and Vector Images

Those of you from the desktop publishing world might know this already, but for all others, here is a brief introduction to the distinction between raster and vector images.

While raster images (bitmaps) store visual information in an x/y-raster, vector images store only a description of the visual information. For example, let's take a circle: If you scan a circle on a scanner you will get a more or less detailed copy of the original, depending on the resolution. But a vector image stores the circle like this: "draw a circle with a radius of 100 points and a line thickness of 3 points". This information is resolution independent because it will always render the best resolution the output device offers, even if the circle is scaled.

So far, the graphics mostly seen on the Web are raster images – you can see vector images only with a Shockwave plug-in from Macromedia. A great feature of this plug-in is that you can zoom in, which makes it ideal for maps, for example. But now it even features animation and sound check it out at Macromedia's Web site.

For the time being, however, we still deal, mostly, with raster images when it comes to Web design.

Color Depth

The dimension of a raster image is set by the number of pixels it has on the x- and y-axis. But there is another dimension and that is the z-axis, also called color depth. For example, 1-bit color depth means that the image can display only black and white, because one bit stores only the values 0 and 1.

The more bits you use for color depth, the more colors ($2^{\text{color depth}}$) can be displayed: with a color depth of 2 you can display 4 colors (2^2) and 8 colors with a color depth of 3 (2^3).

Most designers use monitors and graphic boards that can display up to 16 million colors (16 777 216), which means that the video RAM stores 24 bits of color information for each pixel. Unfortunately, most end users have only 8-bit graphic boards with their computer and

The Resolution

The resolution of a picture for print is around 266 dpi, which means you have 266 raster points (or dots) per inch. In the world of Web design your output medium is the screen, which only has 72 dpi, and a 266 dpi scan would be displayed about 3.5 times larger. To avoid this you need to convert the image in Adobe Photoshop. Select "Image Size" in the "Image" menu and enter in the dialog box the desired resolution, width, and height of your image. You also can choose which algorithm Photoshop should use for the process: select "Bicubic" in the option "Resample Image" for the best result.

thus are limited to 256 colors. What does this mean for you, the designer?

It means that the image that you put on your Web page might get displayed only with 256 colors, even though the image contains much more color information. The computer will make up for those missing colors by dithering them for the display. Depending on your image, this can have quite a drastic effect to the colors in your image, so switch your monitor from time to time to 256 colors to check that your images and pages look okay on a low end computer.

Before I explain how you can optimize your images to 256 colors, let me introduce you to another term that you will hear quite often from now on: the color table.

COLOR TABLE

I don't want to get too technical, even though I know you are burning to read how compression algorithms work. But all you really need to understand about color tables is that they are a way of storing color information and that the GIF format uses this technique.

Before you can save your image in Photoshop as GIF you need to index a color table. You do this by changing the mode from RGB to Indexed in the "Image" menu. In the pop-up menu choose "World Wide Web" as your palette and select "Dither: None" in the Options pop-up menu. Now all the colors in your image get matched to the closest color of the Web color palette and chances are that you see quite a color shift in your image. To reduce this effect you can use "Diffusion Dither", but dithering an image creates a bad compression ratio. Recall that the GIF algorithm compresses the image by looking for runs of same-colored pixels, but with dithering there won't be many of those runs, resulting in a much bigger file size.

Now you are in a dilemma: on one hand you want the image to look good, on the other hand you want to make the file as small as possible.

Instead of dithering the image, you could use an adaptive palette, which means that Photoshop looks for the most common colors in the picture and stores those in an optimized color palette. To create an adaptive color palette, switch the mode to "Indexed" and select "Adaptive" in the pop-up menu of the dialog box.

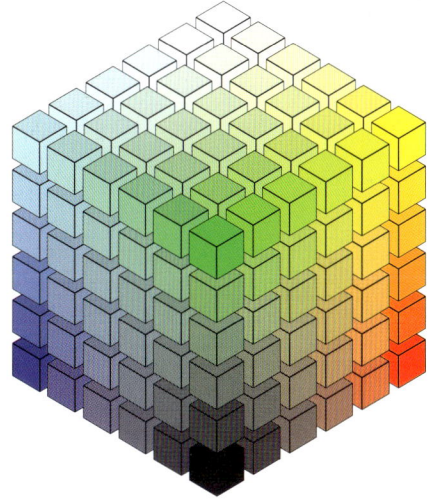

The colors of the Web save color palette will display in a browser without dithering. They are arranged here in a cube (that you see here from both sides).

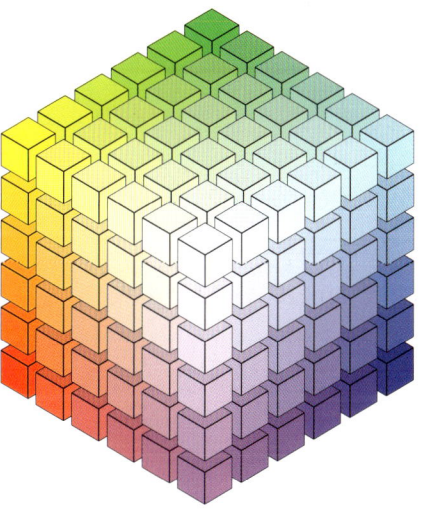

A sidenote: The color table of GIF can store 256 colors with a color depth of 24 bits. In your image file this information requires only 768 bytes. You can calculate the memory for the color table by multiplying the number of colors by 3. For example:
a 7-bit color table stores 128 colors, which will occupy 384 bytes in your image file. You don't really need this information, which was only for the curious.

Images 49

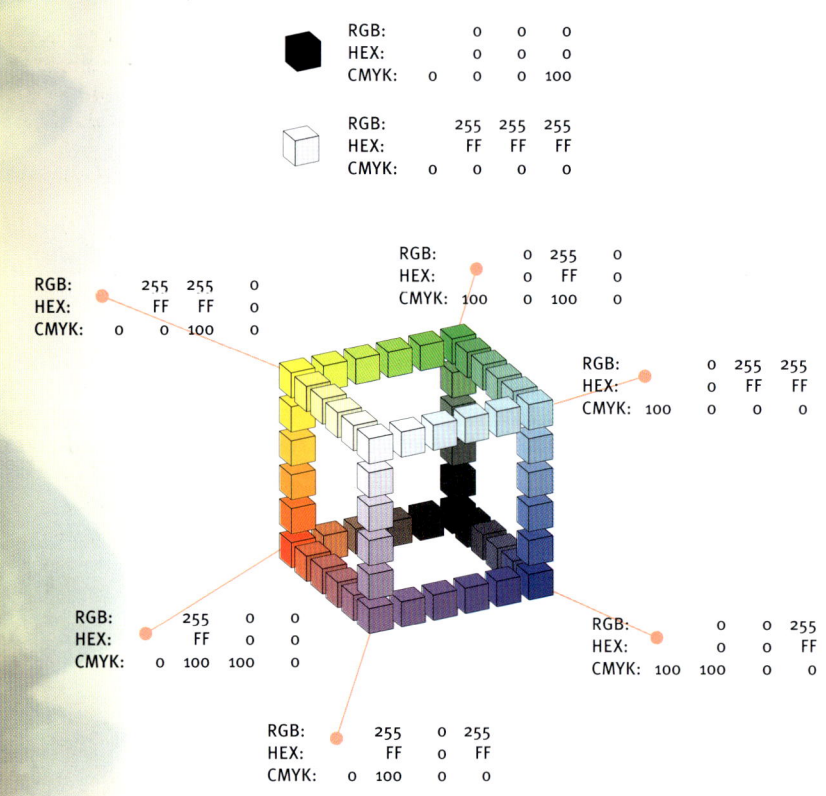

The quality of the image is now good, but you face again the problem that on a low-end computer the colors in your image will shift, because you are not using the Web save color palette.

OPTIMIZING YOUR IMAGES

All Web designers deal with these problems I mentioned before. Preparing images so that they look great on all platforms and every monitor is quite an art. I personally think that the best compromise is to shoot for the middle ground and use an adaptive color palette. This way your image will look excellent on all monitors with millions or thousands of colors and at least good on a 256-color monitor. Of course, you need to double-check: sometimes an image can look really bad on a 256-color monitor and then you need to go back and change the settings.

Another way of optimizing your images is to reduce the number of colors in the color table. The fewer colors in your image, the easier it is for the GIF compression algorithm to compress the file. Most images don't need more than 32 colors, and the trick here is to influence Photoshop to pick the right colors for the color palette (see also the step-by-step story in this chapter).

WORKING WITH THE WWW COLOR PALETTE

When creating or painting an illustration, try to stay with the colors in the WWW palette, because these colors will display without dithering. If you are working with Adobe Illustrator (or any other program that uses a CMYK color picker), use for the CMY channels only increments of 20% (no value for black) and in an RGB color picker, for example in Photoshop, always use for the channels a value that can be divided by 51

PANTONE INTERNET COLOR SYSTEM GUIDE

One of my favorite tools for working with the Web palette is the Pantone Internet Color System Guide. This is a little color book with all the 216 Web colors, listing the hexadecimal code and the RGB and CMYK values. But the main advantage is a color picker (for Macintosh) installed in the system that can be accessed by all programs supporting the Apple color picker, such as Adobe PageMill and Adobe Photoshop.

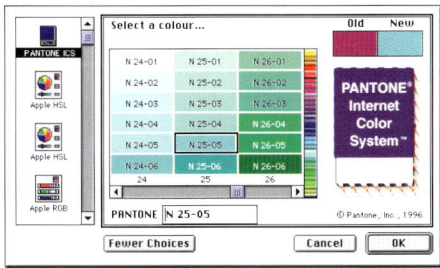

With the Pantone Color Picker it is easy to work with the Web save color palette.

and you will always have a Web save color.

If you are using Photoshop 4.0 and you don't want to bother with typing in the values in Photoshop's color picker, you can create a swatch for the color window. You do this by converting an image from RGB to Indexed: in the dialog choose "Web" as your palette and click "OK". Now that the image is converted, you can go to "Image: Mode: Colortable" and open the color table of the image. What you see is the colortable with the 216 colors used by the WWW. Save it, close the dialog, and open the color palette in the Window menu by clicking on "Show swatches". With "Load Swatches" or "Replace Swatches" in the pop-up menu of the window, import the color table you just saved. Whenever you want to use a color out of this palette for your illustration, you only need to click on one of those colors with the pipette tool to make it the foreground color.

PLACING AN IMAGE

Let's look at the concept of HTML to understand why absolute positioning of images is so tricky.

In a layout program like Pagemaker or QuarkXPress a frame is placed at a fixed position on the page and the text flows around it. However, in HTML, the position is defined by its place in the text itself, and if the text moves, the picture moves. Using tables was the only way to give an image some sort of fixed position. To place an image in your text, you use the IMG tag [03-01].

Whenever you use pictures in your layout, you should also use the ALT attribute. With this attribute you can control what text should be displayed when the user has turned off images or suspended image loading. If you are using navigational elements the viewer would still know where to click or, if you have your logo placed at the top, your company name would still appear.

Another attribute that is frequently used is the BORDER attribute. By default, all images that are also a link get a border to signal that they are clickable and you can specify the width in pixels, but in most cases these borders have no great design and can be turned off by using 0 as the value.

HEIGHT or WIDTH specifies the height or width of the image, either in pixels or as a percentage of the window height. You should always use these attributes because they allow the layout to appear

```
ALIGN="left, right, top, absmiddle,
       absbottom, texttop, middle,
       baseline, bottom"
ALT="AlternateText"
BORDER="pixBorder"
HEIGHT="height"
HSPACE="pixHorzMarg"
ISMAP
LOWSRC="Location"
NAME="imgName"
SRC="Location"
USEMAP="Location#MapName"
VSPACE="pixVertMarg"
WIDTH="width"
```

The IMAGE tag attributes 03-01

If you use ALIGN you can specify the alignment of the image in relation to the surrounding text. The "left" and "right" settings let the text flow around the image, pretty much the way it works in desktop publishing. Top and absbottom aligns the top or bottom of an image with the highest or lowest item in the current line. If there are other images in the line, the top of the current image will be aligned to the top of the highest image on the line (or the bottom, if you use absbottom). Absmiddle aligns the middle of an image with the middle of the text.

PREPARING A GIF IMAGE IN PHOTOSHOP

Optimizing your images is key to creating a fast loading page and reducing the number of colors is one way to decrease the file size. The reason is that limiting the colors in your image makes it more compressible for the GIF algorithm. I use this image to show you step-by-step how to do this in Photoshop.

1 *When you change the mode of an image in Photoshop from RGB to Indexed (menu "Image: Mode"), you have several choices in the option "Palette". The option "Web" will for example shift every color in the image to the next closest color in the Web save color palette. But this is not the best choice, rather select "Adaptive" from this pop-up menu. Now you can enter the desired "Color Depth" and Photoshop will create a palette that displays the image as well as possible with the selected number of colors.*

2 *Here you see the image with a 8-color palette (3 bit) and a 32-color palette (5 bit). The left example obviously has too few colors and the example on the right still uses too many colors. You can see the color palette after you have switched to "Indexed" and then select "Image: Mode: Color Table". If you see too many colors that are close, you are not done. Undo the Mode Change and start over, this time with fewer colors.*

3 *The "Adaptive" color palette creates a color palette based on the histogram of all the pixels in the image. You can influence this by selecting an area that is important to you. Here, for example, I selected the tomato and then switched to 32 colors, and as you can see, the color palettes has now many more shades of red. After adding more areas to the selection, you will get a color palette that displays the image with almost no color shift. Try to avoid dithering the image if possible, because it increases the file size.*

4 *The last step is to export the indexed image via "File: Export: Gif89a". Don't use the "Save as" function, because it produces a much larger file.*
The final image (bottom) with 26 colors and no dither has only 5 779 bytes. This is a reduction of almost 50% compared to the image with a 256-color palette (top) and a file size of 10 648 bytes.

correctly while the pictures are still loading. The consequence of not using those attributes is that the viewer has to wait until every image has been downloaded before the text can be seen. This is because the browser would need to wait for every element before it could determine how the layout is going to look.

Two other tags that go along with the two attributes HEIGHT and WIDTH are VSPACE (vertical space) and HSPACE (horizontal space). They define the margin between the text and the image.

The SRC tag specifies the URL of the image to be displayed. If you are using many pictures, there is the risk that the viewer will abort the image loading process or switch to another site. The LOWSRC tag can help to avoid this because you can specify a low resolution picture, like a bitmap version of your image, to be loaded first so that the viewer sees the complete layout while the high resolution pictures are still loading. Some designers use this tag to create some sort of mini-animation by using two different images, for example an image of a closed door and than one of an open door. The advantage of this

> **EQUILIBRIUM DEBABELIZER**
>
> Besides Adobe Photoshop, another great tool to optimize your images for the web is DeBabelizer from Equilibrium. Many professional multimedia and web designers swear by this name. Unfortunately its awkward interface is difficult to use and the program takes a while to get used to. But its ability to convert graphic formats from many different platforms, its batch processing feature, and its possibility to remap any number of images to one common color palette, called SuperPalette, make it a very powerful tool.

trick is that the first picture gets displayed right away after loading and automatically changes once the second image is loaded – all without any JavaScript programming. If you want to work with JavaScript you can give the image a name with the NAME attribute which JavaScript then can refer to. ISMAP and USEMAP are tags that are used with server-side image maps which will be explained in detail in the next chapter. The following is a typical example of the use of the image tag:

The LOWSRC attribute in this Web Site loads first a bitmap image and then replaces it with a color picture.

Using Transparency in GIF Images

The GIF format allows you to select a color to become your transparency color. In the browser the areas covered by the transparency color display the browser background. Working with this feature has only one pitfall: when composing in Photoshop, the edges of all objects get blended to the background color. This technique is called antialiasing and creates smooth edges by adding intermediate colors. Those intermediate color at the edges will become visible in the browser.

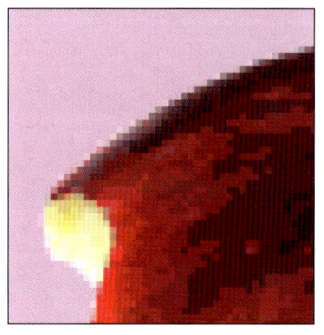

The example above shows how the edge of your image might look in a browser if you have not optimized the edge.

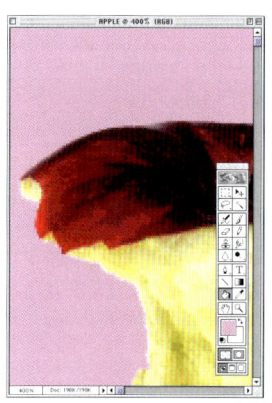

1 To avoid visible edges, give the image the same background color that you want to use in the browser. In Photoshop use the "Paint Bucket Tool" and set the tolerance in "Paint Bucket Options". If you fill now the background of your image, the edges of the object will get blended to this background. When you export the image later, select this color as your transparent color and it will become invisible in the browser and the edges of your object now blend perfectly.

The 50% Transparency Trick

Too bad that GIF has only one level of transparency, but with a little trick you can fake a half-transparent area. I used this trick in the website for the Band Eye2Eye: the shaddows and the plastic in the middle of the CD mix with the background.

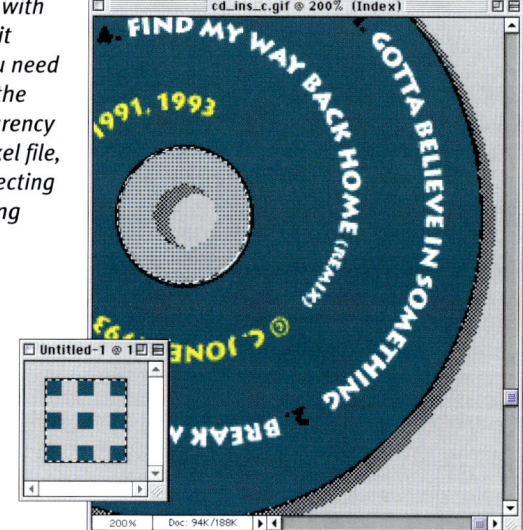

1 I had used this DTP trick very often with print and one day it struck me that it might also work in a browser. All you need to do is create a pattern in which you use the color that later is going to be your transparency color. The example that you see is a 5x5 pixel file, with grey as my croma-key color. After selecting everything I define it as pattern by choosing "Edit: Define Pattern".

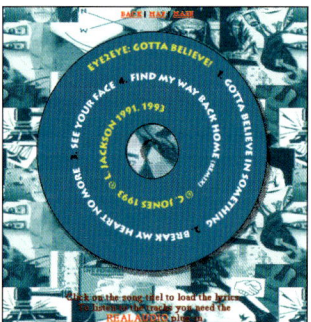

2 I select the areas in the CD that I want to fill with this pattern and select "Contents, Use: Pattern" of the "Fill" function (this function is in the "Edit" menu). Later I saved the GIF with grey as my croma-key color.

```
<IMG SRC="http://www.server.com/
logo.gif" LOWSRC="http:// www.ser-
ver.com/lowlogo.gif" ALT= "WTC: the
Web Technology Company" WIDTH=
"400" HEIGHT= "50" BORDER="0">
```

As you can see, the WIDTH and HEIGHT tags tell the browser the dimensions of the image before it is even downloaded. Because of the LOWSRC tag the browser will first display a low resolution version of the image before it attempts to load the image of the SRC tag, and if the user has turned off images, the text specified in the ALT tag would be seen. You can freely mix JPEG and GIF images as you can see from this example. Browsers that do not recognize the LOWSRC attribute ignore it and simply load the high resolution version. This is pretty much all you need to know to place images in your page. More information on background images can be found in the section Background Tiles. Imagemaps and Image tables also have their own chapter. The rest of this chapter focuses on preparing images for the World Wide Web.

IMAGEMAPS

This feature of the HTML syntax allows the use of an image as an interface for your web site by defining areas of your image as hot spots that link to other documents. In the early days of the Web, the document containing the information about the hot spots had to be placed in a certain location (folder) on the server in order to work properly. This form, containing server side image maps, works basically like this: when the user moves the mouse over an image defined as an image map, the browser sends the coordinates of the mouse to the server. The server then compares this information with the image map file to see if the

METACREATION PAINTER

Formerly known as Fractal Design, MetaCreation offers, with Painter, the best painting simulator on the market. I call it a simulator because Painter really gives you the feeling of painting with oil or chalk on canvas, and I can still remember my excitement when I worked with it for the first time. I wrote the first book on Painter in Germany for version 2.0 but the software has come a long way since then, with some quite dramatic interface changes. It would have been too time consuming to update the book, but I still write step-by-step stories or tests on Painter for the German DTP magazine PAGE from time to time. Yes, I confess, I love this program even though I wish MetaCreation would be more consistent with the interface. What makes Painter such a great tool for Web designers, besides its painting tools, is its support in creating tiles, textures, and interface elements? If you define your image area as tile, Painter will automatically ensure that it will be seamless, or if you need a paper texture as background for your Web page, you can choose among many textures that come with the program. With the 5.0 version MetaCreation introduced a new plug-in called "Bevel World" which allows you to create all sorts of bevels for a selection and has even more parameters than the plug-in "Eye Candy" from Alien Skin for Photoshop. Painter has much more to offer and it is invaluable for a designer. If you don't already have it, check it out.

user is over an area defined as a hot spot. In that case, the server transmits that information and the user's browser cursor changes to a finger, indicating that this part of the image is a link. Once the user clicks on this hot spot, the server links to the new HTML document.

If the server is very busy it can actually take a while until the user gets a response from the server. To solve this problem, image maps were developed that would then be processed by the viewer's own computer, called the client. With client side image maps the document with the hot spots gets transmitted together with the image and the viewer's computer does all the processing. A big advantage for the Web designer with client side image maps is that you can test your site offline, while with server

This interface for the Embracing Humanity website uses an image map to create links to other pages. If you don't have a program like Adobe PageMill, where you can draw the shapes directly onto the image (right, bottom), you can use Photoshop to ascertain the coordinates. Just open the "Info Palette" and you will see the coordinates of the cursor when you scroll over the image (click in the palette to change the measurement to pixels). Use those coordinates then later to create a client-side image map.

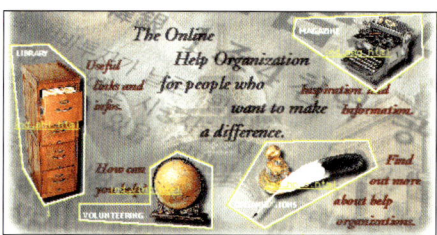

side image maps, you need to install the image map first on the server (HTML authoring programs like Adobe PageMill are able to simulate the response from a server, but creating and installing a server side image map is very inconvenient and I don't expect that you will see many sites with server side image maps in the future).

The only problem with client side image maps is that not every browser understands them (Microsoft Internet Explorer and Netscape Navigator can both handle client-side image maps, which covers the majority of the market) so to make sure that visitors can navigate through your site, you should also include the links at the bottom of your page as traditional text links.

How to Set Up Client Side Image Maps

The image is treated as regular image, either GIF or JPEG, meaning all you need to do is to define this image in the IMG tag as an image map by including USEMAP="#MapName". Because there can be several image maps in one HTML document, the USEMAP attribute tells the browser which map definition should be used. Don't forget the '#' symbol that indicates to the browser that the information is stored within the same document. Without it the browser would look for an external file with that name.

Before getting into details about the tags, let's look at what such a document would look like [03-02].

All the map information is enclosed in a MAP starting and end tag. For each hot spot include an AREA tag with its coordinates and a shape. CIRCLE needs two coordinates. The first pair identifies the center of the circle center and the second identifies a point on the circle's edge. With the RECT attribute the first pair of coordinates specify the upper left corner and the second pair the lower right corner. Finally, the POLY attribute coordinates define the edges of the

continues on page 59

```
<IMG SRC="main.gif" border=0 usemap="#mainmap">
...
<MAP NAME="mainmap">
  <AREA COORDS="100,100,60,100" HREF="/services/index.html"
  SHAPE="CIRCLE">
  <AREA COORDS="10,10,20,60" HREF="/products/index.html" SHAPE="RECT"
  TARGET="_top">
  <AREA COORDS="350,123,467,245,342,54,26,36350,123"
  HREF="/sponsors/index.html" SHAPE="POLY">
</MAP>
```

A client side image map 03-02

How to Create Background Tiles in Photoshop

There are a couple of great programs to create textures, such as TextureScape and Painter from MetaCreation (formerly from Specular and Fractal Design), but you can also create seamless tiles with Adobe Photoshop. Here is how to create and prepare patterns in Photoshop.

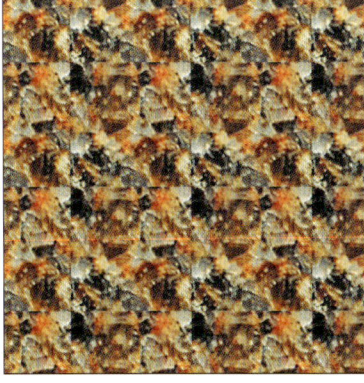

1 *Any selection can be made a pattern: just choose "Define Pattern" in the "Edit" menu, create an empty document and fill the area with the pattern with the function "Fill" (also in the "Edit" menu; pick the option "Contents, use: Pattern"). The result looks like the example to the right: you can see the edges of the selection.*

2 *To make a pattern seamless, you have to smooth the edges with the rubber stamp tool. But first use the filter "Offset" in the category "Other". In the dialog box, enter a horizontal and vertical offset and also click the option "wrap around". Now you can see the edges of the pattern and edit them with the rubber stamp tool. This tool copies part of your image to a different part of your image, rather like painting with your image.*

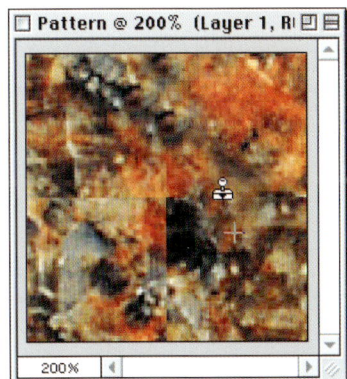

4 *After erasing all the edges, save your image as GIF or JPEG and place it on your HTML page as background image. The result in this example is still very repetitive but at least you don't see hard edges. This technique is great to create paper textures for your browser, but for demonstration purposes this pattern will do it.*
A very popular trick is also to use the pattern function to create a colored sidebar without the use of frames. On the next page is an example from the Web Site "Persistence of the Spirit".

3 *Bring the tool to about 20 pixels from the edge, press the ALT-button on your keyboard and click in the image. Now release the button and click with the tool directly on your edge. The edge will miraculously disappear, because Photoshop is now copying parts of the image over the area where you click with the tool.*

Persistence of the Spirit

Designer: Christopher Stashuk
HTML-Author: James Norris

"Persistence of the Spirit" is a website that captures the spirit of 5 epochs from the late 1700s through 1980 as a thorough historical interpretation of African-American history in Arkansas. Designed like an informal presentation, it uses a photographer's slide motif with handwritten dates on the images to anchor each section. The main story is told through slide images and Historical Narratives articles. Visitors can select a particular chronological section featuring hand-tinted images reflecting the period, covering nearly 300 years of African-American history. Thumbnail images of period pictures – each image can be clicked to view an enlargement and historical caption - are included on a vertical timeline that evolves as visitors scroll down the page. To create the bar in this timeline, James Norris stretched a small image between each picture. This technique reduced the overall download time and allowed the timeline to follow the contours of the browser window, be it minimized or fullscreen.

Another problem that Norris faced related to the background tile image of the site which placed a dark field down the left side of the browser window. He struggled with "placing the elements exactly on the screen in a way in which they would display nicely over the background and also not be influenced by the width of the browser window. We used tables to achieve this, pushing the table with a transparent GIF over to the right side, so that the table wouldn't interfere with the background tile".

polygon with up to 100 sides. If you don't define a shape (CIRCLE, RECT, or POLY) with the SHAPE attribute, the browser will by default treat it as a rectangle.

Another attribute that can be used is TARGET, which is explained in detail in chapter Frames. It basically allows you to specify in which browser or frame window you want a linked document to be loaded.

There is also a NOHREF attribute, that specifies that no URL is loaded when a user clicks an area. This is used to "cut out" one shape from the other.

How to Set Up Server Side Image Maps

A server side image map always consists of two files: the image itself and the file with the image map. Define the image as a server side image map by including the attribute ISMAP into the IMG tag.

The second document contains the information about the hot spot areas and their links and is a plain text document. You need to ask your Internet Service Provider where to put the image map file on the server and which image map file type the Web server requires (i.e., NCSA or CERN). The map file needs the extension ".map" and make sure that the image is contained in an <A> tag that links to the location of the map file, for example: <A HREF="/cgi-bin/ navig.map"><IMG SRC="navig.gif" ISMAP></A>.

Background Tiles

By default, the color of the browser is set to gray, but, luckily, there are several ways to change this to create a better background for your website. The simplest is to set the background color, but you can also use an image as a background. Loading an image as a background, which can either be a JPEG or a GIF, is easy: just add BACKGROUND="image.gif" to the BODY tag. Once the image is loaded, it will be repeated to fill in the whole background of the browser. Because the image is in the background, you can place all your other images and text on top of it. This feature has inspired many Web designers and they have come up with really inventive ideas on how to play with the background (I will discuss those techniques later). If you use a background image, you should set also a background color with the BGCOLOR tag, because this ensures that your page at least looks similar to your idea, in case the image doesn't load for some reason.

Special Effects with the Background

Before frames were introduced to the HTML standard, many designers used the background feature to create a colored sidebar. To do this, create an image with a width of 1200 pixels (or even more) and color the left side of this image. The extreme width of the image is important, otherwise you will see the colored side repeated on the right side. The only way to avoid this is to give the image a width that is larger than the largest monitor. Even though those images are big, they compress very well, especially if they are saved as GIF. The GIF algorithm works well with large areas of the same color and those images still don't need more than 10–20

To create a colored sidebar, Christopher Stashuk used a background image. This image will be tiled by the browser to fill the background. To avoid the site visitor seeing the sidebar repeated on the right side, the background image needs to be wider than a 21-inch screen.

Two pages of the "Persistence of the Spirit" Web site, where you can see the tiling of the background.

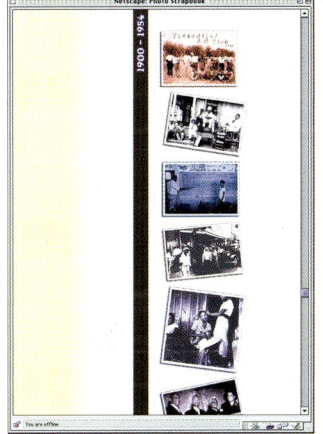

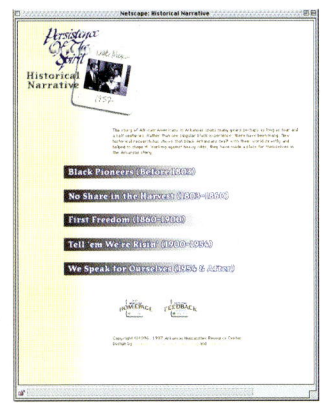

KByte. But keep in mind that those files, even though they compress very well, will be inflated to their real file size once they are loaded in the browser. The resulting memory overflow can cause a browser to crash. Another trick is to use an animated GIF as a background. Internet Explorer 3.0 and Netscape Communicator 4.0 – and this is a pretty new feature – display animated GIFs in the background. So far I haven't seen a Web site that has made use of this feature, but this is more because animated backgrounds weren't possible in the past. If you create something amazing, send me your URL and I will present your site in my next book. Also, let me know if you have used a transparent GIF as background in your site. Because it is possible to control the color of the browser background via JavaScript, you could use a texture with a transparent color and have the background changed. All the areas that are transparent will then display the background color of the browser.

THE PROBLEM OF THE BROWSER OFFSET

Aligning an image with a background image isn't as easy as you might think. The reason for this is that all browsers have an offset, and a picture placed in the upper left corner of your document might get displayed 10 pixels down and to the right. This offset varies with browser and platform. This makes it difficult to place a picture precisely over a background picture, something that would allow for some nice effects. Microsoft Explorer 3.0 allows you to set the offset to zero by including LEFTMARGIN="0" and TOPMARGIN="0" into the BODY tag. Unfortunately, other browsers don't understand this attribute. So if you really need to align an image with a background image, you might be able to fix the problem by writing a JavaScript that checks the browser and the version number and corrects the offset by placing an invisible placeholder in the document.

PRELOADING IMAGES

The more images you put on your page, the longer the download time. You don't need to be a scientist to figure that out. To solve this problem you could preload images, while the visitor is still occupied with reading the first page. One way of doing this would be by writing a JavaScript to tell the onLoad handler to trigger a function that starts loading the images into the cache of the browser. By the time the visitor clicks on the "Next" button, the next page will pop up very fast. But you can achieve the same result with a little HTML trick: just add to the first page some of the images for the following one. To make them almost invisible to the visitor, you scale them down to one pixel by using the HEIGTH and WIDTH attribute in the IMG tag. If you put these images at the very bottom of your page, they are almost unnoticeable to the viewer.

Oaklawn

Designer: Christopher Stashuk, HTML-Author: Nancy Mitchell

Oaklawn is a thoroughbred racetrack in Arkansas. They use their website as a way of posting up-to-the-minute flash results, scratches, and late changes as well as a downloadable daily program including past performances. "Notes & Quotes" gives the reader up-close and personal information about the horses, trainers, and jockeys as they prepare for the races. Visitors to the site are also able to choose from one of 21 electronic postcards that feature shots from Oaklawn, including images from Oaklawn's history, and send them to friends. There are numerous features in the site that are to most visitors not that obvious, like a CGI script that rotates the image on the mainpage each time it gets loaded. Once you click on one of the main sections, you enter a frame-based page, with all the main sections in a navigational bar in the left side frame and all the subsections in the bottom frame. Whenever you click on one of the main sections, a JavaScript changes both the main text page and the navigation for the subsection.

Another big and important task was to create a connection between the computer system at Oaklawn and the website. "We take information from the software that runs their racing office such as workouts and entries and funnel it to the Web, because timely information is important to horse racing fans," explains Nancy Mitchell about the underlying functionality of the site. "That type of information is ported to the Web only during their live season, but the site is fun to visit even in the off-season," says Nancy. "Oaklawn also has an online shopping system, where visitors can add items to their shopping cart and

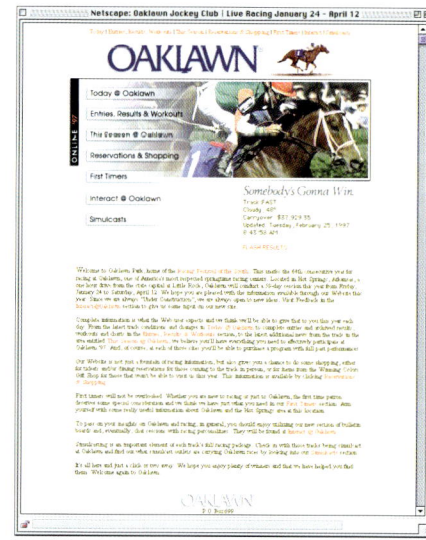

Hit "reload" on the main page to see eight versions of the masthead. Programming rotates the main image so repeat visitors get to see something new each time. The Oaklawn logo also rotates to match the main page image.

receive a cost total once they choose to complete their order."

When Oaklawn approached Aristotle to design the website, they were put under a lot of time pressure, recalls Nancy. "The site has an enormous amount of information, but we did it in less than a month. Getting the site organized was the biggest task. Once we outlined the structure of the site, everything became much easier."

For Oaklawn, the site, which crossed the one-million-hit mark two weeks before the end of the season, has become a great success. How you measure hits can differ from server to server, but "we count hits as how many HTML pages were downloaded. So the average person would look at about seventeen pages," says Nancy. At Aristotle they also keep track of what service the visitor is using when visiting the site. As it turned out, most people accessed it through America Online. "We try to give Oaklawn as much information on the statistics of the site as possible, because it affects their business. We found out, for example, that many people look at the site from work during their lunch break."

One of the eye catchers of the main page is actually a little GIF animation of a running horse. Creating this animation was quite a time consuming job for Christopher Stashuk: "We captured the horse from Beta-SP. Unfortunately the camera was panning while the horse was coming across the path of the camera. After the footage was digitized, I found the centerpoint of each frame – which was a point on the saddle – and repositioned each frame in sure registration. Because the footage of the horse was taped on an actual track, I hand-silhouetted each frame, removing all of the scene's background. However, I left a small portion of the ground underneath which gave the animation a visually supportive anchor." This animation became so popular that many people were downloading this animation and putting it on their personal homepages.

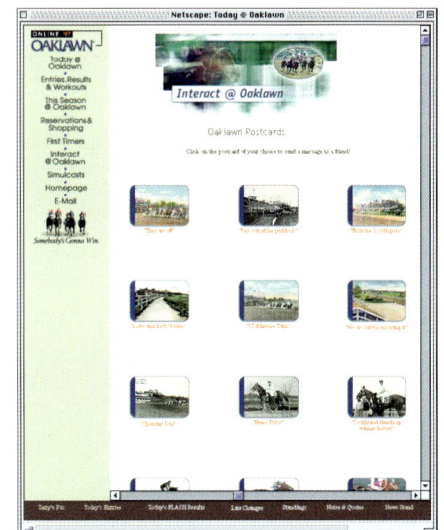

The Postcards section allows users to send a personalized electronic postcard to friends, including an animated postcard promoting the Oaklawn website. Select from one of 21 featured shots including images from Oaklawn's history dating back to an actual postcard from 1909.

The animated horse was developed using actual footage of a horse during a race at Oaklawn.

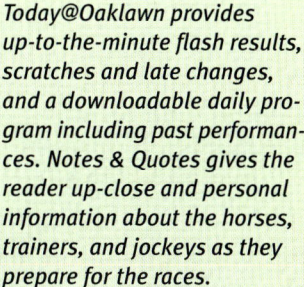

Today@Oaklawn provides up-to-the-minute flash results, scratches and late changes, and a downloadable daily program including past performances. Notes & Quotes gives the reader up-close and personal information about the horses, trainers, and jockeys as they prepare for the races.

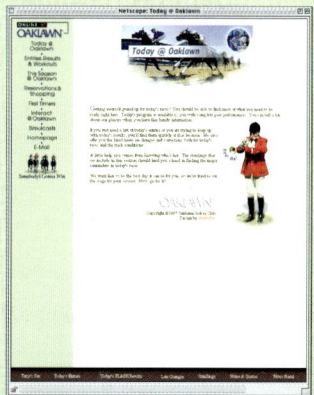

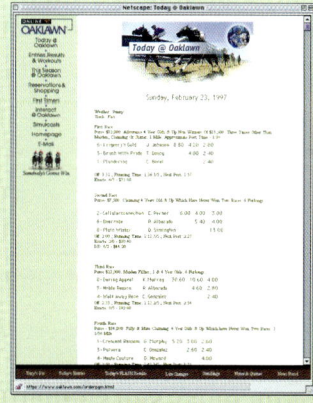

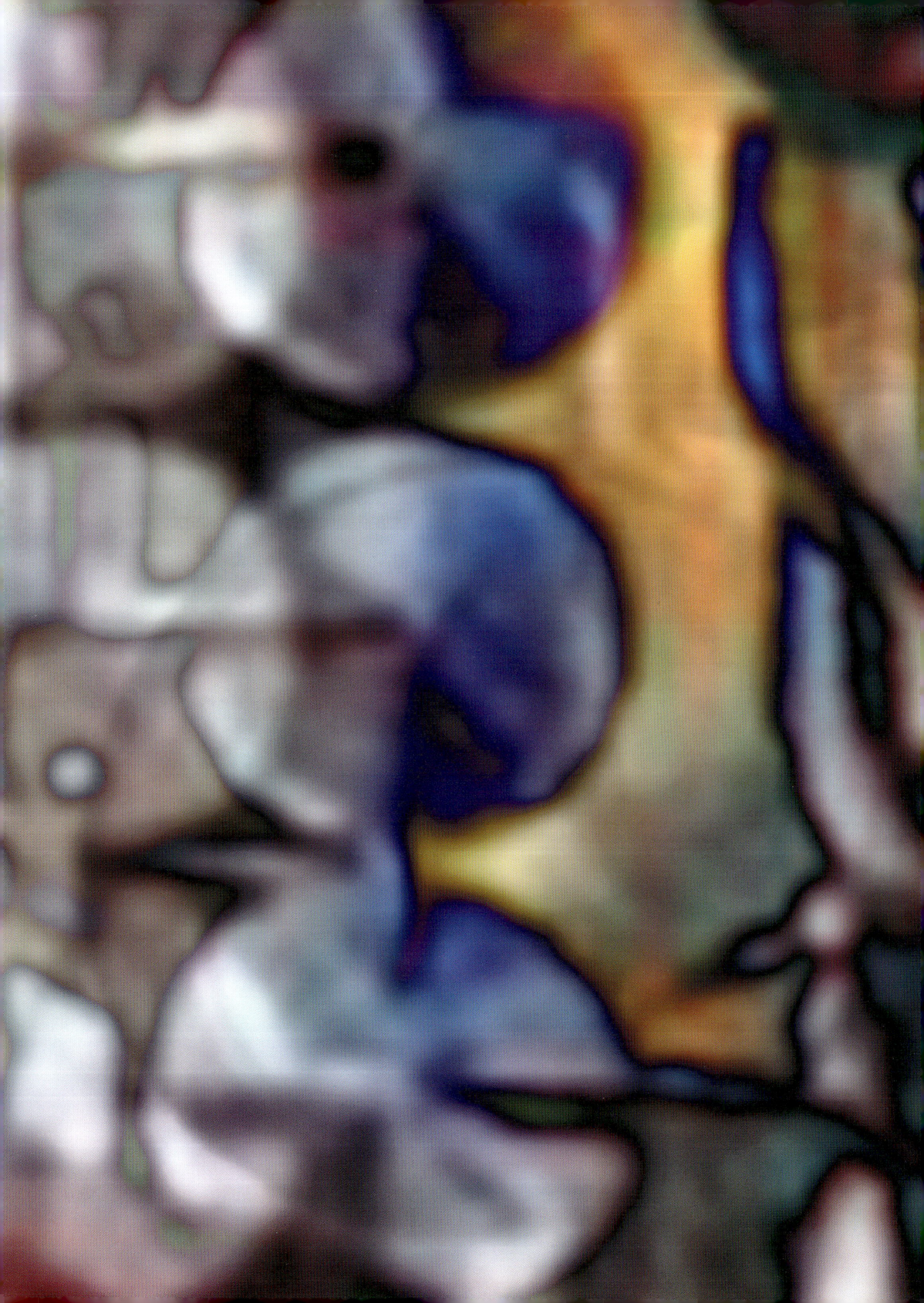

CHAPTER 04

Tables

This HTML extension is one of the most important for designers, because it allows you to have, at least, some control over what your page looks like. Tables can contain anything from text and sound to images (on which see the section Imagetable in this chapter) and, because the borders of a table can be made invisible and can be given a fixed width, most people use tables for layout purposes. Although the basic syntax of tables is very simple, using it can be a little confusing in the beginning, so let us now look at how HTML structures them.

```
<TABLE>
    <TR>
        <TD>1st cell</TD>
        <TD>2nd cell</TD>
    </TR>
</TABLE>
```

A basic table in HTML 04-01

All tables are described as rows into which you put tags for each cell you need. If you want a second row, you just add another row container to your table and include your cells again. The rows and cells are all put in a main wrapper, which is absolutely required, otherwise the table tags will be ignored. A simple table could look like in [04-01].

<TABLE ...></TABLE> is the main tag to create a table and the TR tag defines a table row. The number of rows in a table are specified by how many TR tags are within a TABLE tag. TD stands for table data and are the cells of the row. Before we get into the attributes that each tag can have, let us focus on setting up more complex tables [04-02].

This table consists of two rows, with two cells each. If you left out a cell in one of the rows, it would show up in your browser as a blank space, but we want to look into how to merge two cells.

With ROWSPAN you can create a cell that spans over the specified number of rows [05-03] (of course you can't exceed the maximum of rows you have defined).

As you can see from this example, a TD tag is dropped in the second row, because it is no longer needed. To merge the top two cells you would use the COLSPAN tag and drop the second cell in the first row [05-04].

Now that we have covered the basics of a table creation, let's get into the details of each tag.

```
<TABLE>
    <TR>
        <TD>Upper left cell</TD>
        <TD>Upper right cell</TD>
    </TR>
    <TR>
        <TD>Lower left cell</TD>
        <TD>Lower right cell</TD>
    </TR>
</TABLE>
```

A table with 2 cells 04-02

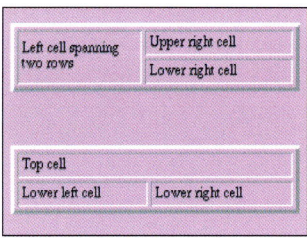

An example of tables with merged cells. To merge cells use the COLSPAN or ROWSPAN attribute. It is important to remember that the ROWSPAN attribute works only top to bottom and COLSPAN only left to right. So, for example, the ROWSPAN attribute needs to be placed in a cell in a top row.

Tables in Navigator 4.0
Netscape has changed (and fixed) the table implementation in Navigator 4.0 and also improved table layout performance. To take advantage of this improved layout performance, you should specify how many columns are in the table as an attribute of the table tag: ‹TABLE COLS=n›.

```
<TABLE>
    <TR>
        <TD ROWSPAN="2">Left cell
        spanning two rows</TD>
        <TD>Upper right cell</TD>
    </TR>
    <TR>
        <TD>Lower right cell</TD>
    </TR>
</TABLE>
```

The ROWSPAN attribute 04-03

THE TABLE TAGS AND ATTRIBUTES

‹TABLE ...›‹/TABLE›: All the other table tags need to be placed between these tags. By adding the BORDER attribute after the start tag, you can control the thickness of the table border. To set the border of your table, type in BORDER ="value", with "value" representing a number of pixels. A value of zero will make the border invisible. You can set the size of your table with the WIDTH= "value_or_percentage" and the HEIGHT ="value" attribute. The value is measured as an absolute value in pixels, with the exception of the width of your table, which can be specifed to be a percentage of the document window. If you don't set values for these attributes the browser will set them automatically. CELLSPACING="value" controls the width of the cell border, and you can make your cell borders look really heavy by using a high value. While CELLSPACING controls the thickness of the border, CELLPADDING="value" sets the amount of space between the contents of the cell and the border. The most compact table is created with this setting: ‹TABLE BORDER=0 CELLSPACING=0 CELLPADDING=0›

‹CAPTION ...›‹/CAPTION›: To create a caption for your table you need to place it outside of any TR, TD, or TH tag. So it is

```
<TABLE>
    <TR>
        <TD COLSPAN="2">
        Top cell</TD>
    </TR>
    <TR>
        <TD>Lower left cell</TD>
        <TD>Lower right cell</TD>
    </TR>
</TABLE>
```

The COLSPAN attribute 04-04

best placed after the TABLE tag. By default the text inside the tag will appear on top of your table. To have the caption under the table, insert ALIGN="bottom" as an attribute to the tag. The caption text is always horizontally centered, but you could align it to the left or right side of the table by placing ‹P ALIGN="left, right"› before the text (inside the ‹CAPTION ...›‹/CAPTION› tags).

‹TR ...›‹/TR›: The table row tag wraps all the TH and TD tags. To add another table row, you simply add another TR tag. If you put any VALIGN or ALIGN attributes into the TR tag, they will act as the default setting for all cells in that row. Possible values for VALIGN are "top, middle, bottom, baseline" and for ALIGN "left, center, right".

‹TD..›‹/TD› and ‹TH...›‹/TH›: For the standard table data you use the TD tag. Every table row needs to have the same number of cells. If you use the ROWSPAN="value" attribute to connect two cells, keep in mind that this cell counts as two cells in the next row. While ROWSPAN connects two cells horizontally, COLSPAN="value" is used to create a cell that spans over two (or more) cells vertically.

The cell contents can be formatted like any other text and can be aligned vertically and horizontally by using

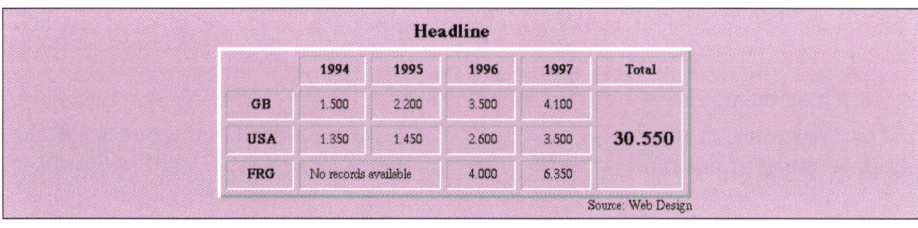

```
<HTML>
    <HEAD>
        <TITLE>Example for a table</TITLE>
    </HEAD>
<BODY BGCOLOR="#CC99CC" LINK="#ff0000" ALINK="#0033ff">

<TABLE WIDTH="450" BORDER="3" CELLSPACING="5" CELLPADDING="5">
    <CAPTION ALIGN="BOTTOM"><P ALIGN=RIGHT>Source: Web Design</CAPTION>
    <TR>
        <TD WIDTH="16%"></TD>
        <TH WIDTH="16%">1994</TH>
        <TH WIDTH="17%">1995</TH>
        <TH WIDTH="17%">1996</TH>
        <TH WIDTH="17%">1997</TH>
        <TH WIDTH="17%">Total</TH>
    </TR>
    <TR>
        <TH>GB</TH>
        <TD><P><CENTER>1.500</CENTER></TD>
        <TD><P><CENTER>2.200</CENTER></TD>
        <TD><P><CENTER>3.500</CENTER></TD>
        <TD><P><CENTER>4.100</CENTER></TD>
        <TD ROWSPAN="3"><H2><CENTER>30.550</CENTER></H2></TD>
    </TR>
    <TR>
        <TH>USA</TH>
        <TD><P><CENTER>1.350</CENTER></TD>
        <TD><P><CENTER>1.450</CENTER></TD>
        <TD><P><CENTER>2.600</CENTER></TD>
        <TD><P><CENTER>3.500</CENTER></TD>
    </TR>
    <TR>
        <TH>FRG</TH>
        <TD COLSPAN="2">No records available</TD>
        <TD><P><CENTER>4.000</CENTER></TD>
        <TD><P><CENTER>6.350</CENTER></TD>
    </TR>
</TABLE>
</BODY>
</HTML>
```

A complete HTML code with a TABLE 04-05

ALIGN="left, center, right" and VALIGN ="top, middle, bottom, baseline". By default the alignment is left and middle and usually the text in a cell is broken up, to fit within the overall cell width. To prevent a line from breaking, use the NOWRAP attribute in the TD tag.

TH stands for table header and is basically identical to data cells. The only difference from TD is that the cell text is always in bold font and has as the default ALIGN="center".

A great new feature is the ability to set a background color for individual cells by adding BGCOLOR="#value" to a TD or TH tag. The color is defined as an RGB color like all other color definitions in HTML (for example BGCOLOR= "#FF0000" is bright red).

It is possible to create blank cells without inner borders. To achieve this make sure there is nothing between the ‹TD›‹/TD› tags. If you want to display an empty cell with borders, put in either a non-breaking space (‹TD› ‹/TD›) or a blank line (‹TD›‹BR›‹/TD›).

BACKGROUND COLOR AND IMAGES

Microsoft implemented some very useful extensions to the table tag in Internet Explorer 3.0 , such as the ability to color the background of a table cell or use a background image for cells, that Netscape Communicator 4.0 is now able to interpret. With BGCOLOR="#nnnnnn" (where nnnnnn is a hexadecimal value) you can set the color of the entire table or of an individual cell, depending on where you place the attribute. For the entire table this attribute must be placed in the TABLE tag, but for an individual cell, in the TD tag. The same principle applies to the BACKGROUND= "name.gif" attribute, that loads an image and places it either in all the cells or only in a single one. Internet Explorer can even color the table borders with the attributes BORDERCOLOR, BORDERCOLORLIGHT, and BORDERCOLORDARK. These attributes must be in the TABLE tag, to work correctly. Netscape Navigator 4.0 can interpret the BORDERCOLOR attribute.

IMAGETABLE

The implementation of tables in HTML has been one of the major steps towards enhancing the design of web sites. Because tables can be made invisible they can be used to position images and text, align forms and create imagetables. Imagetables is a technique in which a larger image is split up into smaller pieces, and put together again in a table to make them look like one big image. This technique is such a

Loading background images into cells and setting the color for border and cells is a nice feature first introduced by Explorer 3.0.

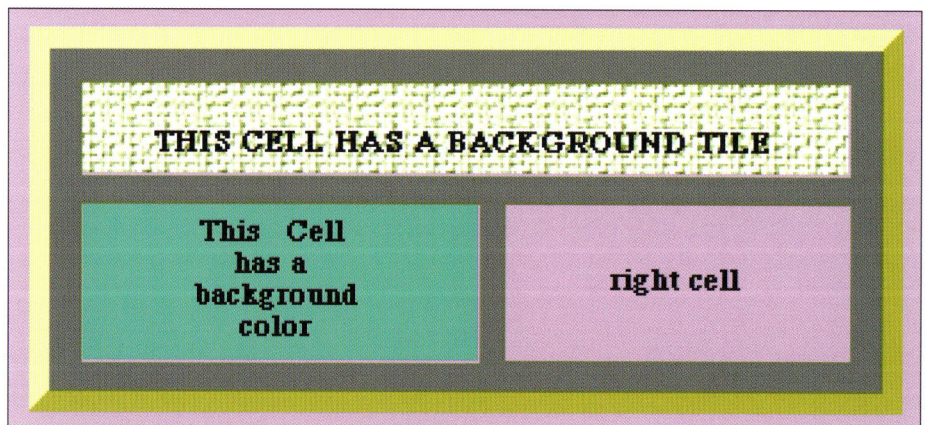

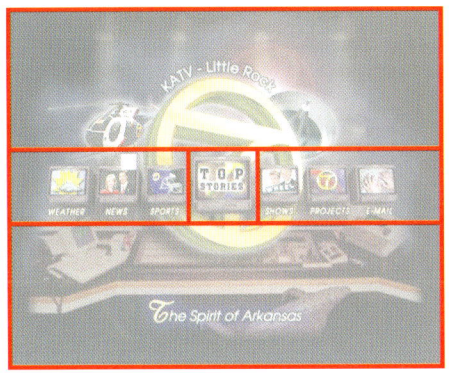

The KATV and the B-98.5 pages use GIF animations in combination with regular images. To the visitor of the site it appears as one large image. This technique is especially helpful, if you want to combine several animations that run parallel: On the B-98.5 homepage are three individual animations, and even though it would be possible to simulate a parallel animation with GIF, it is hardly practical.

great tool to create some advanced designs that it deserves its own section.

A very good presentation of how they can be used for your interface design is the home page of Studio Archetype, a design company in San Francisco. The main page of their homepage looks like one image, but is, instead, composed of several elements. The great thing about their concept is that every time you click a button it brings you to that page and the pushed button in the navigation bar gets exchanged with another image of an engrossed button. This concepts kills two birds with one stone: it doesn't need an image map to process the user input and, also, because only the image of the clicked button needs to be loaded, the next page quickly appears on the user's screen.

Imagetables also come in handy to combine animation with still images. For example, if you would like to have a large image but want to have only part of that image be animated, imagetables allow you to splice up the large image and create animation only in that area and then put everything together again. A good example of this is the radio station B98.5 homepage, designed by Christopher Stashuk of Aristotle. What appears to be one large animation is in fact composed of several little animated segments along with still images (for more on how he created the animation read the chapter Animation).

continues on page 72

Three examples for an image table: Studio Archetypes home page looks very much like a CD-ROM interface – everything is within the constraint of a rectangle. Even though it appears to be one large image, the main page is actually split up in several smaller units that are placed in a table. Any button on the page is a single image with its own link. When the user clicks on one of them, it connects to the corresponding page which uses the same navigation bar, but exchanges the image of the regular button with an image of a pressed button. The buttons are all placed in table cells and enclosed with an ‹A› tag. By default, all images that are enclosed in a link get a colored border. This border can be hidden by setting the border attribute to zero (BORDER="0").

The Sports section features top sports stories of the previous day. It also displays anchor bios, information and game schedules for the Arkansas Razorbacks, the ASU Indians, and the UALR Trojans.

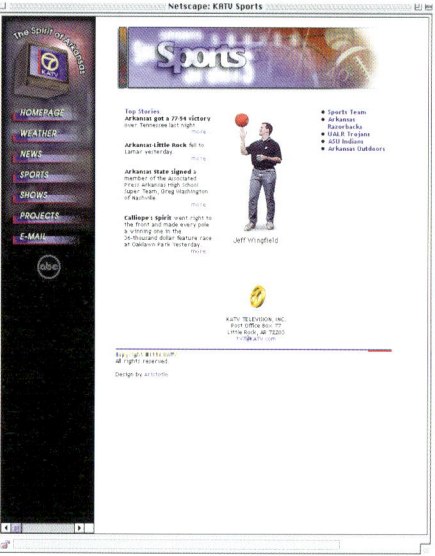

KATV

Designer: Christopher Stashuk
HTML Author: Dina Crane

When KATV Channel 7 began the planning to create a website, Dina Crane and Christopher Stashuk were faced with the challenge that KATV's competitor, KARK was already online. "So our main goal was basically to top their site. A nice compliment we got recently is that KARK revived their website and it looks suspiciously like the Channel 7 website. So they obviously liked what they saw," says Dina Crane. The KATV site features a marquee with the daily weather forecast and also a live picture from one of KATV's weather cameras that faces the downtown area. The live picture is updated every 10 minutes.

The Shows section automatically displays what is airing that night on KATV. There are many other features that make the KATV site a good example of how a

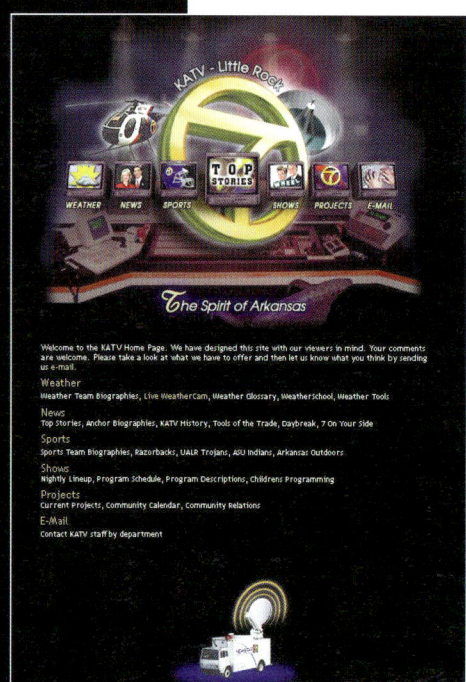

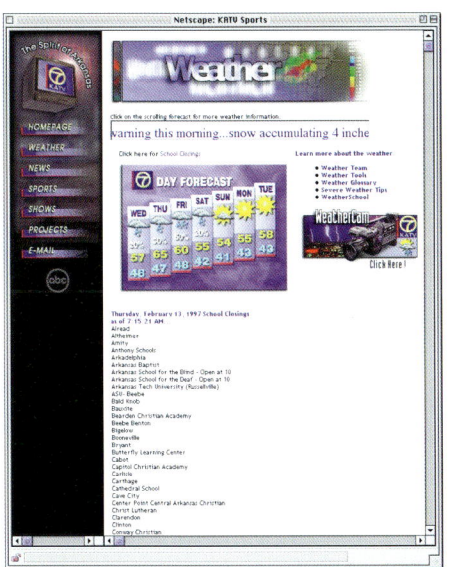 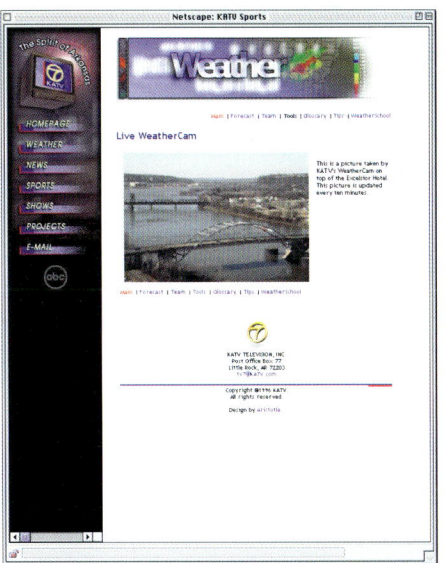

The Weather section contains a live WeatherCam photo updated every 10 minutes, a scrolling marquee of the daily forecast, and a 7-day forecast graphic. New to the weather section is an automatically updated radar image.

television station can provide good customer service through the Internet.

The Aristotle design team is constantly improving the site and its services. Dina Crane and Christopher Stashuk, the art designer, have recently finished work "on a new version of the site in which we made some key changes, like removing a link or bringing popular subsections like 'DayBreak' and 'Seven on Your Side' to the forefront, by making them their own section." The fact that those structural changes were necessary became clear after checking the statistics of the site. "We are monitoring every site on our server to see how many hits every page gets. This gives us the information we need to improve the structure of the site," says Dina. Important to her was realizing "that people were bookmarking interior pages," because this has an direct impact on the information architecture of a site. "We use the main page to inform the visitor about new things and contents, but if the visitor bookmarks interior pages, the whole concept is undermined. Now we are putting the contest page on the main page to make sure that people always visit the main page. This way we make sure that people don't bypass the latest information that KATV wants to present."

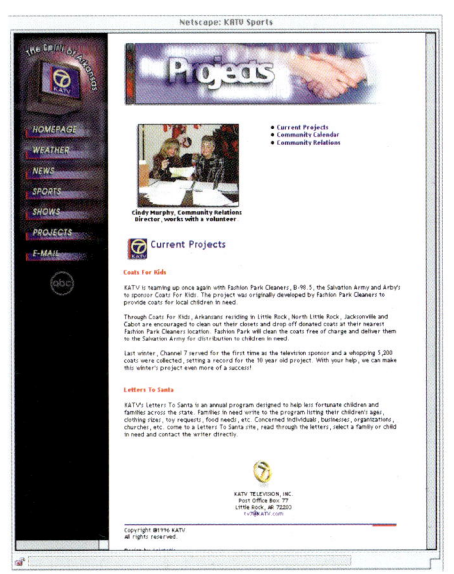

Seven On Your Side contains information on KATV's popular segment featuring: RipOff of the Week, Scam Alert, Case Files, and information on local volunteer programs.

Avoid extra space between the tags:
```
<TD>
<IMG SRC="url">
</TD>
```
Write the code like this:
```
<TD><IMG SRC="url"></TD>
```

The imagetable pitfall 04-06

Make sure that the source code of the table looks like the second example, to ensure that there is no gap between the images.

THE IMAGETABLE PITFALL

To use a table as an imagetable set the BORDER, the CELLSPACING and the CELLPADDING attributes to zero in the TABLE tag. Place the images in the cells, which are represented by the TD tag, calculate the entire width and height of the table and put that information in the WIDTH and HEIGTH attribute of the TABLE tag. Usually that should do it, but when you view your image table in a browser, be ready for a surprise: the images might not align and might have a gap between them. The bug fix is very simple: make sure that the IMG tag follows directly after the TD tag.

In PageMill 2.0 you need to load the saved page into a browsers to see the final result. PageMill 2.0 always displays the images with some additional space between them even though the border is set to zero. Also, delete the space character that PageMill automatically puts into every cell.

THE NOBR ALTERNATIVE

You don't always need to use tables; you can also use the NOBR tag. The NOBR tag is usually used to ensure that a line of text is not wrapped when the viewing of the browser does not allow the display of everything. With the NOBR tag, which is short for "no break", you can make sure that a certain phrase extends beyond the limits of the browser window and that the user has to scroll instead. Luckily this tag also works with images and all you need to do is to place all the images between the starting and end tag [04-07]. It is important that the images are all in the same paragraph, otherwise the browser adds more space between them. If you are using PageMill to create your page, shift-return will put the cursor on a new line without creating a new paragraph.

Now the question remains, what are the advantages and disadvantages of both approaches?

With the NOBR tag you can easily create an "Image table" that even a Netscape 1.1 browser will display correctly, even though it is very unlikely that you need to create a Web page that is so far backward compatible.

The disadvantage is that you can place the images only in horizontal rows, as opposed to a real table where each cell functions as a column in which you can put several images one under another.

```
<P><NOBR><IMG SRC="url"><IMG SRC="url"></NOBR><BR>
<NOBR><IMG SRC="url"><IMG SRC="url"></NOBR></P>
```

The NOBR tag 04-07

In this table are <P> tags, thus adding unwanted space between the images:

```
<TABLE WIDTH="129" HEIGHT="81" BORDER="0" CELLSPACING="0" CELLPADDING="0">
    <TR>
        <TD>
        <P><IMG SRC="url"></P>
        <P><IMG SRC="url"></P>
        </TD>
        <TD>
        <P><IMG SRC="url"></P>
        <P><IMG SRC="url"></P>
        </TD>
    </TR>
</TABLE>
```

This is a correct example of how to place several images in a table cell, which are separated by a BR tag:

```
<TABLE WIDTH="100" HEIGHT="81" BORDER="0" CELLSPACING="0" CELLPADDING="0">
    <TR>
        <TD>
        <IMG SRC="url" ><BR>
        <IMG SRC="url">
        </TD>
        <TD>
        <IMG SRC="url"><BR>
        <IMG SRC="url" >
        </TD>
    </TR>
</TABLE>
```

HTML Frame Code 04-08

Studio Archetype

Interview with Clement Mok & Mark Crumpacker

The Studio Archetype Web Site was designed by Mark Crumpacker and he wanted it to be an example of very straightforward navigation. It is designed to be part of their presentation tool to their clients and he uses it to explain what parallel navigation, global navigation, and local navigation are.

The basic concept behind the site is to enable a global navigation with buttons on top of every page, and to have content surfacing on the homepage to allow visitors to bring up what they think is interesting at that time.

Studio Archetype, based in San Francisco, is one of the most well known Web Design Agencies in America. Among their clients are major software companies like Adobe and IBM, but they also have gained much publicity through projects like 24 hours in Cyberspace which wrote Web history. I spoke with Clement Mok, the founder of Studio Archetype, and Mark Crumpacker, the creative director, about information architecture on the Web.

Studio Archetype started out as a traditional advertising agency, but in recent years it has changed its main focus to the electronic media, especially Web design. How has that change impacted the way you do business?

Clement Mok: When we started with Web design, we already had been doing a lot of CD-ROM projects. At that time we did not have any programmer on our staff, only Lingo specialists. Today around 65% of our business is electronic and the rest is still print. What has significantly changed are the core skills of our employees. Of our 90 people only 40 are really designers, the rest are programmers for Java, or JavaScript or are HTML code warriors.

Mark Crumpacker: We used to have two divisions: we had print and we had interactive. After a while we got rid of that idea, because part of our philosophy is that design is design and it is not discipline specific. It is also easier to attract good designers that way and it is just

more fun having everybody doing everything, because they like the variety. So we broke it up and created one group.

So do you actually see a relationship between print design and online design?

Clement Mok: It depends on what part of the equation you are looking at. I look at it in two distinct ways: communication design, selling a product or articulating something that is of value in a brochure, and product design, where you create the actual product. In the online world there are not such clear distinctions yet, but there are certain parallels between the analog and the digital universes that require a similar mind set and similar thinking. The analog product world is all about creating value. If you now go into the digital world and start to look at an online product, you have to start looking what you can do to enhance the online product or service. So it is important to see that these two worlds have different requirements.

One of the different requirements is certainly that you structure information differently in the online world due to the fact that you have hyperlinks and interactivity. Is this the reason, why you now call yourself information architects?

Clement Mok: We redefined ourselves as information architects because what we are doing is similar to what architects do. A good architect doesn't just design a building, he also looks at all aspects of the location, like the surrounding area or the traffic patterns of the streets; he looks at behaviors and where people go. Architects create great open places in contrast to intimate small areas. The approach to Web design should be similar, like having very large public spaces on one hand as well as very small intimate places. It is important to reproduce this diversity in the digital world.

Mark Crumpacker: In 1995 there was great confusion about what a Web site was and people were thinking about them as if they were a brochure. The convention of pages was a common metaphor to describe the Web and when the sites became larger and more complicated the need surfaced to map these in some way. This is what we call information architecture, basically taking the desired content and organizing it in a logical way. In a lot of cases it takes the form of a printed map and diagram, which we use very often. But now where Web sites have become more and more like software and less like brochures, the information architecture becomes even more complicated. The diagrams have become much more like software plans.

Still, information architecture seems to me a little bit abstract. Can you give me an example how you applied that to a web site?

Mark Crumpacker: A good example would be 24 hours in Cyberspace. The goal was to create a snapshot of a day in cyberspace and it would show how the Internet is changing the life of people all over the globe. We had photographers and writers who would send in their pictures and stories from all continents and we would create the site within a day. That was really a huge volume of information which needed to be orga-

On Studio Archetype's website you find links to projects and clients of Studio Archetype.

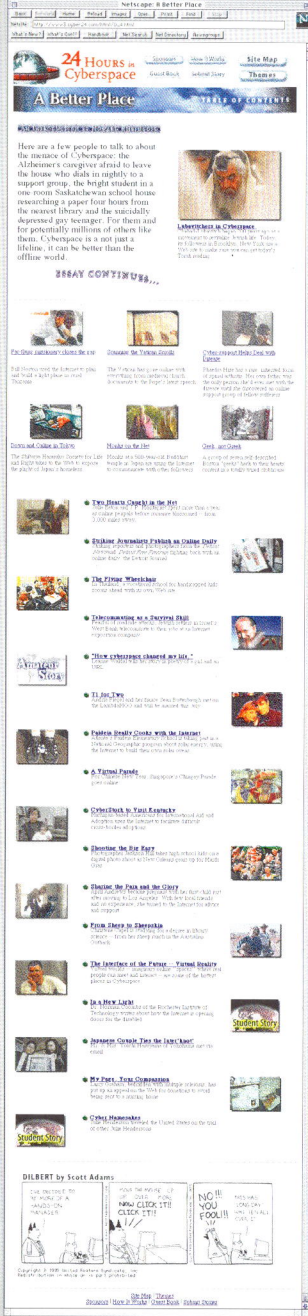

These are screens from the original concept for 24 hours in Cyberspace.

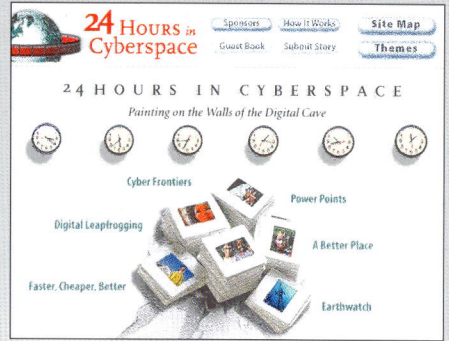

nized in a systematic way. So we went through the information and identified a variety of different page types, from which we created several templates for the pages. Then when the content came in it would be tagged as a particular type of content and then we used the appropriate template.

So basically what you are saying is that classifying the content is Information Architecture?

Mark Crumpacker: That's at least a big part of it. A lot of what we do in Information Architecture is to group similar types of content. When we redesigned the Adobe Web site, we looked at their existing one which had 14 different main categories and we set a goal of having only six categories on the home page. We worked with them on how to group existing types of content together, to make it easier for the visitor to navigate. For example, they made a distinction 'Graphic Design Products' and 'Prepress Products'. We argued that to a designer and user those could easily be the same and could be grouped together to avoid confusion. In the end we reduced the fourteen categories to eight. We didn't quite get the six, but we at least got from fourteen to eight.

Clement Mok: Structuring the information is really the main part of Information Architecture. One of the things that I have been doing in the last two years is explaining to our clients that the Web is not like other engagements that you usually hire design firms. Just because it is displayed in a Web browser, doesn't mean it is like print media. Web design as well as multimedia design has a whole new dimension to it and I have spent a lot of time formulizing the design principles of this new media.

One of the most fascinating things that I realize in this quick developing industry is that the quality of that structuring process is proportional to the quality of the site you end up with. Another aspect of Information Architecture is to design the whole experience that the visitor will have. The American Express website that we created consists of only six main screens, but it took us almost six months to work on. What we were designing was the experience of going through that website. Web design is not just about pages and categories, it is about activities and there is a fundamental change now with websites. Now you create more of an experience for the participant.

Like you were mentioning earlier, that as an architect you create diversity to enrich the experience!?

Clement Mok: Yes, that is right. Web design is not only about pretty graphics! It is about how you can structure the idea and make the website work very effi-

76 Studio Archetype

ciently. If you look at website development it consists of four layers: communication Ddesign, which is for most of the people just simply advertising and it's the thing that we all know from the world of print. Secondly, information design, which is a fancy word for the understanding of structure. Thirdly the graphical user interface, and the fourth piece of the equation is the programming of a site.

So let me ask you then, what is good information architecture to you and what is bad information architecture?

Mark Crumpacker: There are many sites that are clearly architectured in terms of the information, but – and this is typically true for a lot of corporate websites – what happens is that they had been architectured around the divisions of the company. Motorola used to be a good example of that. Their company is broken up into divisions of people working in different cities and they organized their web site that way. But just because cell phones and pagers are seen in different divisions in a company, to a consumer they are both mobile communication. So from an information architecture point of view I see it rather architectured together than split up in different sections. A customer doesn't care if the cellular division is in Texas and the beeper division in Illinois, he wants to communicate when he is on the road. So I think, bad Information Architecture takes into account preexisting structures that are not based around what the user wants.

Clement Mok: A recent project that we have completed was for UPS. They have a website with thousands of pages but at the same time had the challenge not only to manage the maintenance of the site, but also to prevent people from getting lost. When we started to look at it, we realized that the problem was in the structure. It was organized by categories but instead, you start to look at the user model and ask, what are the activities that you want the costumer to engage with? Customers want to go to UPS to track a package, do cost calculation, find out where to drop off a package and call in to schedule a pick up. And essentially what we did was to cluster the website around those specific functions. After we launched the new version, the amount of phone calls to UPS dropped by about 20%, which we believe is a direct result of the redesign.

It seems that this is a common pitfall of information architecture. Do you see any other common mistakes that companies make on their website?

Mark Crumpacker: Often companies are unclear as to what they want to accomplish with their website. The Internet

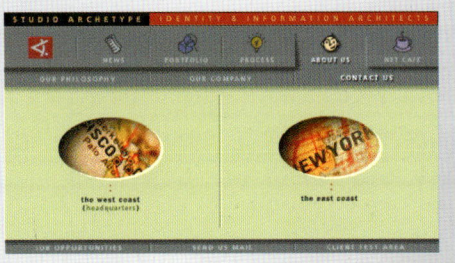

Studio Archetype started out originally as Clement Mok Designs. After renaming the company they also opened an office in New York to server their East coast clients.

THE IBM WEB SITE

Mark Crumpacker: *The intention was to create a page which really felt like IBM and would make an editorial contribution to the world of computing. In the past, their website was basically eight different links to the sections of their company, but we changed that to create something that we call content surfacing. This is where we take one lead story that basically changes every week and you see there a different graphic every week. Then there is another little section for two other news stories. Now when you come to the site, rather then just having eight links, you get a feeling about what IBM is involved in and the links to the different sections are less prominent. So we traded graphics for the eight different sections for IBM making a statement about computing and how it is affecting the world.*

Clement Mok: *With IBM we faced the challenge of coming up with a concept for 120 000 pages. So how do you get your hands around such a large amount of pages, without hiring an army of people? Part of what we did was to install dynamic database publishing, which, to many people, has the stigma of all type and ugly. But it doesn't have to be. What we were trying to do, together with the company called Dynamic Diagram, was to create a context for the information. Instead of just organizing things alphabetically we looked at how to create a dynamic mask, that is where Dynamic Diagram came in.*

Studio Archetype

THE TEN WEB SITE

Mark Crumpacker: When that client came to us and asked us to do their website I went to their existing website and I literally spent fifteen minutes on their site to figure out what this company did. Eventually I figured out that they sold games, and after a little more exploration I figured out they sold games that you can play on the Internet. But I was never able to figure out if those games are for Macintosh or for Windows or how I could get one. They are a software company that sells games that you can play over the Internet, and it's all Windows software. Our objective was to be very very clear on exactly what it is, how you get it, how much it costs and how you actually use it. We did it by using a concept of an underground world where these people live in the sewers. When you go to this site it starts with a manhole cover and they are pirating electricity. You click on the manhole cover and then go down to their world. The first thing you see is a little blinking object that says Start Here. You click on it and it tells you what it is and how to download it and how much it costs and how you play it. We wanted a straightforward interface that gives you the touch and feel of a game.

has been something that has been very difficult for people to identify what the direct benefit to their company is. For a company who distributes software it has been very apparent, for a company who doesn't it might be difficult to figure out. Originally Toyota got a lot of criticism of their website, because they had built a website where they tried to make a cultural statement. There was this whole Jazz section on their site and people where really confused on what Jazz had to do with Toyota. I believe that

Toyota wanted to create content to draw people to their site and I think this is a common mistake: companies believe they have to add this magic word called content to their site to bring people in. People certainly look for content on a company page, but they are looking more for information that relates to the products of the company.

Clement Mok: Another mistake is that they think, let's make some money on the Web. But nobody is really making money on it, because there is no real structure for that. What they overlook is that the web is a great tool to increase productivity. And right now that is the best thing that the Internet can do.

Mark Crumpacker: Have you seen the Ragu Sauce website (www.ragu.com)? It is a site that has won awards. It is a very odd Web site and it basically just talks about eating. People think it is fun, but clearly people are not going to order tomato sauce over the Web. So the ultimate question is, is this the kind of thing that is going to get people to buy more tomato sauce? I don't know the answer, because the companies we work with have more mission-critical problems to solve, like UPS, were we enabled their customers to track their packages and to schedule a pickup. That are direct tangible benefits to the user and those are the kinds of problems we are really interested in solving.

Well, it seems that everybody is eager to get onto the Web in the hopes of increasing revenues. How do you think the Web is going to change the way we do business?

Mark Crumpacker: Only certain companies will figure out how to make the Web a part of their ongoing business and to tie in their presence on the Web to what they are actually doing. I think it will become kind of a bottom line demand of people to have direct access to those companies and sort of skip the retail step in between. This will then force a lot of companies to become much more customer focused. Companies like Intel – which we do a lot of work for – hadn't been a company that sold a lot of stuff directly to the end user. They didn't have a lot of responsibility for their products with the consumer, because they make chips and those go directly into a computer which is made by some other manufacturer which is sold by a retailer. The consumer first sees the retailer and that is their first point of contact. If they then have any questions or issues they would next go to the computer manufacturer, but Intel was even a third step removed from the end user. If there is a problem with a chip or if people have questions, they now went directly to Intel and Intel had to take a look at how they handle those customers. Now, because the customers had this direct line of access to them, Intel had to rethink how they responded to e-mails from customers and shift the focus of the company. Because of the Internet they are not quite so removed anymore.

Are there any more mistakes that you see?

Mark Crumpacker: Another mistake is that many of those companies that go online haven't placed any infrastructure in their company to deal with the actual interaction that they are asking for. So e-mails go unanswered or information on the site is not updated or has been incorrect. Consumers are not willing to accept those kind of things for too long. We have turned down projects in the past because the client wasn't putting in place the proper infrastructure to create the content for the site besides they were underestimating what the demand would be. Very often companies don't realize how much work it actually is to keep a site maintained.

Advertising on the Internet is a big business and is growing constantly. How do you think advertising on the web is going to change?

Mark Crumpacker: We look at advertising as the banners that you pay for to draw people to your site. Those little banner ads are not the most compelling advertisings and I think it is much more interesting when companies sponsor websites.

Clement Mok: Future Web design will be much more participatory, with new ways to engage the visitor. We have to redefine the whole notion of advertising: instead of getting your attention, to holding your attention. If you look at advertising in television how it was done years ago, it was basically just sponsorships. The Comedy Hour sponsored by General Electric was a different model of how to do branding and advertising.

Mark Crumpacker: Have you seen the website You don't know Jack? It is a little trivia game that is very well done and that you can download for free. What happens is that you play this game for few minutes and then the game stops and basically a TV commercial comes on, although it is mostly text due to the bandwidth. But that commercial takes over your whole screen and then it allows

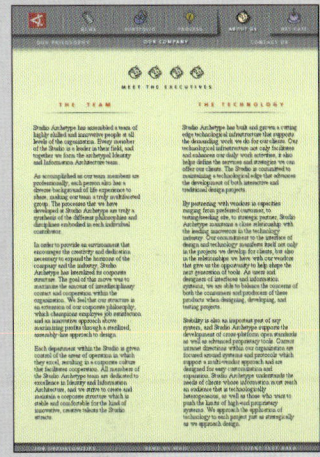

Top: Some background information on Studio Archetype in the "About us" section.

Bottom: Another screen from the Cyberhour.

STUDIO ARCHETYPE — IDENTITY & INFORMATION ARCHITECT

NEWS · PORTFOLIO · PROCESS · ABOUT US · NET CAFE

THE ADOBE WEBSITE

Mark Crumpacker: Adobe is a software company with many products for the graphic designer community. Our basic philosophy in the design of this site was to kind of be all things to all people. If you are coming into the site and you are looking for particular information, like you want to know what the latest version of Adobe Illustrator is, you are able to come into the site and within two clicks you could see a link to the Illustrator page and there are no big graphics in your way. But if you are a designer and you would like to look into the gallery section of the site then you will see more graphics and a more rich-looking environment. So we created different paths based on what we thought people would most like to do in the site. So if you go in the website and click on products, the next screen you would see would be all text with links to all the applications. If you would go into the site and click on the studio section the first thing you would see is a nice photocollage image. We try to create different kinds of experiences for different kinds of people.

you to go back to the game. So it is much more like television all of a sudden.

I think that is a pretty interesting way of doing advertising on the web. People really want to play that game so they sit through the commercials.

Isn't it ironic, that we finally end up again with TV commercials? Anyway, I would like to come back a little bit to Interface design, because this is an important aspect of Web design. How do you think the Graphical User Interface for websites is going to change?

Mark Crumpacker: I think web design will become much more like application design and right now it is very often just a simple metaphor of pages that is very conventional and where you hop from one place to another. But with the new extensions to HTML, there is the opportunity to make something much more like a CD-ROM, where your whole experience is within one screen and you never get the sensation that you hop to another page, you just draw different content onto your screen. The effect of that is that you have to be good at designing interfaces that people understand, because you are trying to put much more information in a smaller area and it becomes an application development problem instead of a 'layout of individual pages' problem. I think that people who are really experienced in user centered interface design will be the ones who are really good at it and it will become increasingly difficult for designers who are coming from print to catch on.

Clement Mok: I think even a step further and could imagine three dimensional spaces like virtual reality. An Interface where you walk through a virtual world and hear ambient noises and see information in a three dimensional way. Something that just would enrichen the experience of being online instead of looking at flat pages.

... which reminds me of Tikkiland, a virtual world at the MTV Online site, where you can walk through a scenery and meet other people like in a chat room. Mark, you were saying that you think that designers that come from print will find it more and more difficult to catch on, simply because Interface design will become more and more important. I am curious as to your point of view on what you think is good interface design?

Mark Crumpacker: It's all again based on usability and how intuitive it is to the user. What we are looking for are basic user interaction metaphors that are widely understood by people. We can look at existing type of applications to see what are the conventions and then try to reuse those same kinds of conventions.

I think what is also very important in good interface design is to ensure that the interface works for every possible visitor. When we design an interface we try to accommodate every possible scenario that the user could go through and actually go through a process where we try to break our design. We design them to fit 480 by 640 screen environments and then we decide which modem speed and how many colors the potential visitor might be using. Then we try

to break the design and look at what kind of frustration the user might have and then fix those things.

I see a lot of sites that are designed for screens that are very big or that are too advanced, working only with Netscape and Shockwave and you are wondering how many people can actually see that. Or another thing is that designers do really tricky things with the Interface and then expect the user to understand what they mean, but they don't.

It seems that you do a lot of beta testing to check usability?

Mark Crumpacker: We do a lot of beta testing here ourselves where we just put people in front of the screen who have never seen the site before and watch how they interact. The basic scenario is that we create a prototype and then we give the user a task to find a place in this application, videotape them and then check how long and how many moves it takes them to find that information. Then we start reducing things from there.

When we go into a focus group, we do different kinds of testing. We test if what we have built is what the visitor expected and if it is appropriate, based on what their expectation of that company is. It is important to us to find out if they are surprised at the way the information was presented.

And then there is a third type of testing, which is our Quality Assurance, where we try it on different platforms and browsers and where we have the user try to break the application.

Thank you very much for the interview. I have only one more question for you,

Clement. Your involvement with the Web is getting stronger and stronger. You even started a software company that develops a Web layout program called Fusion. Do you think that you might abandon the print world?

Clement Mok: No, that was my first love and it will always be important to me. The reason why I do love print is that it is about validation and has the authority of power. Publishing on the Net is easy and there is no former criticism. On the Internet everybody can publish. The other thing is that the Internet has no memory. Things disappear very fast, nobody has documented what has happened three years ago, but you can go through a book that is 100 years old and still get a notion of the mindset at that time.

Studio Archetype

CHAPTER 05

Frames

One of the problems with large documents is that any table of contents or navigation buttons placed at the top of a document are out of reach once the user has scrolled down the window. One way of solving this problem is to use frames, which allow the browser window to be segmented into smaller, independent units. In the beginning, there were a couple of drawbacks of using frames. For example, borders could not be made invisible. Fortunately, this has been fixed, because it isn't easy to create a great design, with grey borders cutting through your artwork.

Another disadvantage of using frames was that you needed to provide an alternative document, in case the browser of the user wasn't frame capable. Although this is still an issue, most people access the Internet with Microsoft's Explorer or Netscape's Navigator and they both handle frames very well.

Before I go into the design aspect of frames, let me explain to you the HTML syntax for frames.

FRAME DOCUMENT

A frame based site always consists of at least three documents: one document for the layout of the frames, and two (or more) for the content of each frame. These documents are regular HTML documents, although the file for the frame layout isn't, it is a meta-document format. Instead of a BODY container, the frame document uses a FRAMESET container. This container describes the frame layout and defines which documents are loaded into which frames [05-01].

To understand what a Frameset is and how it works, here are two examples. One for a vertical frameset [05-02] in which the main browser window is divided in a smaller frame on the left side and a larger one on the right side. The COLS attribute – which is short for columns – specifies that these frames are arranged vertically.

For a frame based Web site you need at least three documents: the frameset loads the other two documents.

```
<HTML>
    <HEAD>
    </HEAD>
        <FRAMESET>
        </FRAMESET>
</HTML>
```
A standard Frameset 05-01

```
<FRAMESET COLS="25%,75%">
    <FRAME SRC="cntrlbar.html">
    <FRAME SRC="main.html">
</FRAMESET>
```
Example for a vertical Frameset 05-02

```
<FRAMESET ROWS="25%,75%">
    <FRAME SRC="banner.html">
    <FRAME SRC="main.html">
</FRAMESET>
```
Example for a vertical Frameset 05-03

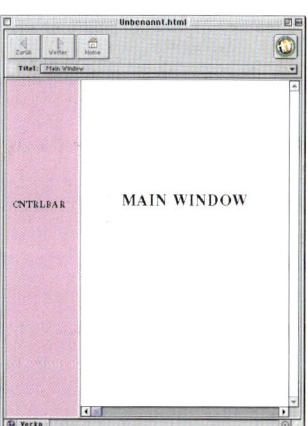

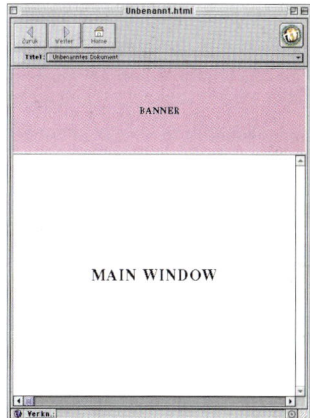

The Aristotle homepage uses four frames. A JavaScript determines which browser and version the user has and loads then an optimized version to compensate for the different browser offsets.

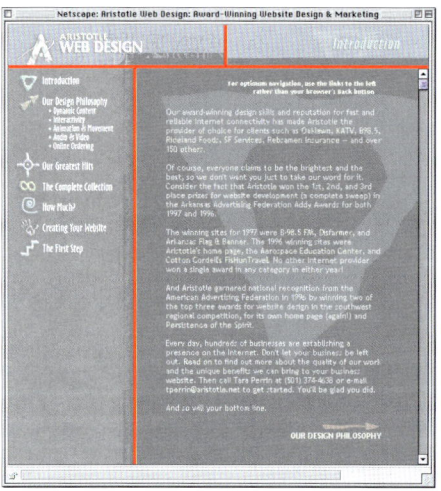

The same example with a horizontal frameset would look like in [05-03]. This time, the window of the browser would be divided into a smaller top frame and a larger bottom frame, loading the document "banner.html" into the top frame and "main.html" into the lower frame (FRAMEs without SRC attributes are displayed as a blank space of the size defined in the FRAMESET tag).

Defining Frame Sizes

The ROWS and the COLS attribute consists of a list of values that specify the size of the frames in percent, absolute pixel values, or relative scaling values. Because the user monitor might not be large enough to display all the frames, it's possible that a frame might get scaled, even though it was defined with a fixed height or width.

For every additional row or column you want to add, just add another value to the list. The value of a row or column can be given a fixed size (in pixel) by simply putting in a numeric value. This type of frame should always be combined with one or more relative size frames, otherwise the browser might override these values to match the user's maximum monitor size.

One way to avoid this is to use a percentage value for the frame, which must be between 1 and 100. If the value is larger than 100, the percentages are scaled down to sum up to 100%.

Another way is defining them as relative-sized frames. This is done by typing a single '*' character, which is then interpreted by the browser as a command to give this frame all the remaining space. The good thing about this feature is that you can add a value before the '*' character to give that particular frame more relative space. For example: "*,3*" would give the first frame 1/4 of the available space and the second one 3/4.

Defining the Margins of a Frame

There is the possibility of controlling the size of the margins for each frame individually by adding a MARGINWIDTH or MARGINHEIGHT attribute after the SRC tag. The value for these two tags are set in pixels, cannot be less than one, and must be specified so that there is space for the document contents. So, for example, if you had two frames and set

---

The Three Ways to Define Frame Sizes

1. Three columns, the first and the last being smaller than the center column, defined in percent: ‹FRAMESET COLS="30%,60%,10%"›
2. Example for 2 rows, the first being fixed height, with the remaining space assigned to the bottom row: ‹FRAMESET ROWS="50,*"›
3. Example for 3 rows, the top frame with fixed height, the bottom frame with 15% of the total available space and the remaining space assigned to the middle row: ‹FRAMESET ROWS="50,*, 15%"›

```
<FRAMESET ROWS="25%,75%">
    <FRAME SRC="cntrlbar.html"
    MARGINHEIGHT="20" MARGIN-
    WIDTH="20">
    <FRAME SRC="main.html">
</FRAMESET>
```

The MARGIN attribute 05-04

one frame to 60 pixel and the MARGIN-
HEIGHT to 30 pixel, there could not be
any visible contents in this frame, because the value for the MARGINHEIGHT
counts twice (2x30). In any event, the
MARGINHEIGHT and MARGINWIDTH are
optional so you do not need to specify
them. The browser uses its default setting for these values if they are missing
[05-04].

Scrollbars in a Frame

By default a scrollbar automatically
appears in a frame if the frame can't display the whole contents at once. But
this can be disabled by setting the attribute SCROLLING to "no", in which case
you never see a scrollbar, even if some
content is hidden. The opposite is to set
it to "yes" to have the scrollbar always
to visible. The SCROLLING attribute is
optional and must be placed in the
FRAME tag [05-05].

Disabling Resizing

Frames can be resized by the user, but
most of the time you want to prevent
the user from doing this because it is
out of your control and can easily dest-
roy the design. Setting the NORESIZE
flag disables the resizing feature. Always
use this attribute, because frames are
resizeable by default. The NORESIZE
attribute has no value, you just add it
into the FRAME tag [05-05].

Invisible Frame Borders

Microsoft's Internet Explorer was the first
browser that gave the designer the option of making the frame border invisible. Use the attributes shown in [05-06]
in the FRAME tag of your HTML document, and the frames will be invisible
for both browsers, IE 3.0 and Netscape
Navigator 3.0 and up.

```
<FRAMESET ROWS="50,*,15%">
    <FRAME SRC="cntrlbar.html"
    SCROLLING="no" NORESIZE>
    <FRAME SRC="main.html">
</FRAMESET>
```

The SCROLLING & NORESIZE attribute 05-05

Common Mistakes

To make sure that the frame document
works properly, don't use any BODY tags
in the document, exept inside the NO-
FRAME tag. Additionally, avoid any other
tags that would normally appear between the BODY tags before the FRAME-
SET tag, otherwise the browser will
ignore the FRAMESET tag. The only tag
you can use within the FRAMESET tag is
the NOFRAME tag, which displays a message to the user if their browser isn't
frame capable. The NOFRAME tag can
also be used to provide an alternative
home page, so, for example, if your
frame based home page consists of a
navigation bar and a main frame, you
could place a combination of the navigation elements and the main page inside the NOFRAMES tag. Because a
frame-capable Internet client ignores all
tags and data between the NOFRAMES
tag, you would see the alternative home
page only if the browser doesn't understand the FRAMESET tags [05-07].

It is important to know that if you edit
attributes in the FRAMESET document,

```
<FRAMESET ... FRAMEBORDER=0 FRAMESPACING=0 BORDER=0>
    ...
</FRAMESET>
<NOFRAMES>
    <BODY>
    Viewing this page requires a browser capable of displaying frames.
    </BODY>
</NOFRAMES>
```

Invisible FRAMES and the NOFRAMES attribute 05-06

```
FRAMESET
    FRAME COL
    FRAME COL
    FRAME COL
/FRAMESET

FRAMESET
    FRAME COL
        FRAMESET
            FRAME ROW
            FRAME ROW
            FRAME ROW
        /FRAMESET
    FRAME COL
/FRAMESET
```

Nesting FRAMES 05-07

To nest a frame you replace a FRAME tag (top) with another FRAMESET tag (bottom).

while viewing it in the browser, you need to reopen the FRAMESET document in the browser to see the changes! Pushing the Reload button in Netscape, for example, will only reload the content of the frames, not the FRAMESET document itself.

Nesting Frames

With this technique you can create any frame layout you want by combining row and column frames. To do this, you nest a FRAMESET tag inside another FRAMESET tag. The new FRAMESET definition is then placed inside the corresponding frame. Let's say, for example, you have created a document with three column frames. Now, to add three subframes in the middle frame, you need to replace the second FRAME COL with another FRAMESET tag. Inside that FRAMESET tag you define your row frames [05-07].

This could go on and on. To subdivide one of the row frames, replace that tag with another FRAMESET tag. In this way it is possible to create any layout you want. Understanding this concept can be very helpful and in [05-08] you see an example of a typical Frame document.

Naming and Targeting Frames

Each frame in the browser window can be named (by default all windows are unnamed), which allows you to target a specific frame in a frameset. This is important, so that the links in a control bar can trigger the loading of a new page in a different frame.

When you name your frames, begin with an alphanumeric character and assign a name to a frame by including the optional NAME attribute into the FRAME tag.

There are several ways of targeting a window. The most common is inclusion in an A tag. You simply add TARGET="window_name" to the syntax of the ‹A› tag. When the user presses the hyperlinked text, the page will be loaded in the target window. If you want all (or

```
<HTML>
    <HEAD>
        <TITLE>The FRAME document</TITLE>
    </HEAD>
<FRAMESET ROWS="70,*">
    <FRAME SRC="top.html" NAME="top" SCROLLING=NO>
        <FRAMESET COLS="125,*">
        <FRAME SRC="control.html" NAME="control">
        <FRAME SRC="main.html" NAME="main">
        </FRAMESET>
</FRAMESET>
<NOFRAMES>
    <BODY>
    Viewing this page requires a browser
    capable of displaying frames.
    </BODY>
</NOFRAMES>
</FRAMESET>
</HTML>
```

A typical FRAME document 05-08

most) links in a document to be targeted to the same window, you could define a target in the BASE tag. This is particularly helpful if you have a control bar or a table of contents and want all links to open in a main window. By adding ‹BASE TARGET="window_name"› into your HEAD tag of the document with the hypertext links (not the frameset document), the BASE TARGET establishes a default TARGET. All links will automatically open in this window unless you add a TARGET attribute to a link, because this overrides the default target. The TARGET attribute can also be used in the AREA tag of the client-side image map.

Another use for the TARGET attribute is found in the FORM tag. If you submit the information of a form to the server, the result of the form submission will be displayed in the same window. To force the display to a different window, add the TARGET attribute to the FORM tag.

Special Target Names

There are some predefined target names that trigger certain actions and these all start with an underscore character. The first one is: **_blank**.

Usually a link opens a new document in the same window. If you provide links to other web sites on your home page, a drawback is that the user is suddenly on a different site and might not come back to your site. To avoid this, it is very helpful to open the link in its own browser window. In that case the user will still have your home page in a separate window, even though he is exploring the other site.

Another helpful target name is: **_self**. This target links into the same window as the anchor.

The **_parent** target name is a little difficult to explain, but looking at how a frameset is defined will make it much clearer. Complex frame layouts are a combination of several nested FRAMESET tags, where each subframe is like a child of another frameset. With the _parent target, you can erase a frameset and have the new page loaded in the parent frame of the nested frameset. Still sounds complicated? It isn't. Just imagine that you have a control bar and a main window. The main window is subdivided into two frames and usually a link in one of those subframes will load

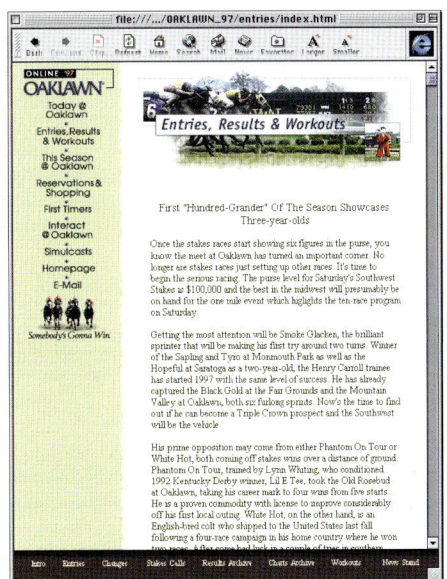

To each section of the Oaklawn website (in an invisible frame on the left side) has several subsections that are all displayed in a subframe (bottom). The subsection is controlled via a JavaScript: clicking on a main section loads two documents: one in the main window and one in the bottom frame.

```
<FRAMESET COLS=25%,75%>
    <FRAME SRC="controlbar.html" name=control>
    <FRAME SRC="mainwindow.html" name=main>
</FRAMESET>
```

Loading another FRAMESET document 05-09

```
<HEAD>
    <--! Main Window with Subframe -->
    <BASE TARGET="_parent">
</HEAD>
<FRAMESET ROWS=80, *
    <FRAME SRC="subcontrol.html" name=subcontrolbar>
    <FRAME SRC="products.html" name=submain>
</FRAMESET>
```

The document "mainwindow.html" 05-10

the linked page only in the subframe. If the target is _parent then the loaded page will eliminate the other subframe in the main window and use the whole space.

There is also a target that allows you to eliminate all frames and subframes at once and display the page in the full body of the browser window: **_top**. If you put <BASE TARGET="top"> in the HEAD section of your document, it will prevent your page from being opened as a subframe in somebody else's page.

CONTROLLING TWO FRAMES WITH ONE ANCHOR

While loading one page into a frame using the TARGET attribute is easy, loading two pages in two different frames at once seems to be much more challenging, because there is no direct HTML tag for this. Many Web books will say that doing this requires some JavaScript, but there is a simple way to do this in HTML. It is possible to use <BASE TARGET ="_top"> to prevent your page from being opened in a sub-frame and it occurred to me that it must be possible to use the "_parent" target in the BASE tag to load a document in a sub-frame and have it automatically erase all previously placed frames. This is exactly the case and it allows for some great interface design. Imagine a layout with a vertical control bar and a main window. Because every section in your control bar has

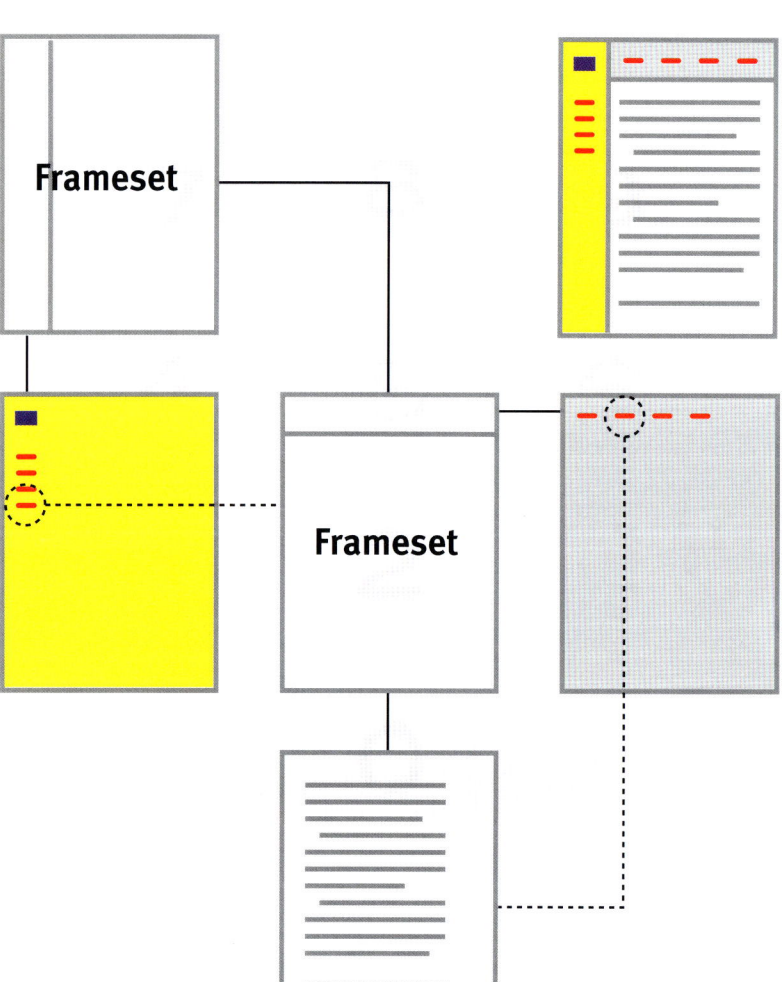

This diagram shows an alternative way to control the loading of two documents with one click: The first frameset loads another frameset document. Important is, that the links of the main section always link to a frameset that has the base target _parent (see dotted line). All the links in the subsections link directly to the HTML document and use the target attribute to load it into the main window.

several subsections (e.g. the section "Shop" might have the subsections "Product1", "Product2", you want to have a sub-frame with the links to those products displayed at the bottom of the main window. All you need to do is link your sections in the control bar to a frameset document that divides the main window and automatically loads the sub-control bar. This technique won't work correctly unless you add <BASE TARGET="_parent"> between the HEAD tags to all the frameset documents.

The frameset document that loads the control bar and the main window is shown in [05-09]. All the links in the control bar have TARGET="main", to open all the other frameset documents in the main window.

All the sections link to a frameset document [05-10] that loads two documents: a main window and a sub-controlbar. In this frameset document you must insert <BASE TARGET="_parent">. If you use a Web authoring program you might need to insert this tag manually by opening the frameset document in a text editor.

This technique solves the majority of interface design problems you might have, but it doesn't solve all of them, in which case you need to program a solution in JavaScript.

Aristotle

Interview with Christopher Stashuk and Elton Pruitt

Christopher Stashuk is the art director at Aristotle, a website design company in Little Rock, Arkansas, that has created many award winning websites for local and international businesses, organizations, and government agencies. Together with Elton Pruitt, the HTML author of that site, he developed the Aristotle Web Design homepage.

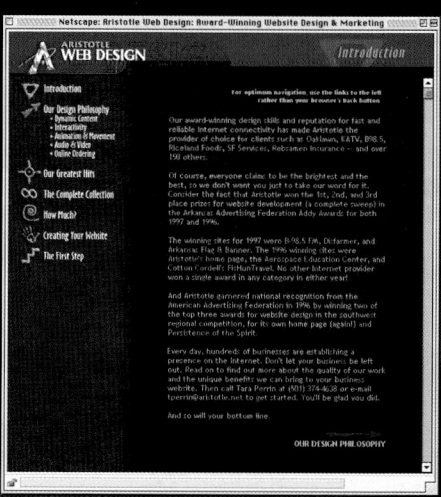

What was your main goal, when you designed the Aristotle website?

Christopher Stashuk: We wanted this site to present our view on good Web design and also show what is possible, so we used a balance of some of the older and newer technology with GIF animation in the right hand corner and JavaScript in the side bar to illuminate the icons when you scroll over them. The whole site is frame-based, but to make this not so obvious, I designed the art within each frame to closely relate. For instance, the blue tab from the upper frame is incorporated into the upper portion of the lower frame tile. Instead of a frame that ran straight across, the effect allows for a nice overlapping feel that you don't usually get with many frame-based sites. I also didn't want the background tile of the links frame to be visually repetitive, so I made it tall enough to assure that the pattern of the flat areas and edge were unique.

Elton Pruitt: One of the challenges we were faced with in developing our Web Design site is that in Internet Explorer the site looked great, but in Netscape the section headers were offset from the top of the browser window, causing the animated headers to extend into the black portion of the background tile. To avoid this, we wrote a JavaScript to detect the browser and platform and then load different pages optimized for each browser version. There are actually three versions of what you see: one for Internet Explorer 3.0 and two for Netscape 3.0, because Netscape for Windows has a vertical offset of 1 pixel and Netscape for Macintosh has a vertical offset of 8 pixels. Another thing is that we wanted to use Cascading Style Sheets to gain more control over the appearance of the site. At the time, Cascading Style Sheets were only supported by Internet Explorer 3.0. So we used Netscape's SPACER tag – which is not recognized by Internet Explorer – to approximate the same indent on the paragraphs for Netscape.

Designing for the web means working with limited color palettes. How do you make sure that your sites look good with the 216-color palette?

Christopher Stashuk: Usually I don't use that web safe 216-color palette, because it doesn't give me the results I am looking for. A lot of people will religiously use that palette, but I don't because of the significant color limitations it imposes. What I am religious about is careful testing to assure that my adaptive palettes perform well in 256 colors in both Mac and PC environments.

I assume you work with Adobe Photoshop or do you work also with other programs?

Christopher Stashuk: I use Photoshop for the majority of what I do. Sometimes I also use DeBabelizer for batch processing, but for extremely limited color palettes, I most often establish the colors in Photoshop first. When I was supervising the art on a 3DO game for Electronic Arts, I used DeBabelizer heavily. DeBabelizer's super palettes, scripting, and automatic file renaming functions, make it an excellent choice for the processing of large quantities of images. For the majority of my 3D modeling and animating I use Autodesk 3D Studio.

Everybody has a little different way on how to approach the creation of sites. How do you usually start working on a new project?

Christopher Stashuk: We usually meet with the client and figure out what they want for their Internet presence. In the initial stages, I come up with a main page sketch that sets the tone of the look and feel for the whole site. That sketch is a nice intermediate step for me. Most often, I work up the sketches by hand, not on the computer. The sketch is a nice vehicle to help the client visualize the ideas and creative focus. From there, we move directly towards the digital creation of the main page, which we use as a milestone for the process. We use it to get the approval from the client on all aspects of design – color, typography, and overall layout. Once we have the main page completed, the rest of the site is created based on the look and feel that we have established. Working with the HTML authors, the overall concept and the navigation of the site is decided. It is here that we try to plan on the use of frames, non-frames, Java, QTVR, etc.

Web design is advancing very fast and I am curious on what your perspective on Web design is.

Christopher Stashuk: As a designer I hope there will be more parity between the browsers. Right now we deal with a competitive war between the browser leaders. I hope that we will see the leading browsers become more parallel in the essentials that relate to the display issues surrounding HTML and design.

Elton Pruitt: This is pretty much the same for me. I am really looking forward to a standard, where you can design your page and know that it will display the same way in both browsers.

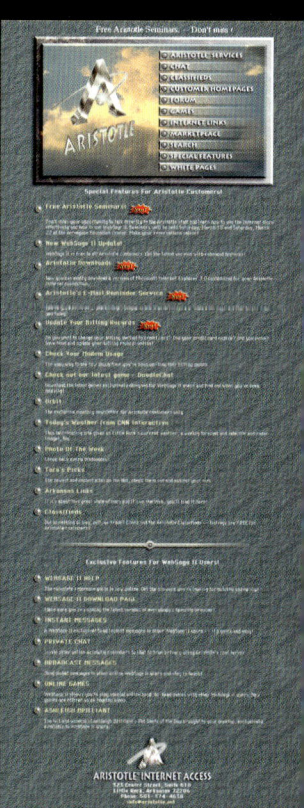

Aristotle is not only a Web Design Agency, but also an Internet Service Provider.

CHAPTER 06

GIF Animation

From the beginning of the Web's popularity, Web designers have wanted to add animations to their websites. Although plug-ins are now available, Gif-Animation is still the most popular way of bringing animation to the Web. The reason is simple: Netscape 2.0 or higher and Explorer 3.0 can read an animated GIF file without any plug-ins. No struggle for the visitor to a site to get the right plug-in before the site can actually be seen. Even if the browser doesn't support GIF animation, it will certainly support GIF files, because the GIF graphic format is the standard format for online graphics and, at least, the first (or last) picture of your animation will be seen in the browser.

Another reason for the popularity of GIF animations is that the software to create these animations is inexpensive or – in case of the Macintosh program GIF Builder – even free. It's too bad that GIF doesn't support sound or interactivity – then it would be too good to be true (actually GIF does support some simple interactivity like a stop, but this is not supported by the browsers). For those features you need Shockwave, developed by Macromedia, which allows the embedding of little Director applications on your site.

The GIF89a History

The GIF89a graphic format specification was created in 1989 and had been around for several years before it was picked up by the web community. Netscape was the first browser to support GIF-animation, but, not being documented, it took some time before the first animations appeared on the web.

GIF animation works like cell animation: the file contains several pictures that are layered on top of each other. GIF stands for graphical interchange format and was developed by CompuServe, but the compression scheme of GIF, known as LZW (Lemple -Ziv -Welch), is patented by Unisys. A few years ago Unisys announced that it would collect royalties from everyone using LZW compression. That caused a major upset in the computer community, because the GIF standard, seen as being public domain, had become widespread. However, end users, online services, and non-profit organizations do not pay this royalty.

What Programs Can You Use?

The following is a list of some programs which can be used to create GIF animations. One of the most popular programs for the Macintosh is:
- **GIFBuilder**

This program is used by most designers who work with Macintoshes, because it is easy to handle and also because Yves Piguet, the programmer, put it out as freeware. You can download the latest version directly from the Internet.

• **GIFmation**

GIFmation is a commercial software program available from BoxTop. If you want to check it out before you buy it, just go to their website (www.boxtopsoft.com) and download the demo version. If you are working with Windows, you can use:

• **GIF Construction Set**

This is one program for Windows to create GIF animations. It has some nice features like creating rolling text or generating transitions between the pictures of a GIF animation.

	Frames					
22 frames	Length: 16.50 s		Size: 410x170		Loop: forever	
Name	Size	Position	Disp.	Delay	Transp.	
Frame 1	410x170	(0;0)	N	50	1	
Frame 2	96x114	(50;25)	B	–	W	
Frame 5	98x104	(255;35)	P	–	▪	
Frame 6	97x77	(55;38)	U	150	–	

GIFBuilder's Frame window allows you to set most of the options by clicking on the entry. You can set some of the options for individual frames or for all of them. To change the options for only one frame, select the frame and double click the entry. To change them for all the frames use "Select All" from the "Edit" menu first.

The top line of the Frame window displays the number of frames the entire animation has and the total length in seconds. It also displays the settings for the image size and the Loop mode. If you click on "Size", the dialog for the frame size appears and you can set it from minimum size to fixed size, depending on your intention. Loop: Clicking on this entry opens the Loop dialog.

How to Use GIFBuilder for Macintosh

Yves Piguet has done a great job with this software because it's easy to use and has nice features, such as "Frame Optimization", that crops each frame to reduce file size, and others.

GIFBuilder can import PICT, GIF, TIFF, or Photoshop 2.5/3.0 files. If you are using System 7.5 (or higher) with Drag Manager installed, you can drag the files from the Finder into the Frame window. Otherwise use "Add Frame" in the File menu and load the images individually.

Arrange the order of the frames by selecting the frame with the mouse and hold the mouse button on the second click to drag it to the right position. A horizontal line displays the position where the frame would be placed after release. Clearing a picture is just as easy: choose "Clear" in the "Edit" menu or hit backspace. The next step is to set the graphic options in the Options menu:
• pixel depth
• color palette
• dithering

Using those features in GIFBuilder may not be the best choice because Photoshop provides much better control over those settings, especially if you create an adaptive color palette. With an adaptive color palette you can limit the number of colors that are used, thus making your image much smaller.

If you create the color palette in Photoshop you need to save the color table in the "Image: Mode: Color Table" dialog in Photoshop before importing the images into GIFBuilder. Then in GIFBuilder load this color table ("Options: Colors: Load Palette"), and your images will look exactly the same again.

GIFBuilder also offers the possibility of using the standard Macintosh system palette ("Colors: System Palette") or a 25-color grayscale palette. If you are using "Best Palette", GIFBuilder creates an adaptive color palette which can be limited in its color depth ("Options: Depth"). This will most likely result in a color shift and you can improve the quality by using the option "Dithering", but this always makes compression for the GIF algorithm harder, giving you a larger file size. The 6x6x6 color palette is the Web save color palette of 216 colors and displays the same on both Windows and Macintosh.

"Remove Unused Colors" eliminates all colors in the palette that are not used in the image. This gains some file saving, but it is advisable to do all the color palette reduction in Photoshop, because it provides much better control over the results.

Optimizing the Animation

To create animations with very efficient file sizes, there are a couple of things you need to know. First, full-size images are not needed for each cell and step of your animation; you can also place images that are cropped and contain only the parts of the image that change. GIFBuilder has a function that does this automatically, called Frame Optimization, and you can find it in the Options menu. If you mark this option, GIFBuilder will go through every cell and compare the current picture with the previous one, cropping it to just those areas that have changed. This is particularly interesting if you convert a Quicktime Movie with GIFBuilder: if the movie has a static background, GIFBuilder will crop each cell to only the parts that change (the option "Frame Expansion" by the way, does the opposite of this function: it adds to a cropped cell the entire background).

With Frame Optimization you can save a lot of file space, but, depending on the animation, you can sometimes get even more if you do it manually. To see why and how, take an example: imagine you want to create a banner advert, and on the right side you have a logo that flashes and on the left you have an object or text moving towards your logo. Frame Optimization would always crop around both elements, but, because they are almost at opposite ends, you also get all the static background between.

With the option "Frame Optimization", GIFBuilder crops the next cell to the parts that are changing. In this example, only the face will be kept.

But if you crop the object and the logo in Photoshop and import them together with the background into GIFBuilder, you can then move those elements independently without adding the static background. Now, here is a little trick: You still want both images to appear simultanously and so the frame delay for one of the elements must always be set to zero. To the human eye, it almost looks like the frames are displayed simultaneously, but the file size is minimized because it now contains only three images: the background, your logo, and the other element.

Transparency and Disposal Methods

Another important feature is transparency and the disposal method. With GIFBuilder the transparency can be set for each cell individually. This can be done in the Frame window by selecting the cell and than clicking on the transparency entry or by selecting it in "Options:

With the zero delay trick you can have two cropped cells appear like one image.

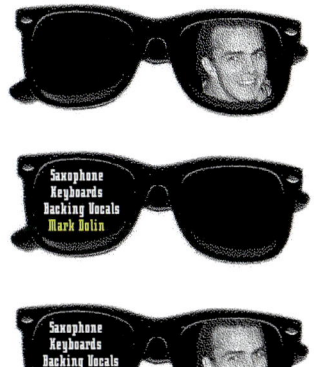

Christopher Stashuk worked from a clip art EPS of the diver for this animation for the B98.5 Web site. The legs and arms were animated in Illustrator, the parachute in 3DS.

Transparent Background". The four settings are "No", "White", "Based on first pixel" and "Other". "No" and "White" are self-explanatory. "Based on first pixel" uses the pixel color in the upper left corner as the transparency color. This makes a lot of sense because often you have an element in the center of an image and want the corners to be transparent and this option picks this color automatically for you. If you need a different color, select it in a color picker that you get by choosing "Other".

You can set a disposal method for each frame, which is only important in animations where transparency is used. The disposal method specifies what is seen through the transparent areas of the frame and you can choose between "Unspecified", "Do not dispose", "Restore to Background", and "Restore to Previous".

"Unspecified" is the standard method for images without transparency and it can be used to replace one full-size frame with another.

"Do not dispose" is mostly needed in conjunction with the "Restore to Previous" setting and ensures that this frame is not disposed by subsequent frames.

"Restore to Background" displays the background of the browser at the transparent areas of the frame, unless you have set a different background color in GIFBuilder.

"Restore to Previous" uses the last frame that was set to "Do not dispose" to fill in the transparent areas of the current frame. This feature is used a lot because it allows you to import one image as background and have an transparent image animated on top of it.

In each frame, the transparent areas will be replaced with the background image or the last frame that had been set to "Do not dispose". Unfortunately this last setting might not work correctly in Netscape 3.0 and you need to view your animation in the browser to make sure it looks the way you want.

Looping

In the GIF standard you can specify if and how often your sequence should loop. When you open the dialog in GIFBuilder, subtract one from the total number of loops you want, because the initial sequence is not taken into account giving you a run of the initial animation plus the number of loops you set in this dialog. To have it loop forever, just select "Forever" in the dialog box.

Creating Animations with Director

GIFBuilder is certainly a great program, but it doesn't support many animation tools so using Macromedia's Director for the animation process might be a good choice. Director is optimized to animate sprites and you can export the final result as a PICT sequence that can then be loaded into GIFBuilder. When setting up the stage, use a very small stage and animate your sprites using a very low frame rate. Then export the animation as a PICT sequence, import all the PICTs into GIFBuilder and use "Frame Optimization" to minimize the file size.

A Simple Animation Using the META Tag

There is a simple way to create an animation by using a tag called META. With this tag you can specify another HTML page to be loaded after a certain length of time. This can be used to create an animation or a rotating banner ad. For example, you can split your page with frames into a top frame for the ad-

B-98.5

Designer: Christopher Stashuk, HTML Author: Nancy Mitchell

The DJ of B 98.5 – Craig O'Neill – welcomes visitors with a sound file to the Website of B98.5 as animations of the station's mascot, the radio signal tower, and the loudspeaker catch their attention. The nine sections of the site feature GIF animations ranging from a parachutist to a barrel-rolling biplane, and a contest advertising blimp. They were combined with static images to create one large image by using invisible tables.

"This was one of our very quick jobs. We did it in about a week, which was possible because they were open to anything we wanted to do," recalls Nancy Mitchell. Another supporting factor was that "they knew they needed a Web presence. All the other radio stations were getting online so they had to get online too," says Christopher Stashuk.

B-98.5's website ended up as an award winning one. The site is designed in a cartoon style because B98.5 wanted their site to be a fun site. "B98.5 is a radio station whose number one audience are women of all ages. They are number one in that demographic and their morning radio guy is very popular. Because they are number one with women, they have special programs for children, including a club called 'KURBY'. B 98.5 wanted to make sure that the children's aspect of their company was included on the website, so we included online registration for them. They also have a link section and a schedule section that they keep up to date with their appearances around the town," says Nancy Mitchell, explaining the structure of the site.

Most of the advanced features of the site are not visible to the visitor; they mostly deal with the differences between Netscape and Explorer. Says Nancy: "We had some difficulties with the schedule page and we had to fix this by providing two versions: one for Netscape and one for Internet Explorer. Internet Explorer 3.0 will allow you to have an animation and a JavaScript on the same HTML source code line, Netscape 3.0 for some reason wouldn't. We also wanted to use some background sound and so we have quite a few pages that are customized to the Internet Explorer and Netscape browsers."

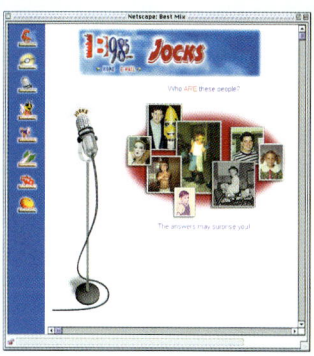

The Jocks section has a photo collage of the DJs in their younger days. Clicking on any of the photos will reveal the identity and give a short bio of that person.

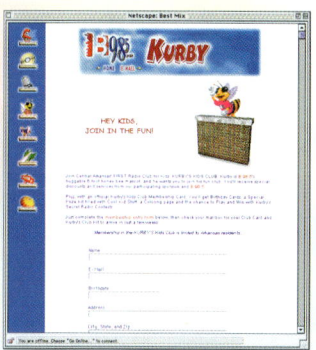

KURBY is the B 98.5 mascot and is the sponsor of a Kids' Club. The Kids' Club members receive discounts at area merchants as well as lots of gifts from the station. Visitors may sign up their children online and a package will be mailed to them.

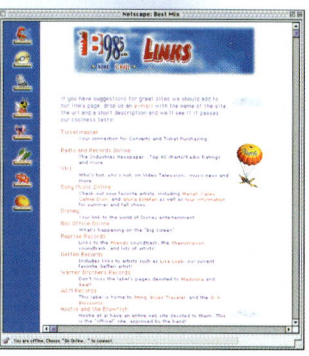

The Links section provides visitors with a few of the sites that the B 98.5 staff finds enjoyable.

In this animation from the B98.5 homepage, the animation runs forever, but you can also specify a limited number of runs.

vertising and a main frame for the content. In the top frame you load an HTML page with a placed advertising banner, and that uses the META tag. In this example the HTML page specified in the CONTENT attribute is loaded automatically after 30 seconds [06-01].

```
<HEAD>
<TITLE>Advertising Banner</TITLE>
<META HTTP-EQUIV="refresh"
CONTENT="30,URL='http://www.ser-
ver.com/ad2.html'">
</HEAD>
<BODY>
    <IMG SRC="ad1.gif">
</BODY>
```

Animation using the META tag 06-01

How the Rotating KATV Logo Was Created

Christopher Stashuk from Aristotle explains how he created the GIF animation on the KATV website.

1 *Working in Autodesk 3DStudio, I began by making a 3D mesh of the KATV logo. After setting up a 360 degree looping animation, I played with how many frames to employ and settled with 11, just enough frames to give some fluidity, but still short enough to ensure a small file size. I rendered out the frames with the background set as white (the website background color) and clicked on the alpha channels option. This features saves an alpha channel for each frame and allows for masking the logo when editing in Photoshop.*

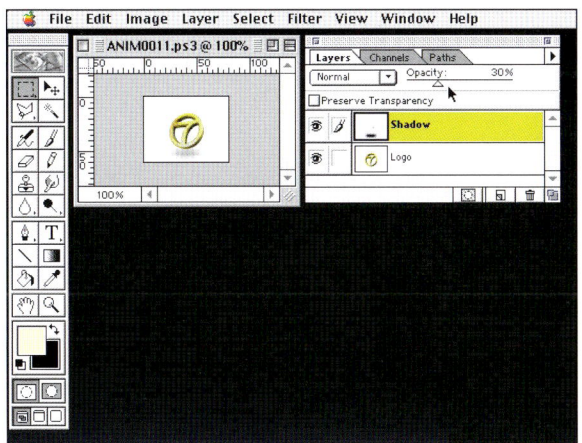

2 When creating a GIF animation with a 3D program, I rarely ever go straight in to cropping or compressing the files. I usually add some subtle touch and also do some type of enhancement, such as sharpening particular areas of the image. As I was evaluating the frames, I decided that a soft shadow resting beneath the logo would be a nice touch and would allow the animation to interact with the background of the site instead of just floating there. I began with the image tweaking first. In the case of this animation, I wanted the golden look to really be rich and was unhappy with the somewhat muted look of my rendered frames, so I used "hue/saturation" and an "unsharp mask" adjustment to enhance the image. With an "Action" sequence in Photoshop I automated the process of loading a frame, making the color change, and then performing the sharpening. Next came the addition of the shadow. After making a few variations (expanding and contracting widths) of a realistic looking shadow, I dragged the appropriate shadow layers to the individual logo frames. With the realistic positioning of the foreshortened shadow, I was then left with a shadow layer that partially overlapped the bottom of the logo. This was solved by loading the frame's alpha channel and making this into the shadow layer's mask.

3 I played with indexing the palette at several depths. I finally settled on the use of a 6-bit palette – more than I might have expected, but the diffusion of the shadow, as well as the shimmers in the gold, demanded this number of colors. I then saved my palette as a loadable CLUT (Color Look-Up Table). What made creating this animation so easy was the fact that white – my future croma-key color – wasn't part of the logo.
After determining the tightest crop that would still include the entire image on each frame, I ran the 11 frames through an Action sequence in Photoshop, that loaded my predefined CLUT (converting them to a global index palette) and cropped the frames (using canvas size).

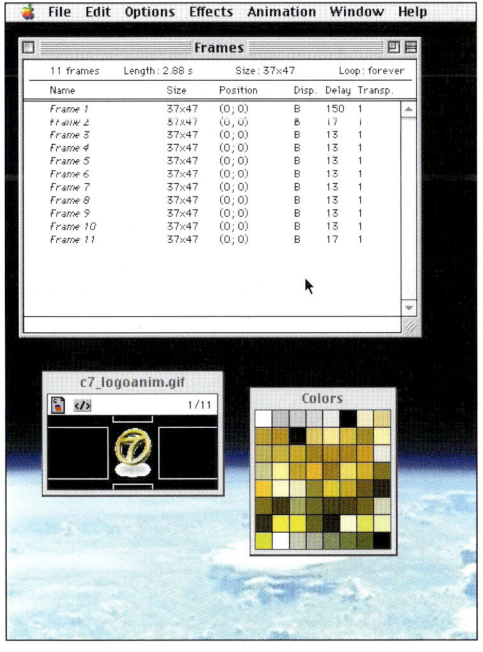

4 Finally, the frames were imported into GIFBuilder. The background for the KATV site is a large (900 x 747 pixel) tile that is predominantly white with a ghosted image of their logo. Because of this background, it was necessary to make the animation transparent, otherwise you would see the confines of the animation. I played with the timing between the frames and wanted the logo to settle into a fixed position before continuing on to loop, to keep the animation from being a noxious, mind-numbing loop. I chose a 3/4 view on one of the frames as my return point and gave it a hold of 150/100 of a second and for all other frames 13/100 of a second. The animation's cycle seemed stiff, so I added the subtle touch of 17/100 of a second timing to the frame just prior to and after the holding frame. Though a small adjustment, this "ease to" approach makes a big difference in the final product and makes for a nice anchor to the site's interior pages, being only 8KByte in file size.

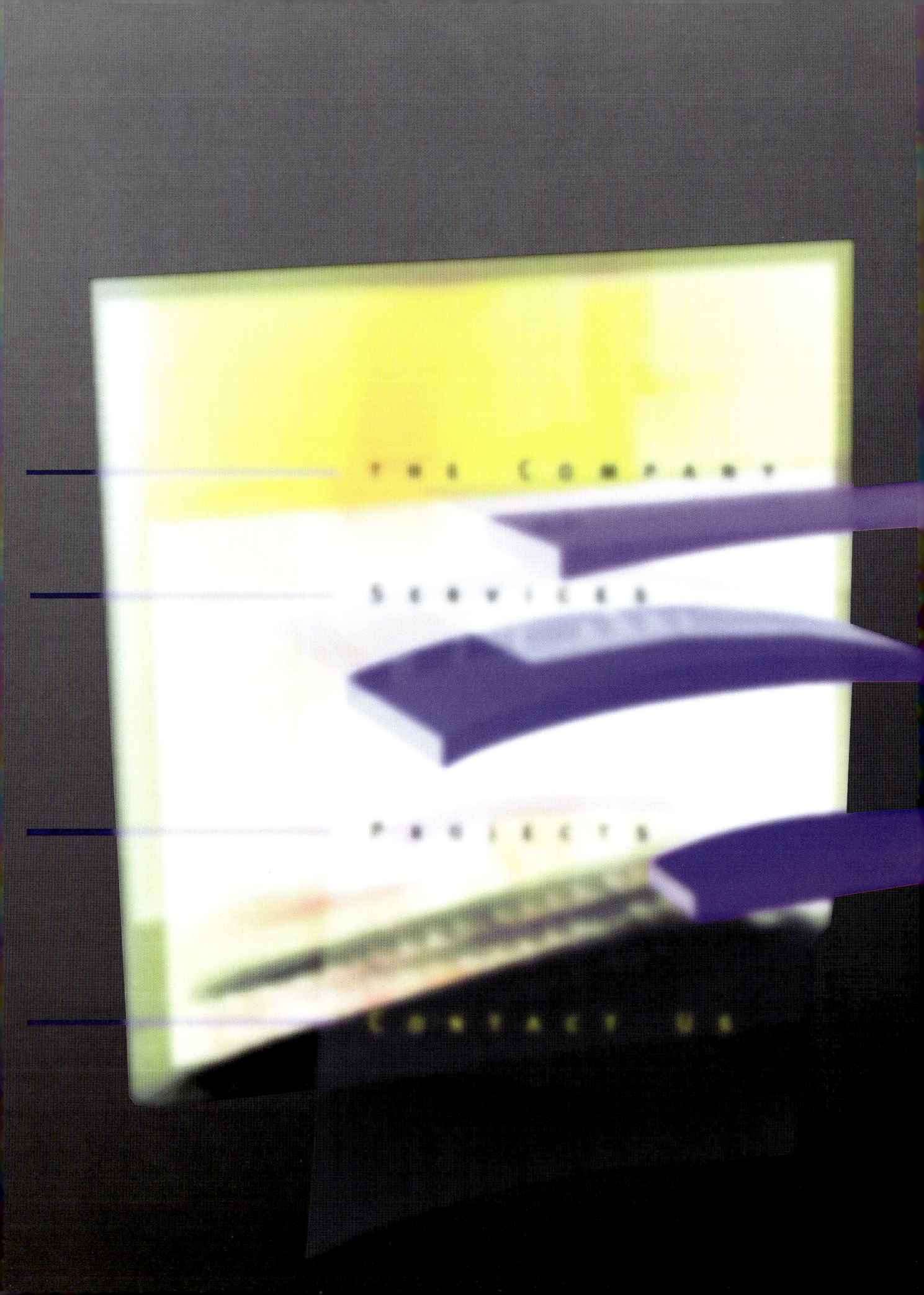

Avalanche

**Interview with Peter Seidler
Creative Director and Co-founder**

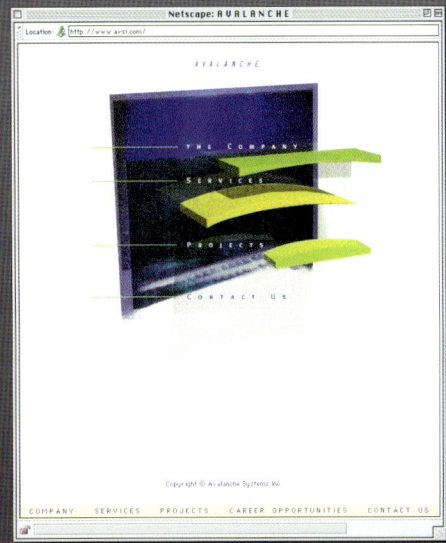

Avalanche was founded in New York in 1994 by Peter Seidler and Michael Block, his partner, and is today one of the largest interactive agencies in America. Among their clients are many major record labels and television networks as well as top Fortune 500 companies.

I spoke to him about his view on information design and how the Internet is going to impact the recording industry.

Prior to Avalanche you had an interface design company, now you are doing Web design. What do you like about those two media?

Peter Seidler: When I went to the California Institute of Arts, which is in the desert north of LA, I concentrated on how to move information through a system, something that is nowadays called information architecture. Ever since then I have always tried to create an enjoyable, easy to use Interface which is also the main challenge in designing for the Web.

Information Architecture has become quite a buzz word since the Web became such a success. What is Information Architecture for you?

Peter Seidler: Fundamentally it comes down to understanding the body of information that needs to be communicated, who is communicating it and who is receiving it and then building a framework in which that can happen with pleasure, ease, and usefulness. It's a very customized process and when people ask me what my favorite site is, I ask them what their favorite word is, because we are only beginning to distinguish one kind of electronic experience. They don't realize that there are numberless electronic experiences that have yet to be defined. So what's good for one event, is not good for another.

Can you give an example of that?

Peter Seidler about the Carnegie website: How do you represent this great space and hall with its great interior? To solve this we spent a few days there, walking around in the basement and behind the stage. We had a photographer who shot key features of the architecture to give the viewer the experience of being there and then created a site where we composed the photography along with very lyrical typography. The client really liked the result and it is interesting to see that this site is beginning to influence the other marketing materials that Carnegie Hall is putting out. Another thing about the Carnegie Hall site is that there is an extensive database, where you can view their program, check how many seats are still there, and finally go to the online ticket office and buy tickets. Our goal was to keep the informational aspect of the site very subtle, so we built all the transaction capabilities but kept it low key.

Peter Seidler: When we created the site for FAO Schwarz, the driving concept was to enable the user to experience it as an interactive toybox and move through this space with a sense of play. We carried that all the way through to the transaction process which is the intention of the site: to have users buy things online. Everything was focused on achieving that, but the way we did it might not work with a different client or with a different site.

How do you make sure that your Information Architecture really works and how do you approach a project?

Peter Seidler: We have a Quality Assurance division where we test the sites that we create. Beta testing of your product is standard in the software business, but it is a novelty in the new media business. We are creating new models for production, because it is bringing together media issues and software issu-

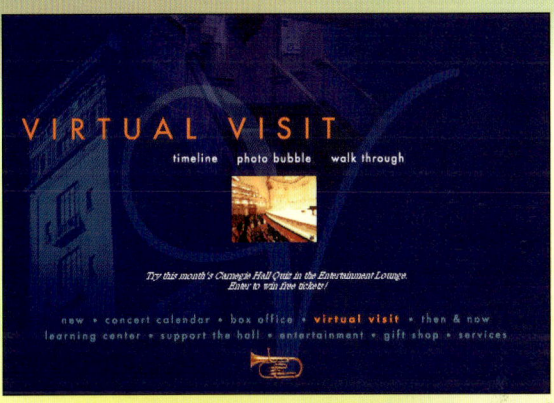

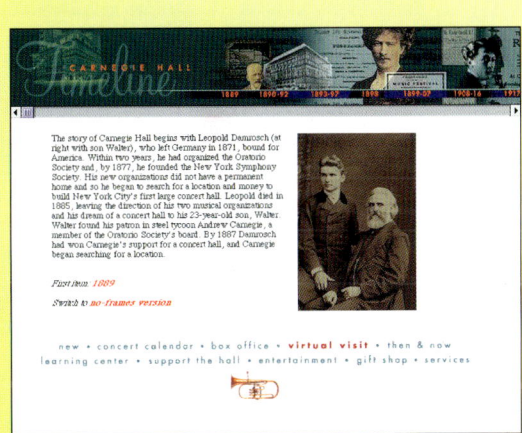

In the virtual visit section you can explore the Carnegie Hall and read about the history in the Timeline section.

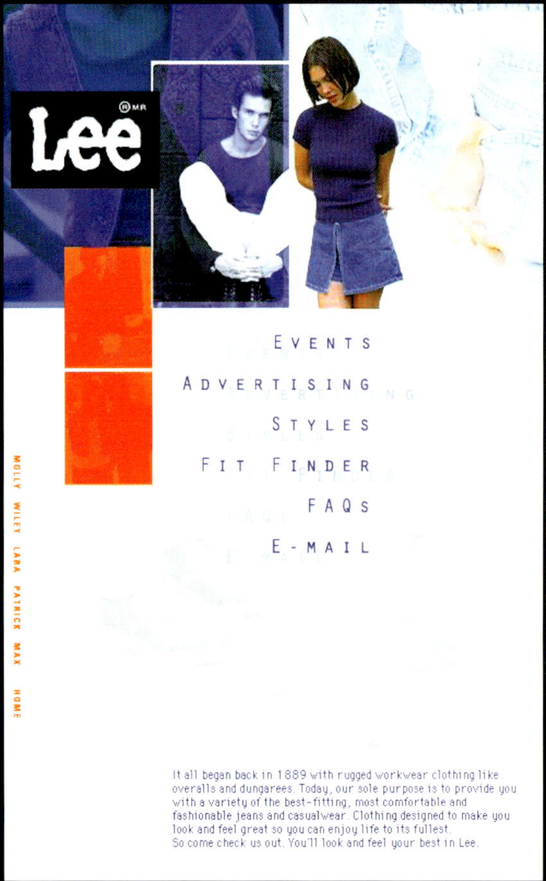

Lee

EVENTS
ADVERTISING
STYLES
FIT FINDER
FAQS
E-MAIL

MOLLY WILEY LARA PATRICK MAX HOME

It all began back in 1889 with rugged workwear clothing like overalls and dungarees. Today, our sole purpose is to provide you with a variety of the best-fitting, most comfortable and fashionable jeans and casualwear. Clothing designed to make you look and feel great so you can enjoy life to its fullest. So come check us out. You'll look and feel your best in Lee.

Ferry Boat
(MoV File:1.5mb)
Sand Dune

LEE JEANS: This was one of five different brand sites we built for the VF Corporation. Lee wanted to reposition their brand and target a younger audience, so we gave the site a little edgier and wilder design to aim for a more college age audience, says Peter Seidler.

es. And one of the things that make web design different from print design is that you need to incorporate beta testing of your site. This will become more and more important because Web design projects are becoming more and more technical.

In terms of working with the client, we have an early phase that involves understanding what their project considerations are, including the audience, identity, etc. As we get acquainted with the client's issues, we build a more focused proposal. We write a project specification which covers all the technology issues, the business issues, what the buildout is, and then the scheduling along with the creative brief.

How long does this process usually take?

Peter Seidler: This can range from four weeks to nine months. One of the longest projects we have been working on is the Warner Music label site.

You have many clients from the media industry and in particular music labels like Warner or Electra. Is there any particular reason for that?

Peter Seidler: No, not really, other than that the music industry has embraced the Internet since the very beginning, because the Internet is a great distribution channel for music as it is for software. One of our earliest sites three years ago was for Elektra Entertainment. It was just before background color and CENTER tags were allowed in HTML, so it used the most primitve HTML. Our approach is not necessarily to deploy the most recent technology, but to do something that is a smart fit at that time. But that also means that we have to maintain a site and right now we are doing the Version 2.5 of the Electra site.

You said that the music business has embraced the Web as a new distribution channel. How do you think the Web is going to impact the music business?

Peter Seidler: The Web is going to impact every business, but businesses that have products that can be transmitted electronically will see the most impact. Five years from now it will be quite easy to get all your music from the Internet and the music industry is aware of this. All major music companies are doing a

lot of thinking right now on how to use the web for their purpose. They either aggressively embrace it or they are just trying to understand it, but it is clear that it is going to shake up the music industry in a big way. One thing is that you will be able to get unreleased tracks from an artist that you like through the Internet, that normally wouldn't be profitable for the record label to publish. For example the record company of Peter Gabriel might have different versions of a Peter Gabriel song in their archive that they now could make available. This could be handled through the Internet with a micro charge, where you can buy the song to play five times over the Internet or pay for downloading it to your hard drive. These ideas open up new possibilities for the record labels to make money with already existing material and that's why they are so eager to get on the Internet.

You also do a lot of work for TV networks and movie companies. One of the sites you created was for the movie Lost Highway, and what I liked about that site was that it makes no use of buttons.

Peter Seidler: I've always hated buttons. I think people are much smarter than that, they don't need buttons, and if possible I avoid them. The exciting part of the Lost Highway site is that we wanted to recreate the nonlinear nature of the film. So we build a rudimentary intelligence into the interface: when you click on text, you get more text, when you click on pictures, you get more pictures. In a very basic way it has its own intelligence that respond to your input.

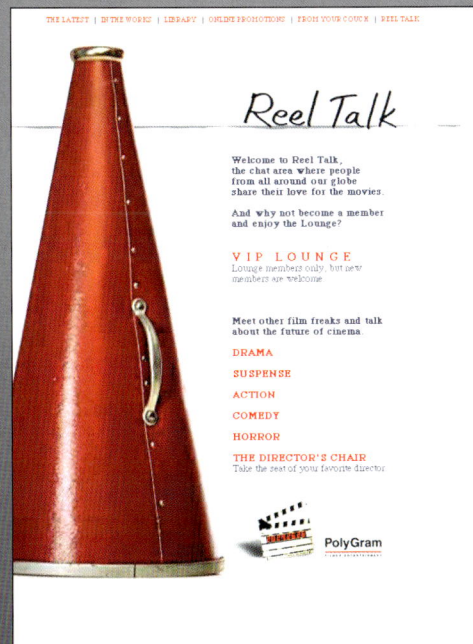

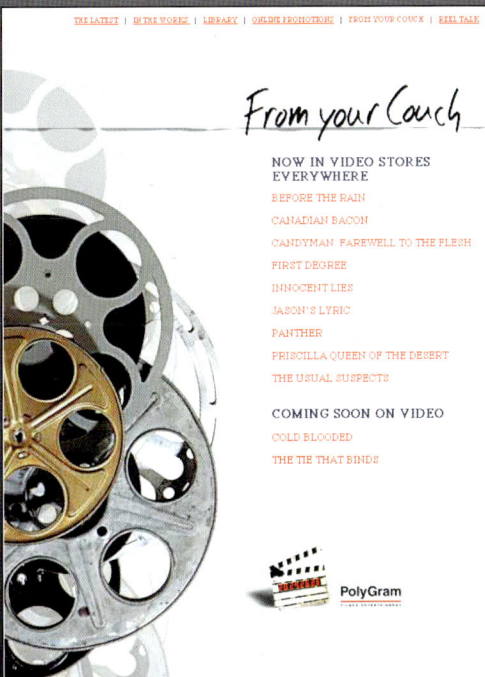

POLYGRAM FILMED ENTERTAINMENT
Peter Seidler: This site was built to reflect the strong point of view that Polygram Filmed Entertainment has. We set up a photography shoot and gathered an assortment of well used film equiptment to show the real life details of film production.

Chapter 07

Cascading Style Sheets

The only way to specify a font in HTML is the FONT tag, which allows you to specify a list of fonts as your preference. But it was clear that this was not enough, so in search of a solution, the Cascading Style Sheet extension was created. With Cascading Style Sheet Level 1 (CSS1) you can set the fonts, colors, or white space of your text and redefine the HTML tags. This means that you can still use the regular structural tags like ‹H1› or ‹P› (Heading or Paragraph), but include formatting information for these tags in a style sheet. If the browser doesn't understand CSS, it will at least interpret the structural tags as usual. This was actually one intention of the creators of CSS: instead of creating more HTML tags for the display, they wanted to ensure that HTML would remain a structural language.

Implementing a CSS into your Web site is very easy, because you can place the specification in an external reference file and link to this file in every page of your Web site. The advantage to this is that any changes to the CSS file will change the appearance of the whole Web site.

There are actually three ways you can implement a style sheet: beside the linked style already mentioned, there are inline styles and embedded styles.

```
<HTML>
<HEAD>
<TITLE>CSS Test</TITLE>
    <LINK REL=STYLESHEET TYPE="text/css"
    HREF="http://www.server.com/my_style_sheet" TITLE="my_style">
    <STYLE TYPE="text/css">
    @import url(http://www.server.com/additional_styles);
    H1 { color: blue }
    </STYLE>
</HEAD>
    <BODY>
    <H1>This Headline is blue</H1>
    <P STYLE="color: red">This paragraph is red.</P>
    </BODY>
</HTML>
```

Three ways of implementing CSS 07-01

An inline style is included within an HTML element and might look like this: ‹P STYLE="margin-left: 20%"›, which creates a paragraph with a left margin of 20% of the browser window. While this inline style is only effective for this tag, you can also create an embedded style sheet, which is effective only for one page. To embed a style sheet, use the STYLE tag in the head of the file (between the HEAD tags), which allows you to override a linked CSS.

The example [07-01] shows the three ways of implementing a style sheet:
1. Import a style sheet as an external file by using the LINK tag or by using the CSS '@import' notation;
2. Place a STYLE tag inside the HEAD tag; and,
3. Set the STYLE attribute in the P tag. To be downward compatible put all the CSS definitions inside comment tags. This ensures that a browser that doesn't understand the STYLE tag will not treat the definitions as standard text.

As you can see in this little style sheet [07-02], the definition is placed inside a comment tag, to make sure that non-style sheet browser don't try to interpret the information. If you put this style sheet inside the HEAD tag, every H1 tag in the document will be in red. If you save this style sheet externally, you can import it in every page of your site with the LINK tag.

Another important tag is SPAN, because it allows you to give only a word or a sentence a different appearance. For example, to show a word in a different color, enter ‹SPAN STYLE="color: red"›word‹/SPAN› in your HTML source code. Depending on the situation, you could use an inline tag like EM, which is used to emphasize a word or a sentence within a paragraph and redefine it to gain the same effect. This way the word will still be emphasized in a non-CSS browser.

COMBINING STYLE SHEETS

You can combine a linked style sheet with embedded or inline style sheets. The styles included within an HTML tag (Inline styles) have the highest priority, followed by embedded styles and then linked styles. This cascading affect allows the child styles to modify the display of the parent, very much as in a layout program like QuarkXPress or Pagemaker, where you can format a paragraph, but then still give single words a different appearance. For example, marking a paragraph with ‹P STYLE= "background: #660033"›Top Ten‹/P› gives the appearance of highlighted text to this particular header without affecting any of the other formatting.

A CONDENSED GUIDE TO THE CSS1 SYNTAX

Designing simple style sheets is easy and I want to list here some of the main features and how to implement them, so that you can start using CSS1 in your Web site. Much more is possible than I can list here and if you want to get deeper into it, you should download the specification from the Internet (http://www.w3.org/pub/WWW/TR/REC-CSS1). But also check out the home pages of Netscape and Microsoft, because not all of the CSS features are supported.
Font-family: Values are separated by a comma to indicate that they are alternatives: BODY { font-family: arial, helvetica, sans-serif }. In this example, "arial" and "helvetica" are font families, but the last value is a generic family name. The following generic families are de-

```
<STYLE TYPE="text/css">
<!-- H1 { color: red } -->
</STYLE>
```
Using Comment tags 07-02

fined and you should always offer a generic font family in your list as an last alternative:
- serif (e.g., Times)
- sans-serif (e.g., Helvetica)
- cursive (e.g., Zapf-Chancery)
- fantasy (e.g., Western)
- monospace (e.g., Courier)

If the font name contains white space it should be quoted: BODY { font-family: "Gill Sans", sans-serif }

Font-style: The font-style property selects between normal, italic and oblique faces within a font family (H1, H2, H3 { font-style: italic }). The only problem is that there is no universal standard for classifying fonts. Slanted text may be labeled as Italic, Oblique, Slanted, Incline, Cursive, or Kursiv.

Font-variant: With font, variant you can set small caps. This is an example for an H2 element in small caps: H2 {font-variant: small-caps}.

Font-weight: You can set the font weight as normal, bold, bolder, lighter, and as a numerical value. These are set in hundred increments from 100 to 900, where 400 is equal to normal and 700 equals bold: H2 { font-weight: 700 }. The "bolder" and "lighter" values select font weights relative to the weight inherited from the parent: STRONG {font-weight: bolder}.

Font-size: The font size can be set as an absolute or a relative value [07-03]. For the relative value you can also use the keywords "larger" and "smaller".

Font: The font property is a shorthand for setting fontstyle, fontvariant, fontweight, fontsize, lineheight, and font-family at once [07-04].

The first entry (12pt/14pt) sets the font size and the leading, the comma-separated list defines the desired font.

Color: This property describes the text color of an element. There are different ways to specify the color:
P { color: red }
P { color: rgb(255,0,0) }
P { color: #FF0000 }

Background-color: This property sets the background color of an element.
H2 { background-color: #FF0000 }

Background-image: It is possible to place a background image with this property [07-05].

Background-repeat: This determines how and how often a background image is repeated. The possible values are: repeat, repeat-x, repeat-y, no-repeat. If you use repeat, the image gets repeated in both directions, while repeat-x and repeat-y limit it to the horizontal or vertical direction. To have the background image displayed only once, use no-repeat [07-06].

Word-spacing & letter spacing: For both properties, you can set a spacing:
H1 { word-spacing: 0.4em }
BLOCKQUOTE { letter-spacing: 0.1em }

Text-decoration: This property allows you to set some decorations. You can

continue on page 114

```
P { font-size: 10pt; }
BLOCKQUOTE { font-size: larger }
EM { font-size: 150% }
EM { font-size: 1.5em }
```
The font-size attribute 07-03

```
P {font: 12pt/14pt Helvetica, Arial, sans-serif}
```
The font property 07-04

```
BODY { background-image: url(image.gif) }
P { background-image: none }
```
The background image 07-05

```
BODY { background: url(image.gif);
background-repeat: repeat-y;}
```
Background repeat 07-06

INSTALLING CSS WITH BBEDIT

BBEdit is a great text editor and it is the perfect tool to do some final scripting for your website. The reason is, simply, that you can define your own HTML tags, which then makes it easy to implement features that your HTML authoring program doesn't know. But most of all I appreciate its "Find&Replace" feature because this feature allows batch-processing across multiple files. This makes it great for implementing CSS into your website within minutes.

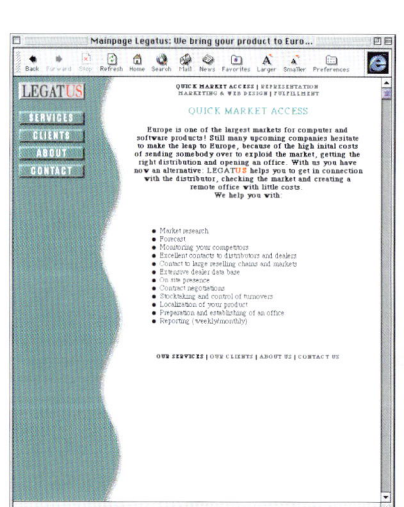
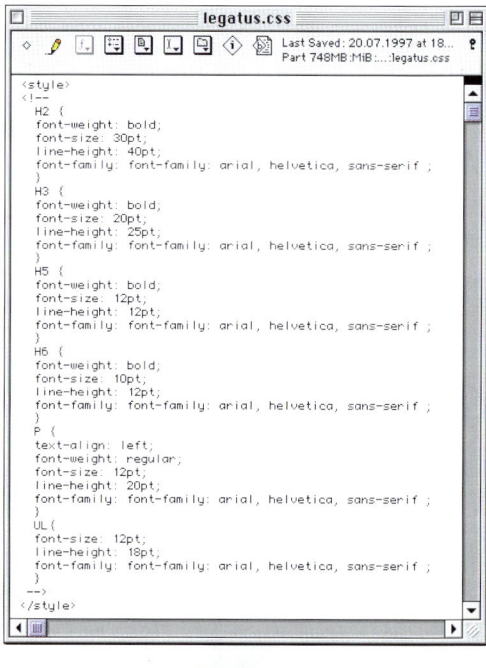

1 To implement CSS into the Legatus website, I used an external style sheet linked to in all the pages of the site. To do this I created a new file and entered all my definitions for the headline and the paragraph tag and saved it as "legatus.css". It is important that you don't forget the STYLE tags, the comment tags (‹!-- --›), and – after each entry – the semicolon (;).

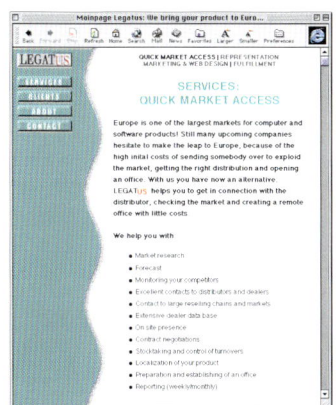 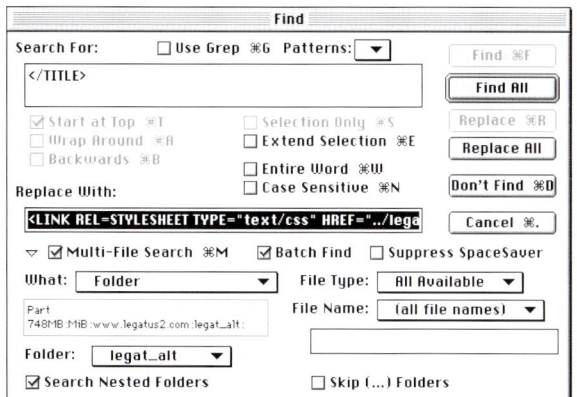

❷ *I opened "Find" in the "Search" menu and entered ‹/TITLE› in the "Search For" field. In "Replace with" I entered ‹/TITLE›\r‹LINK REL=STYLESHEET TYPE="text/css" HREF= "../legatus.css" TITLE="legatus.css"› and checked the "Multi-File Search" and the "Search Nested Folder" Option. After selecting the folder, BBEdit looks in all the text files for the ‹/TITLE› tag and replaces it with the string above. This feature is particularly helpful to implement style sheets in an existing site with hundreds of pages. The "\r" in the string is only for formatting reasons, because this signals BBEdit to insert a return at this location.*

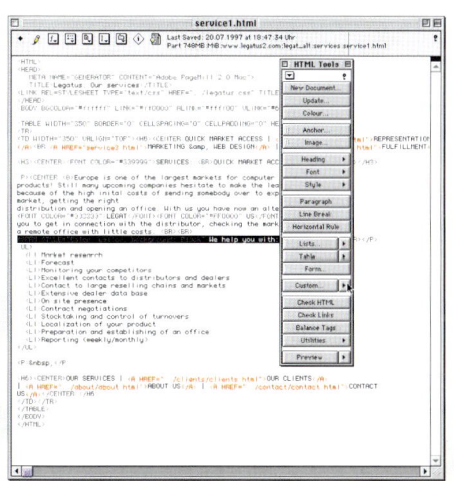 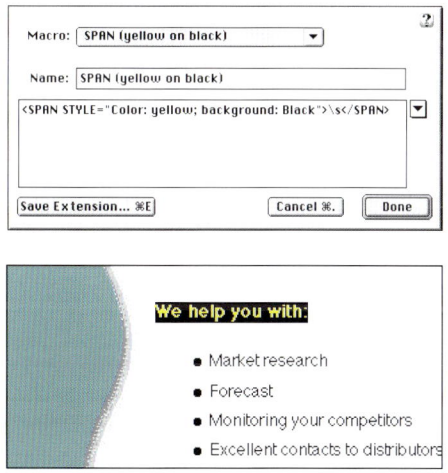

❸ *In BBEdit you can define your own HTML tags and I used this feature to define the SPAN tag, which allows me to insert CSS formatting in the text. To do this, click on "Custom" in the HTML Tools window, select an "Undefined" macro, then choose "Edit". I entered ‹SPAN STYLE="color: yellow; background: black"›\s‹/SPAN› and named this macro. This macro defines yellow text on black background and because I used "\s" in the string, the macro now allows me to select a text and have the starting and ending tag be placed at the right position before and after the selected text.*

Cascading Style Sheets 113

choose between: none, underline, overline, line-through, and blink. A nice use of this property is to specify the appearance of links:
A:link, A:visited, A:active { text-decoration: none }
Vertical-align: You have the following values to affect the vertical positioning: baseline, sub, super, top, text-top, middle, bottom, text-bottom, and 'percentage'.
Text-transform: Choose between capitalize, uppercase, lowercase, and none.
Text-align: With this property you can define how the text is aligned: choose between left, right, center, and justify. For example: P { text-align: justify }
Text-indent: Indentation for the first line is now possible without any tricks. Just use this property and set its length. It is also possible to use negative text-indents or a percentage value of the parent: P { text-indent: 3em }.
Grouping declarations: You can give several tags [07-07] the same properties by putting them in a semicolon-separated list.
Comments: They are similar to those in the C programming language:
/* this is a comment! */
Links: It is also possible to set the colors of links.
A:link { color: red }
A:visited { color: blue }
A:active { color: yellow }

BACKWARD COMPATIBILITY: BLENDING TWO WORLDS

The FONT tag was one of the first attempts to give the designer some control over the fonts in the layout. This tag will sooner or later be redundant, but if you want to ensure backward compatibility with older browser version, you should consider using it together with CSS. If the browser doesn't understand CSS, it will at least interpret the FONT tag [07-08].

In the FONT tag, you specify a list of fonts that the client's browser should look for in order of your priority. If one of the fonts is installed, the browser will use this font to display the text. Unfortunately there isn't much choice. Because you have to restrict yourself to those fonts that are commonly installed (which are only the system fonts that come with the Macintosh and Windows operating systems), use the combination "Helvetica, Arial" or "Palatino, Times" to be on the safe side. Together with the SIZE attribute, you now have pretty good control over the appearance of the site in case a browser has no CSS.

H1, H2, H3 { font-weight: bold;
font-size: 10pt;
line-height: 15pt;
font-family: arial, helvetica }

Grouping CSS 07-07

<FONT FACE="fontname, fontname, fontname" SIZE="x">
This is text</FONT>

The FONT tag 07-08

CHAPTER 08

Shockwave

Creating Shockwave was a very smart move on the part of Macromedia, because it allows the designer to create advanced multimedia applications with the popular multimediaprogram Director and then embed them in their websites. Macromedia has emphasized Shockwave a lot so it's no wonder that the Shockwave plug-in is so widespread, and installed in many browsers on Windows and Macintosh.
In future the Shockwave technology might become part of the browsers, but for now you need the Shockwave plug-in to view Shockwave movies. If you are working with Director 5 you also need the program Afterburner to convert standard Director projectors into Shockwave applications, while with Director 6 this is done directly from the program. This chapter gives background information on how to create and optimize an application Streaming Shockwave, the new version of Shockwave. With Streaming Shockwave the viewer no longer needs to download the application entirely before anything can be viewed. The viewer can start the application right away while elements like audio and graphics are being downloaded in the background.

Streaming Shockwave will certainly have a big impact on the Web because of its many advantages over traditional HTML pages, such as true WYSIWYG, the multimedia features, and a powerful programming language.
Programming is an important part in the creation of Shockwave applications, but Director 6 makes this much easier. Even if you have almost no programming experience, you can create a simple interface and functionality without too much knowledge of the Director tool Lingo. In Director 6 simply choose from a list of behaviors to create "interactive buttons" that change their appearance when you click on them or control the navigation. So if you haven't yet worked yet Macromedia's Director it's worth consideration.

HOW TO PREPARE A STREAMING SHOCKWAVE MOVIE

Coming up with a good concept for a Streaming Shockwave application requires as much thought as creating a standard website, simply because you are still dealing with the same issue: the bandwidth of the Internet. This means that you have to think about the order in which to introduce the cast members of your movie so that there is no bottleneck where too many images are transmitted at the same time, forcing the user to wait. Greg Knoll, Art Director at Dennis Publishing (see interview), creator of the online version of the CD-ROM magazine Blender, usually uses a text intro for the stories, because while the user is engaged in reading the intro,

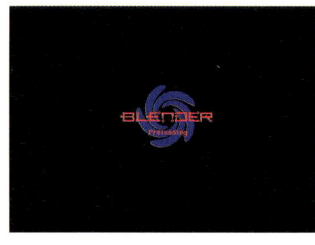

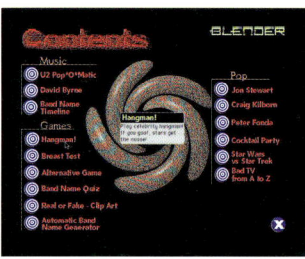

Blender, the CD-ROM magazine from New York, uses now Streaming Shockwave for their Web Site.

The behavior palette in Director 6 makes it much easier to create interactive buttons that are highlighted automatically, or to display a custom "wait" icon, like a watch cursor. Those elements are very important for a Streaming Shockwave application because they engage the user, giving the impression of response while cast members are downloaded in the background. Also playing an audio message or a background sound could help to make the waiting time more interesting.

the elements can be downloaded in the background. Another way to avoid the waiting time is to introduce the elements stepwise, because one way Director determines the order in which the elements are streamed is by their appearance in the score window.

Another important factor is to think about how to compress the elements. One advantage of Director is that you can use bitmap cast members that can be colored individually without using more memory. For example, you can create a headline with a drop shadow with the same element. All that is needed is to place the bitmap text twice in the stage window and color both differently. Reusing the same cast members is key to smooth Streaming Shockwave applications, because once downloaded they remain in memory until you quit the application or leave the page where it is embedded.

Another great thing in Director is that you can define geometrical shapes that need almost no memory. So try to use as many of these as possible instead of bitmap images.

Shockwave downloads the cast members in the order in which they appear in the score window, but as you know, it might very easily happen that the user jumps ahead in the score. Any missing cast members will then be either ignored or displayed with a placeholder. One way of avoiding this is to make sure that the user can't jump so far ahead in the score, but another way is to use Lingo. In particular the behavior "Net Hold Until Frame Ready" might be very helpful. Behaviors are new to Director 6 and they automatically create Lingo for you; all you need to do is to enter the parameters. The "Net Hold Until Frame Ready" behavior creates, for example, a Lingo script that makes sure all elements in a specified frame range are downloaded before continuing with the movie. But there are many more behaviors or Lingo commands that help you to determine if files have been downloaded already or that preload cast members, which can also help to improve your Streaming Shockwave application.

Using Audio in Your Shockwave Movie

Did you buy Director 6 in a bundle package together with SoundEdit 16? Lucky you, because this program is a big help in creating audio for Shockwave or Director movies. Additionally, it has some features that you don't want to miss (in case you usually work with another sample editor).

One of those features is that you can synchronize cast members to audio. Jason Pearson, Creative Director and Cofounder of Blender magazine, used this feature to create a party scene for Blender, where the lips of the guests are synchronized to the sound of their voices. You can see the result on many of the Blender CD-ROMS, but also on their

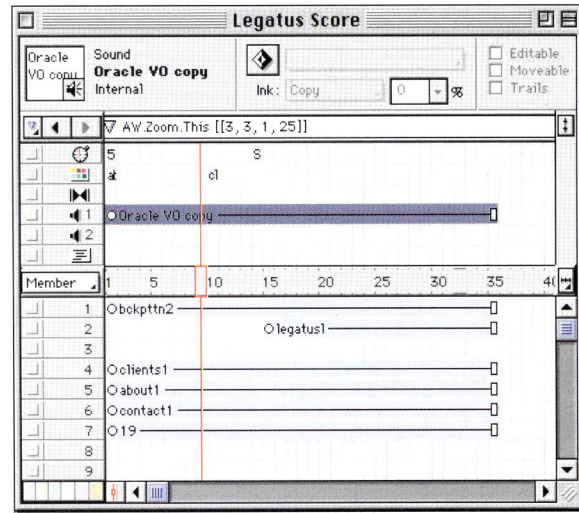

web site (www.blender.com), where you can download a Shockwave projector (you have to download a universal main application from which you then access the content. This main application is also on the CD-ROM with this book).

To synchronize the Director movie to an audio file, simply set all cue points in SoundEdit 16 where you want action to appear and save the sound as an AIFF or QuickTime file. In Director you need to display the tempo channel, which can be shown by clicking on the "Hide/Show Effects Channels" button in the score window. The top channel with the stopwatch icon is the tempo channel and in this channel double click on the cell directly before the sprite that you want to synchronize. In the dialog box that appears, select the Option "Wait for Cue Point" and then choose the cue point in the pop-up menu. What now happens is that the playback head will stop in the score window until the audio file has reached the cue point and will then continue playing.

Another nice feature of SoundEdit 16 is the batch processing of sounds, which means you can convert several sound files to another format at once, a feature that even some expensive sound editors don't have. In the chapter on Audio you can read more about sound editing and processing. If you only have SoundEdit 16 you can try to enhance the quality of your sound by using the "Normalize" and the "Equalizer" effects.

"Normalize", a function found in the "Effects" menu, searches for the loudest peak in the sound and then raises the volume until this peak reaches the maximum dynamic.

With the Equalizer effect the high frequencies in your sound can be raised to compensate for the loss of clarity and crispness you get when the sound is downsampled. You can also select the option "Boost Highs" in the Sound Format dialog box , found in the "Modify" menu, which will do this automatically for you. Downsample your audio material as low as possible, such as 11 kHz and 8-bit, for example. To finally create a streaming audio file you need to import the sound into the Score Window of Director and there select the "Shockwave Audio Settings" in the Xtra menus. In the dialog box choose as low a bit rate as possible. You won't hear the results right away, because they are

If you are working with Sound-Edit 16 from Macromedia, you can set markers in an audio file that trigger the change of cast members in Director. This effect can be seen in the Party Scene of the CD-ROM magazine Blender: the lips of the cartoonactors are synchronized to the audio.

only effective when you save the Director movie as a Shockwave file.

To test the application and the streaming audio, first embed the Shockwave application in an HTML page and view it through your browser to see and hear the effect (if possible, upload everything to the server and test it there).

There are only two things left that you need to know: the first is that all the audio files imported into the Sound Channel are part of the application, which means they are not real streaming audio. They are streamed as cast members, but streaming audio really means that the audio file is played as it is downloaded. To have real streaming audio you have to create a special cast member with an Xtra that links to an external file. Streaming an external audio sound is simple: choose "Insert: Media Element: Shockwave Audio" and type in either the URL of the audio file that you want to link to or click on the button "Browse" to select it from your hard drive (this newly created cast member needs to be placed in the regular channels, not the sound channels).

The second thing you need to know is to include the Shockwave Audio Xtra with the movie. To check which Xtras are used by your movie, go to "Modify: Movies: Xtras" and get a list, which should also include the SWA Streaming Xtra.

When your Director movie is finished, save it with "Save and Compact", choose "Xtras: Update Movies", and select the option "Convert to Shockwave Movies". The option "Back Up Into Folder ..." creates a backup of your original movie file in a folder that you can specify here. After clicking on "Okay", your movie is updated to a Shockwave Movie including all the required Xtras.

Embedding a Shockwave Application into Your HTML Page

There are two tags that can be used to place a Shockwave application. The most universal one is EMBED (the other one is OBJECT). EMBED is understood by Netscape Navigator and Microsoft IE and a standard tag would look like this: ‹EMBED SRC="ShockwaveMovie.dcr" HEIGHT="200" WIDTH="250" NAME="MyMovie"›. The height and width attributes are important but the NAME attribute is only needed if you want to interact between the HTML pages and the Shockwave application with JavaScript. Use the NOEMBED tag to display alternate information or an image for the people with a browser that doesn't support this tag and use the attribute

```
<OBJECT CLASSID="clsid:166B1BCA-3F9C-11CF-8075-444553540000"
CODEBASE="http://active.macromedia.com/director/cabs/sw.cab#version=6,0,0,0"
WIDTH="640" HEIGHT="480" NAME="theNameOfTheMovie">
<PARAM NAME="SRC" VALUE="Movie.dcr">
<EMBED SRC="Movie.dcr" WIDTH="640" HEIGHT="480" NAME=theNameOfThe-
Movie" PLUGINSPAGE="http://www.macromedia.com/shockwave">
</OBJECT>
<NOEMBED>
This page requires a web browser that can display objects.
</NOEMBED>
```

Embedding a Shockwave Application 08-01

PLUGINSPAGE to link to the page where the user can download the right plug-in in case it hasn't been installed. There is a way to use both tags, OBJECT and EMBED: change in this example [08-01] all the HEIGHT and WIDTH attributes to your values, also the NAME attributes. Exchange "Movie.dcr" to the URL of your movie and you are all set.

Blender

Interview with Greg Knoll

Be a guest at the Blender Online Cocktail Party and hear the latest rumors.

Blender is one of the most successful CD-ROM magazines on the market. Created in New York by Dennis Publishing, Blender focuses mostly on pop culture and presents music and movie reviews as well as interviews and games. Their Web site in the past relied mostly on HTML and JavaScript. Now they have decided to create a site that gives visitors more of a feel of the CD-ROM itself. The reason is simple "we already have the

There are no surprises, nothing moves, everything is in place.

content from our CD-ROM and all we need to do is to adapt it to the Web. With Streaming Shockwave we are now able to load the graphics and the other elements on demand", says Greg Knoll, one of the designers at Blender, who is now responsible for adapting the interactive stories to the Web. "We use JavaScript on our website to determine if you have the Streaming Shockwave plug-in. If you don't, you can download the player by itself and start it from the desktop". Because the application does not contain any graphics or sound, it is relatively small and can be downloaded quickly, something that is a big advantage over earlier versions of Shockwave, where all the data needed to be downloaded first. "It also allows us to black out the entire screen and give it a more Blender-like feel. Every story takes you about 15 minutes to go through and Shockwave is pulling the graphic files from the Web even in the idle time and this is why you don't have the experience of waiting for the content. By the time you get to the next page, the files had already been downloaded," says Greg on the advantage of Streaming Shockwave. "Another trick that we use is to start the stories or games with a text intro; this way we have some time to download the files while the user is occupied". Greg sees a big future for Streaming Shockwave, because "the

The main screen of Blender Online looks like the CD-ROM interface.

great thing about designing with Shockwave is that you put it out on the Web and it is cross platform. There are no surprises, nothing moves, everything is in place. With traditional Web design you have to check your pages in multiple browsers and on the several platforms, something that Shockwave has made obsolete".

This new approach has many advantages for Blender: besides better layout and design features than traditional HTML, it allows also for new ways of placing advertising. "With a Shockwave player we have the ability to present ads based on the user profile, like where did the visitor spend how much time, and where did he click." This profile is created by the application that runs on the client side, something that Greg Knoll thinks has a big advantage: "Why should you process the information on a server that is thousands of miles away?

With a shockwave player we have the ability to present ads based on the user profile.

Even the worst computer on the client side is faster than sending the information to a server and processing it there. We are writing now an advertising engine that makes decisions based on what the people have seen already. That makes it possible for example for a user to see an advert twice, based on the booking of the ad. After he has seen it twice, he is not going to see it again."

Using Streaming Shockwave has another advantage for the advertiser, "it allows for full screen advertising with soundtrack on the Internet, something that you didn't really have up to now and also gives you effects, like big screens sliding in, that you can't do with traditional Web design."

Last but not least, using Streaming Shockwave is faster than designing HTML pages from scratch. "It takes the designer about eight hours and the programmer about four hours to adapt a story from Blender to Streaming Shockwave." Most of the work is "compressing the audio and making it streaming audio files," says Greg. Another part is "learning how shockwave compression works, because it is not as simple as with GIF, where you just get rid of the colors and then it compresses much better." But still, eliminating colors is one of the keys and "we work hard on knocking down the graphic files and making them 1-Bit or 4-Bit. If you look at the images on the CD-ROM you see that they are all dithered to make them look better. For the Web we made them flat, because this way they compress better," he continues.

Important with Streaming Shockwave is also to keep the bandwidth of the user in mind. Greg has set himself a limit of "8 KByte per second for streaming audio and about 10 KByte per second for the graphics, because even with a 28.8 KBaud modem you don't get usually the full bandwidth and we want to make sure there are no interruptions".

Blender is certainly one of the pioneers of bringing the richness of Multimedia CD-ROMs to the Internet. But Greg Knoll has more ideas for Blender-Online than just putting the magazine out on the Internet. "What we are working on is the ability to chat. Because the Shockwave application runs on the client side, you have a much faster response time than with a server and the traditional Post or Get command. We also try to get on some multi-player content, where several people can participate in a game".

All this effort is geared towards an independent product. "There is a three part approach to Blender-Online: it is a marketing tool for the magazine, it is another revenue source as far as advertising goes, and for Dennis Interactive it is an example of what we can do. The CD-ROM market is not what it used to be, so we are moving more and more in the direction of an online content provider."

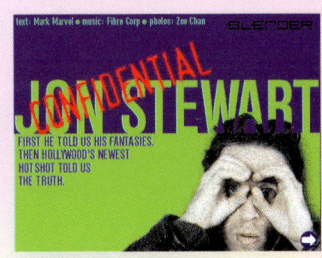

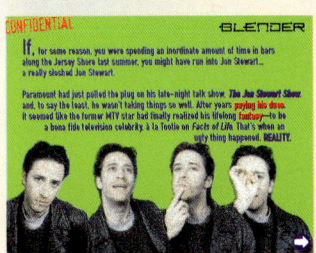

Memory for adults: the kids game was adapted and you have to match breasts.

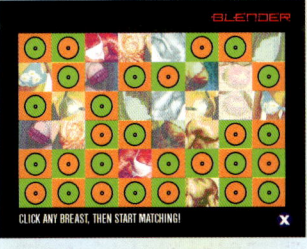

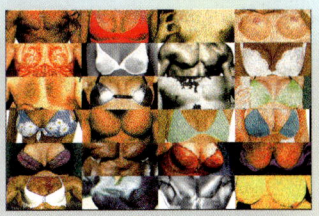

CHAPTER 09

JavaScript

Many designers don't like programming, but designing for the Web will become more like multimedia design than designing for print media. This requires basic knowledge about Java and JavaScript, since they allow for much more interactivity than regular HTML. In this chapter I want to give you some ready-made scripts that you only need to adapt slightly for your pages. All you need is some basic knowledge of how to implement Java and JavaScript, but let me first explain the difference between them to avoid confusion due to their similar names.

JAVA AND JAVASCRIPT

Developed by Sun Microsystems, Java is a programming language, while JavaScript is a scripting language. The difference is, simply, that with Java you can create applets that work as stand-alone applications or are embedded in your HTML page, while JavaScript is only used to make your page more interactive by assigning little programming scripts to elements, like changing pictures based on the user input. Java and JavaScript are similar in their syntax, and information can even be controlled and shared between JavaScript and Java. But although they are both easy to learn and use, Java is still a programming language which requires some familiarity with programming languages like C++ to create your own applets. JavaScript is easier to learn and implement into your Web page. If you have ever worked with Basic, it shouldn't be too difficult to learn JavaScript. In this chapter I will present some JavaScripts that can be used in your own Web site to get a feel for it.

HOW TO IMPLEMENT JAVA AND JAVASCRIPT

Programs written in Java are called applets and you can find many ready-made applets on the Internet that can be used for free. To embed a Java applet use the APPLET tags and specify the parameters of the applet with the PARAM tag [09-01].

In this example an applet for an interactive button is embedded with the dimension 100 by 25 pixels, and all the necessary information – such as the value of the parameter named "button" – are handed over to the applet. To implement a Java applet into your page you need to know which parameters are required, and this information is usually placed as a comment inside the source code. Because Java is also transmitted as text, you don't need any additional software to read or modify the code.

To return to how you can enhance your Web site with JavaScript: As with

Some browsers can't interpret Java and will display an empty rectangle instead. To avoid this, you should always include an image within the APPLET container that will display if the applet wasn't loaded.

```
<APPLET CODE="ChangingImage.class" WIDTH=100 HEIGHT="25">
<PARAM NAME="button" VALUE="button_regular.gif">
<IMG  SRC="alt_image.gif">
</APPLET>
```

The APPLET tag 09-01

Java, you can also find many tutorials on the Internet that explain how to program JavaScript as well as offer many helpful scripts that only need to be copied and placed inside your HTML page.

To implement a JavaScript on your page, you need to place the script inside the SCRIPT tags [09-02].

```
<SCRIPT LANGUAGE=javascript>
<!-- ... here you place the script -->
</SCRIPT>
```

The SCRIPT tag 09-02

```
<A HREF="http://www.server.com" onMouseOver = 'button.src="image2.gif"' onMouseOut = 'button.src="image1.gif"'>
<IMG NAME="button" SRC="image1.gif" BORDER=0 WIDTH=100 HEIGHT=25></A>
```

Interactive button 09-03

```
<HTML>
<HEAD>
<TITLE>JavaScript Banner</TITLE>
<SCRIPT LANGUAGE="JavaScript">
//this script rotates a banner ad
var counter = 0
var timer
var imgs = new Array()
    for (var i = 1; i <= 3; i++) {
        imgs[i] = new Image()
        imgs[i].src = "banner" + i + ".gif"
    }
    function banner_animation() {
        counter = (counter < 3 ) ? (counter + 1) : 1
        document.banner.src = imgs[counter].src
        timer=setTimeout("banner_animation()",5000)
    }
</SCRIPT>
</HEAD>

<BODY BGCOLOR="ffffff" onLoad="banner_animation()">
<IMAGE SRC="banner1.gif" NAME="banner">
</BODY>
</HTML>
```

Rotating Banners/Images 09-04

Placing the script between comment tags (<!-- ... -->) ensures that the script won't get displayed in browsers that don't understand JavaScript.

INTERACTIVE BUTTONS AND POP-UP MENUS

One of the best uses for JavaScript is to trigger an image change. This can be used for many things, such as buttons that change once the cursor is brought up over them, or for displaying a little descripion of the link as a pop-up image. Another use for this might be a banner ad that changes every fifteen seconds. The two commands needed are onMouseOver and onMouseOut. To script the change, simply name the image and specify two different image sources. For an interactive button that gets highlighted automatically if the user scrolls over the button, see [09-03].

In this script the image in the IMG tag was named "button" with the NAME attribute. Now this image can be addressed with JavaScript. In the link to this image the source for the highlighted button was set to "image2.gif".

What looks like text is actually an image: the yellow buttons are replaced with red buttons via JavaScript.

Every time the user brings the cursor over the image, the onMouseOver event handler changes the image (image2.gif) and the onMouseOut event handler brings it back to the original when the cursor is outside the image boundaries. How you name your images doesn't matter and you can use this for as many images and buttons as you like, but it is important that the images have the same size, otherwise they get scaled to the dimensions specified in the IMG tag or to the dimensions of the first image.

Rotating Banner

Many Web sites make money by displaying a banner ad at the top or the bottom of their page. It might be a nice feature to have those banner ads rotate so that every ad gets displayed for several seconds. This can be done with JavaScript, which has the advantage that it is easy to change the ads that are run. Simply drag the ads into a folder and name them properly. This script can also be used to create animations, with the benefit that making changes to the number of images shown is very easy and the sequence can then be controlled by user input. Use this script for example to create an online portfolio and let JavaScript change the displayed image. The only important factor here is that the images have the same dimensions, otherwise they get scaled to the dimensions of the first displayed image.

To change the number of banners displayed [09-04], change in the line "for (var i = 1; i <= 3; i++)" the number 3 to the number of images you have. Also change the number 3 in the line "counter = (counter < 3) ? (counter + 1) : 1". All banners must follow a naming convention that can be specified in the line "imgs[i].src = "banner" + i + ".gif"". In

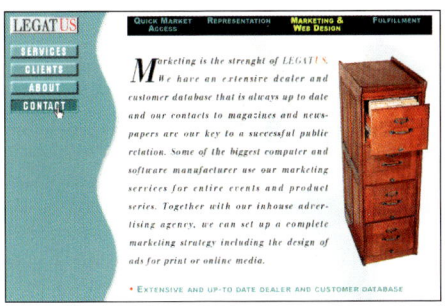

Another example for an interface with buttons controlled by JavaScript.

```
<HTML>
<HEAD>
<TITLE>JavaScript Banner with rotating link</TITLE>

<SCRIPT LANGUAGE="JavaScript">
//this script rotates a banner ad
var counter = 0
var timer
var imgs = new Array()
    for (var i = 1; i <= 3; i++) {
    imgs[i] = new Image()
    imgs[i].src = "banner" + i + ".gif"
    }
    function banner_animation() {
        counter = (counter < 3 ) ? (counter + 1) : 1
        document.banner.src = imgs[counter].src
        timer=setTimeout("banner_animation()",5000)
        if (counter == 1) {
        newLocation="http://www.web_address_1.com"
        }
        if (counter == 2) {
        newLocation="http://www.web_address_2.com"
        }
        if (counter == 3) {
        newLocation="http://www.web_address_3.com"
        }
    document.links[0].href=newLocation
    }
</SCRIPT>
</HEAD>

<BODY BGCOLOR="ffffff" onLoad="banner_animation()">
<A HREF="www.web_address_1.com">
<IMAGE SRC="banner1.gif" NAME="banner" BORDER=0>
</A>
</BODY>
</HTML>
```

Rotating banner/images with a rotating link 09-05

A scrolling banner in the status bar of the browser. With the script in [09-06] you can create your own text banner.

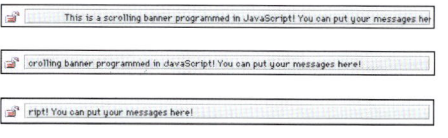

this example, the images are all numbered with the prefix "banner" and the extension ".gif". The animation is triggered after the loading of the page by placing the onLoad event handler in the BODY tag and the time between each banner is set to five seconds (5000).

Having a rotating banner ad is great, but in most cases banner ads are combined with a link. Then it is possible with a few lines of code, to have the banner ad always linked to a different URL [09-5]. To do this, place the image inside an ‹A› tag and add to the function a command that changes the link to a new location: "document.links[0].href= newLocation". You might need to change the zero in brackets because this number addresses the first link on the page and doesn't work if there is a previous link. The variable "newLocation" is defined in a couple of "if ...then" routines.

SCROLLING STATUS BAR

Scrolling text always attracts a lot of attention and it is possible, via JavaScript, to display scrolling text in the status bar of the browser. This is a great way to inform visitors of special events or offers that you have. The following little script allows the speed of the banner to be controlled by changing the value for the variable "banner_speed" and the message, by changing the variable "message". The "banner_main" function is then triggered after the loading of the page by adding the onLoad event

```
<HTML>
<HEAD>
<TITLE>JavaScript: scrolling text in the status bar</TITLE>
<SCRIPT LANGUAGE="JavaScript">
var banner_position=0;
var banner_speed=10; //this value defines banner speed
function banner_main() {
   var message="This is a scrolling banner programmed in JavaScript!"
   +" You can put your messages here!"
   var k=(100/message.length)+1;
   for(var j=0;j<=k;j++) message="         "+message;
   window.status=message.substring(banner_position,banner_position+100);
      if(banner_position++==message.length){
      banner_position=0;
      }
   setTimeout("banner_main()",1000/banner_speed);
}
</SCRIPT>
</HEAD>

<BODY BGCOLOR="ffffff" onLoad="banner_main()">
</BODY>
</HTML>
```

Scrolling text in the status bar 09-06

handler, but it could be triggered by any other event, such as the event handler onMouseOver or onClick. This way you could display a banner text if the user brings the mouse over a link or after one link has been clicked [09-05].

Opening a New Window

JavaScript can also be used to control browser windows and, this can be a nice tool to create a navigational window from which you then control the main window. In this example the navigational window is loaded automatically after the loading of the main page by writing the event handler onLoad into the BODY tag. This event handler triggers a function called "openWin()" that contains the command "window.open" with some specifications, such as which document to load (web_page.html), the name of the window (name_window), and most importantly the appearance of the window. With "status=no,width=200,height=300,toolbar=no,directories=no,menubar=no" all the browser window elements such as the toolbar are hidden, and with the attributes "width" and "height" the dimensions of the browser window are set [09-07]. Important note: do not add a space after the commas, or it may not work. Finally the command "self.name" assigns to the main window a name, which is then used in the navigational window to address it by using the attribute TARGET in a link (e.g., <A HREF="page.html" TARGET="main">).

Loading Several Pages with One Mouse Click

In the chapter on frames I explained how to load in a framebased web page several pages with one mouse click. Here I want to show you how to solve the

```
<HTML>
<HEAD>
<SCRIPT LANGUAGE="JavaScript">
    function openWin(){
    var newWin=window.open("web_page.html","name_window",
    "status=no,width=200,height=300,toolbar=no,directories=no,
    menubar=no")
    self.name = "main"
    }
</SCRIPT>
</HEAD>
    <BODY onLoad="openWin()">
    </BODY>
</HTML>
```

Opening a HTML document in a new window 09-07

same problem with JavaScript. The basic principle is to create a function that triggers the page load into each frame and then have a link call this function. Calling a function with a link is an important feature because it allows for nice effects. In the line "<A HREF="JavaScript:loadFile('page1.htm','page2.htm')">click here</A>" you see how you address a function with a link: the HREF attribute addresses JavaScript and the function "loadFile". Inside the parentheses you

```
<HTML>
<HEAD>
    <SCRIPT LANGUAGE="JavaScript">
        <!--
        function loadFile(document1, document2) {
        parent.frame_name1.location.href=document1;
        parent.frame_name2.location.href=document2;
        }
        // -->
    </SCRIPT>
</HEAD>
    <BODY>
    <A HREF="JavaScript:loadFile('page1.html','page2.html')">
    click here</A>
    </BODY>
</HTML>
```

Loading several pages with one click 09-08

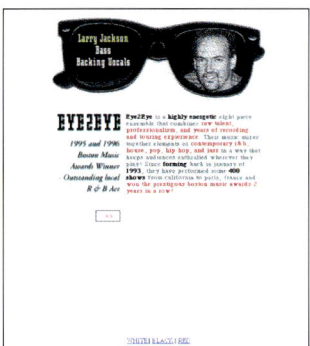

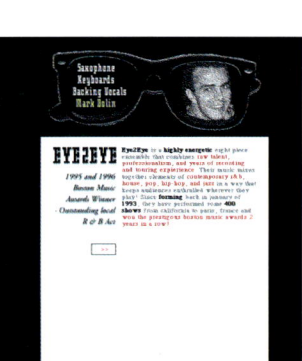

In the homepage for Eye2Eye, a music band from Boston, I created a website to feature the band and its CD releases. One of the section is called "BIO" and features background information about the band. I wanted to give the visitor the chance to customize the color of the background so I created a framebased page and a function that would trigger color changes in all the frames except the middle one.

see the documents that are handed over to the function and that are going to be loaded after clicking on this link. The function receives those variables and assigns them as the URL address, which means that you need to place the absolute or relative URL here. Replace "frame_name1" and "frame_name2" with the names of your frames and this script should work correctly [09-08].

Changing the Color of a Page

Every attribute of your Web page, such as the color of the background or the color of the links, can be addressed and changed with JavaScript. Here now a nice gimmick which allows the user to customize the background color. In this example a link calls the function "change-Color", which consists only of one com-

```
<HTML>
<HEAD>
    <SCRIPT LANGUAGE="JavaScript">
        <!--
        function changeColor() {
        document.bgColor="red"
        }
        // -->
    </SCRIPT>
</HEAD>
    <BODY>
        <A HREF="JavaScript:change-
        Color()">change the color</A>
    </BODY>
</HTML>
```

Changing the Color of Pages 09-09

mand line: document.bgColor="red". If you don't want to use the 16 standard color names, just use the regular syntax (#nnnnnn) to assign an RGB value. Other color properties that can be set are foreground color (fgColor), color of links (linkColor), color of links when clicked (alinkColor), and the color of followed links (vlinkColor). Unfortunately, many of those properties don't work with the Netscape browser, but this might change in the future [09-09].

CREATING BUTTONS WITH EYE CANDY

One of my favorite plug-ins for Photoshop is the filter collection Eye Candy 3.0, formerly known as "The Black Box", of Alien Skin Software, because here you have numerous standard effects right at your fingertips which would take much more time to create using the traditional techniques. Now that you know how to create interactive buttons with JavaScript, I want to show you how to design buttons with Eye Candy.

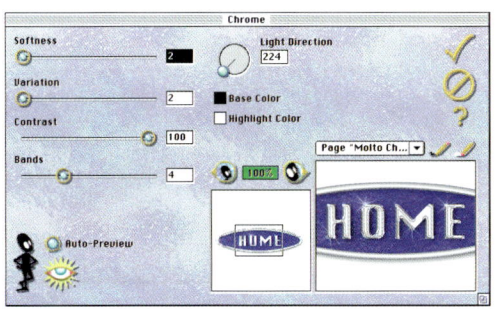

1 *Although not much Photoshop knowledge is needed if you have Eye Candy, you do need some basic knowledge on how to work with selections as well as the channel palette. To get this button with a chrome edge I loaded a texture, selected an area and deleted all the redundant parts by inverting the selection and pressing the delete button on the keyboard. Then I inverted the selection again and saved it in a channel (#4), duplicated this channel (#5) by selecting #4 in the channel palette and clicking on the pop-up menu in the palette. With "Select: Modify: Contract" I contracted the selection and filled it with black. The result is now an ellipse with a 10 pixel white border. After selecting the RGB channels in the channel palette I loaded the channel #5 as selection ("Select: Load Selection"). With this selection and the chrome filter of Eye Candy I created the chrome effect. It is even more authentic if, in addition, you use the filter called "Drop Shadow". This filter creates a drop shadow for any selection and gives this edge the needed 3D touch. The same filters are used for the text in the button and a fine border was given the selection by using "Edit: Stroke".*

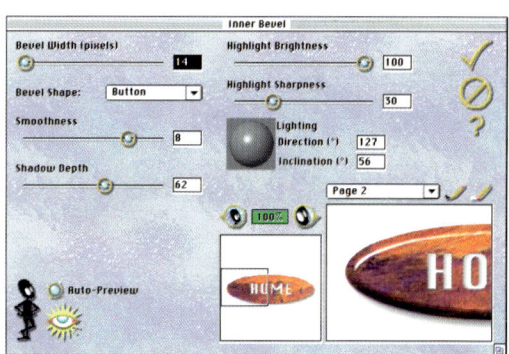

2 *To create a three-dimensional button you can also use the "Lighting Effects" filter in Photoshop, but you need some knowledge on how to create this relief channel in order to create beveled objects. Eye Candy makes it much easier to create buttons with a bevel because it provides four bevel forms in the filter "Inner Bevel". All you need to do is to select them in the Bevel Shape Option and then set the other parameters like Light or Shadow Depth.*

JavaScript

CHAPTER 10

Music & Audio

To make your web site a true multimedial experience, you need sound and video. Unfortunately, both are really hard to transmit due to the bandwidth of the connection that most users have. But advances are being made and audio will become more and more common.

So far there are two methods for delivering audio over the Web: files that have to be downloaded before playback, and audio that plays during download (streaming audio).

The first method gives you, in general, better control over the sound quality and doesn't require any plug-in because both Internet Explorer and Netscape Navigator can play these files through the browser. The problem is that the download of a long audio file might take too long for the visitor, in which case you should use streaming audio.

INSTALLING A SOUND FILE

There are several ways of implementing sound into your Web page. If you don't want to use a plug-in, you can use the ‹BGSOUND› tag of Internet Explorer 3.0 or use the standard ‹EMBED› tag, which both browsers understand. The ‹EMBED› tag plays audio files in WAV, AIFF, AU, and MIDI formats.

```
‹EMBED SRC="music_file.mid"
AUTOSTART="true" WIDTH="144"
HEIGHT="60" LOOP="1"›
```
The EMBED tag used for a MIDI file 10-01

WAV (.wav): This format is the standard audio format on an IBM-compatible running Microsoft Windows.
AIFF (.aiff) is the standard audio format on Apple Computers and is good for music and high quality sound.
AU (.au) was developed by Sun, has a poor sound quality, but a small file size.
MIDI (.mid): If you are a musician, you are probably familiar with this format, because it is used to record music with a sequencer. For non-musicians let me explain what MIDI does and how it works.

MIDI stands for Musical Instrumental Digital Interface and all modern electronic instruments are equipped with this interface, because it allows transmission of the musical information, like notes and duration, from a musician playing on a keyboard. This information can be recorded and arranged in a sequencer program on a computer and later be send back to a musical instrument.

The advantage of this technique is that it doesn't require much memory. This also makes it an interesting solution to create background music for your Web page, but, because MIDI is not an audio format, it requires an installed sound card on a PC or an installed QuickTime Music system extension on a Macintosh.

The best way to put sound or a MIDI file on your page is using the EMBED tag, because Netscape 2.0 and higher support sound in EMBED tags but none

```
<EMBED SRC="music_file.mid"
AUTOSTART="true" HIDDEN="true"
LOOP="1">
```
The HIDDEN attribute 10-02

```
<NOEMBED>Your browser doesn't
support EMBED! To listen to the
background music, please click <A
HREF="bgsound.aif">here.</A></NO-
EMBED>
```
The NOEMBED tag 10-03

```
<META HTTP-EQUIV="refresh"
CONTENT="20; URL=bgsound.wav">
```
The META tag used for audio 10-04

of them support the BGSOUND tag (Internet Explorer 3.01 and higher support BGSOUND and EMBED> tags).

An example of a sound file placed with an EMBED tag is [10-01]. You need to use the right extension, depending on the file type. In this example a MIDI file is loaded and the attribute AUTOSTART="true" automatically plays the sound after it is completely downloaded. If this attribute is set to "false", the sound will only play when the user hits the "play" button in the control panel. This control panel is visible if you set WIDTH and HEIGHT to the given numbers. Smaller numbers will display an incomplete image and below WIDTH="0" and HEIGHT="2", the console will not be displayed at all. If you want to hide the control panel, you need to set the HIDDEN attribute to "true" [10-02].

Finally, the LOOP attribute tells the browser how many times you want the sound to be played, and this attribute can be an integer or true/false. Using "true", the browser will continue playing the sound until the stop button on the console is clicked.

For all the browsers that don't support EMBED, you can insert a NOEMBED tag into your page and place a link inside it [10-03]. All the browsers that do support the EMBED tag will hide everything between the NOEMBED tags, otherwise the user will see the link inside the <NOEMBED> tag.

But there is also another way to play a sound file and that is by using the META tag. This tag can be used to refresh a page after a certain time, but also to play a sound file [10-04]. The tag needs to be placed inside the HEAD tags at the beginning of your document and, in this example, the background sound is loaded after a period of 20 seconds. Best of all, the file will automatically open in a new window with its control panel.

SOME TIPS ON HOW TO RECORD AUDIO

If you have a Macintosh PowerPC you can also digitize external sound sources without needing any other hardware. To obtain the best possible fidelity when recording digital audio, it is important to record your audio signal at the highest possible level without introducing clipping. If your sound clips, the signal is louder then the dynamic range of the analog/digital converter and you will get a distorted sound. This is something that can't be fixed later, so it is really important that you pay attention to this when you record.

When you record audio into your computer, always use the maximum available resolution, because a much better quality will be obtained if you do all the signal processing with your sound in CD quality and then convert it to a lower setting. The CD quality standard is 44.1 kHz at 16 bit and for a regular pop-song this means between 40-60 MByte of data. There is only one Web site that I

MACAMP is a program for the Macintosh, that can create and write MPEG.

know of where you can download a complete song that way, and that is the David Bowie homepage (a fast T1 connection is recommended). As long as the majority of web surfers only access the Internet with a 28.8 modem, CD quality will not be available for the standard user, so you need to lower the frequency rate to 22.05 kHz, 11.025 kHz, or even 5.664 kHz to make it available for a broader audience. With 22 kHz and 11 kHz you still get acceptable quality. At 6 kHz the sound quality is similar to a telephone – okay for voice, but not enough for music.

While the frequency sets the quality on the time axis, the bit rate sets the dynamics of your sound, so another way to reduce the data in your audio file is to convert it to 8 bit. A good setting for streaming audio is 22.05 kHz/8 bit, if you expect your visitors to have a 28.8 connection, and 11 kHz/8 bit, if the majority has a 14.4 modem.

Optimizing Audio for the Internet

Before making any conversion from a high fidelity sound to a streaming audio file, you should optimize the audio for the Internet. In the software programs Peak or Cubase VST you can perform some enhancements that partially com-

continues on page 138

Audio Formats for the Web: MPEG Layer 3

MP3 or MPEG layer 3 is a very advanced audio format that provides almost CD quality sound files at reasonable file sizes. The compression ratio is up to 12:1. The resulting files are bigger than RealAudio files in best quality mode (17:1), but also superior in sound. MPEG layer 3 compresses sounds by removing parts that are inaudible, retaining the full frequency and dynamic spectrum. Streaming of MP3 files is incorporated in the file format, but requires high bandwidth connections, such as ISDN. Right now files are mostly posted for downloads. On the Macintosh you need special player programs like Vamp, MacAmp, or SoundApp and a Power-PC to play those files. 680X0 machines cannot play the files without additional hardware. On PCs you need at least a 486 CPU and a soundcard, and a Pentium 133 CPU is highly recommended WinPlay, WinAmp, or MuseArc are player programs for this platform. To create an MP3 file on the Macintosh, you can use MPecker Encoder 02ob5, a freeware utility for PowerMacs. The common settings for MP3 files are 128 kbps and Joint Stereo Encoding. MP3 retains the high quality of the source material, so no prior processing is really necessary. The use of Waves' L1 maximizer still gives most material more of a modern, powerful edge. Macromedia's Shockwave audio format also uses MP3 algorithms. To create Shockwave audio use Macromedia's SoundEdit 16 2.0 or higher, Director, or Authorware.

Warner Music Latin

Peter Seidler, Co-founder Avalanche, New York

One great example for a Music website is the Warner Music Latin site. It features Video clips and RealAudio Sound and was designed by Peter Seidler from Avalanche: "The Warner Music Latin is a trilingual site and you can switch between those languages throughout the whole site. From the design point of view what I wanted to accomplish there was to literally get some local music flavor. We sent disposable cameras to all of Warner Music Latin's offices in South America, even offices with only three people, like in Chile. We gave them a list of things we would like to see, stuff on their desks, the view outside their door, pretty ordinary scenes, with the request to send us back the cameras. Part of the reason we did it that way was that there was not a one hundred thousand dollar photo budget and we couldn't send a professional photographer. So we received all those disposable cameras from all over South America, developed the pictures, scanned the best ones, colored it red in Photoshop and used those images as background patterns. When you view the Brazil page you get a very subtle touch of the country because you might see in the background an everyday scene, maybe just the view of a bus, but the special thing is that it is a particular bus. It is the bus that was standing in the street right in front of the Warner Music office in Brazil."

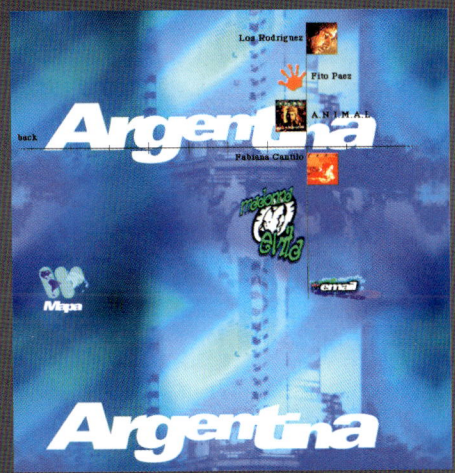
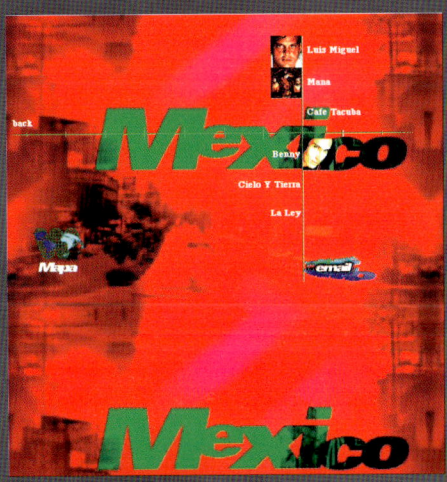
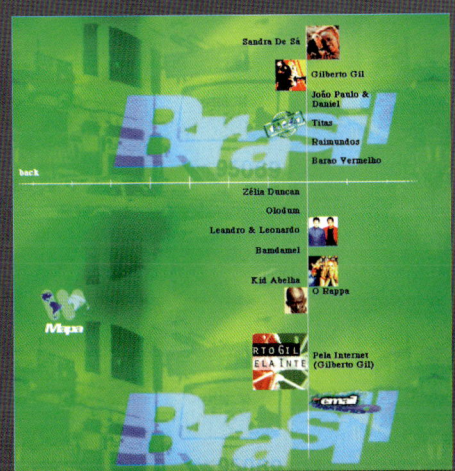

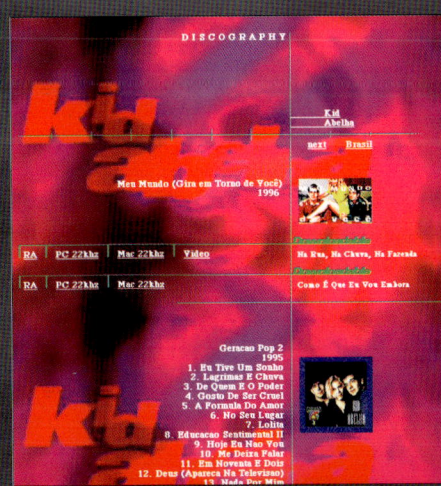

In each country you can select a national artist and hear a demo track or see a music video.

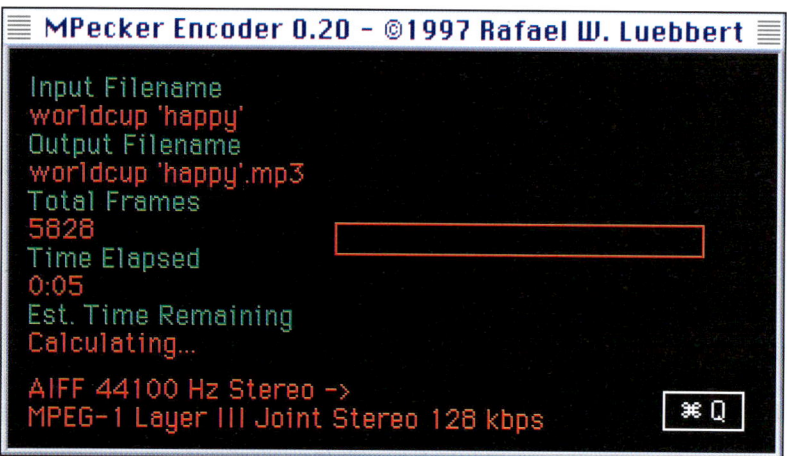

The program MPecker for the Macintosh allows you to encode MPEG-1 Layer III audio files.

The RealAudio Player is available as free plug-in for Macintosh and Windows.

AUDIO FORMATS FOR THE WEB: REALAUDIO

This file format is very popular because it allows almost instant access to very long sound files such as songs, interviews, or even live transmissions, thanks to streaming technology. The RealAudio algorithm uses high compression rates ranging from about 17:1 to 170:1, which are based on CD quality audio. A three-minute song can be reduced to as little as 180 KB of hard drive space compared to the nominal 30 MB in CD quality. There is a definite deterioration in sonic quality when using these high compression ratios for slower modems. However, the resulting low continuous data rate necessary for those files provides realtime audio access for modems as slow as 14.4 Kbps. Low bandwidth files like these require special preparation to avoid sonic artifacts such as distortion, dull sound, or high noise levels.

pensate for the loss in quality. Here are the main tools:

Normalize: This is a function available in almost any audio editor and all it does is look for the highest peak in a sound file and then raise the volume of the whole audio file until this peak reaches the maximum possible dynamic range.

Compressor: A compressor goes a step further and compresses the dynamic range between the highest peak and the parts with low volume. The final audio file will sound much louder but has an almost linear level.

Equalizer: Because many users listen to the audio files through their computer speaker, the sound loses many of the higher frequencies. With an equalizer the high frequencies can be raised to compensate for the loss.

USING REALAUDIO

RealAudio from Progressive Networks is a plug-in that allows you to listen to an audio file in real time. This is a fantastic feature and has become one of the most commonly-used plug-ins. You can not only download the plug-in, but also the necessary encoder, at their website at www.realaudio.com and then create your own streaming RealAudio file.

In the encoder select a frequency response and a target speed (e.g., 28.8 KBaud Modem, Mono) before you convert the file. The result might have about 500–600 KByte in file size, but will still sound good enough for a reasonable hearing experience. To integrate this sound file into your Web page, create a link to this file with an ‹A› tag. But here comes the surprise: if you click in the browser on the link, the audio file gets downloaded first to your hard drive before it opens with the RealAudio Player plug-in. This is obviously not a streaming audio file, so what went wrong?

Here is the trick: to have it be real streaming audio you need to create a metafile, which is a text file that merely contains the URL of the actual audio file. The link in your HTML document links to this metafile, which then links to the audio file. This sounds more complicated than it is, nevertheless it is still a drag, because you need to upload everything to your server before you can check if it works correctly. Here again is the whole setup:

1. In the HTML document create a link to a metafile with the extension ".ram" (e.g., ‹A HREF="audiofile.ram"›).

2. Create a metafile, a plain textfile that you save as "text with linebrakes", with the URL of the RealAudio file location (e.g., "http://www.yourserver.com/myfolder/audiofile.ra"). This is no typo, the extension of the audiofile needs to be ".ra"!

3. Put the audio file at the location that you specified in the metafile and everything should work.

STEINBERG CUBASE VST

As mentioned before, audio files are not the only thing that you can hear in a browser. MIDI files can also be integrated into your Web page. One of the best software to create music – and soundfiles – for the Web is Cubase VST from the German software company Steinberg.

Cubase VST is a sequencer program combined with hard disk recording system which allows you to record and edit audio files. This combination of sequencer and audio editing makes it a nice tool for all sorts of music production for the Internet.

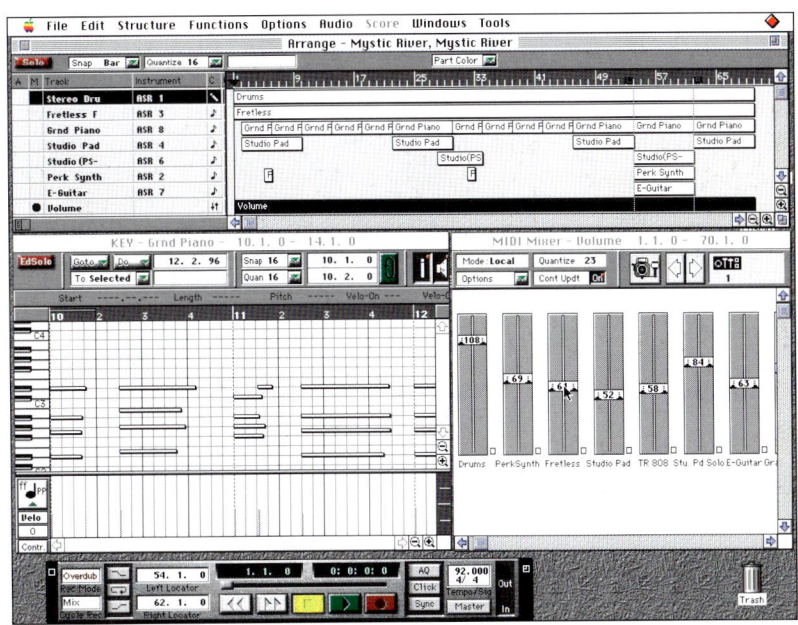

The arrangement window and some of the edit windows of Cubase VST.

If you are interested in creating MIDI files for the Internet, you need to know what General MIDI is. This standard had been developed by the Japanese keyboard company Roland to ensure that you can listen to a MIDI file and have a sound experience that is at least similar to the idea of the composer. Maybe this sounds confusing, but it isn't if you remember that the MIDI file doesn't store any information about the sound, but stores only note information. This

Cubase VST is a sequencer combined with a hard disk recording system. In this screen you can see the Audio Mixer Window.

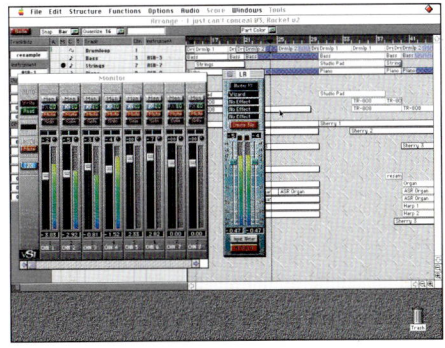

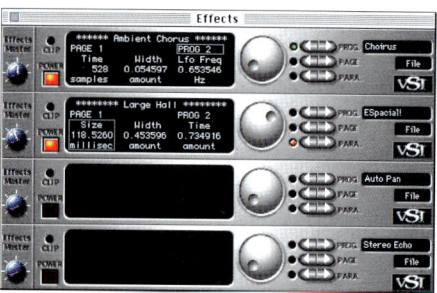

In the effects window you can simulate up to four effects that you can route to different audio tracks.

circumstance used to require the listener to have the same sound module as the composer, but, because this wasn't practical, the General MIDI standard was defined to specify which sounds a sound module needs to have. So in a General MIDI sound module, for example, drum sounds or bass sounds are always stored in the same program numbers. The composer can now store a program change number with his song knowing that whatever General MIDI sound module the listener might have, it will be a similar sound to the one on his sound module. To create a MIDI file for the Internet, you need to have such a sound module with General MIDI standard and set the program changes in the sequencer before you save it. If you are working with a Macintosh, you can use the sounds of the Quicktime Music extension by addressing them via OMS.

Bias Peak

This software package for the Macintosh is a pure sound file editor, with great features that make it even more suitable for preparing sound for the Internet than Cubase VST. One reason is that it can write RealAudio files directly. This is also possible with the free RealAudio Encoder, but Peak also allows you to embed URLs in your sound file. Now you can have a sound file change the pages in the browser.

But there is more to Peak than just this: it can read soundfiles directly from a CD. If you need to create a site for a music band, for example, that wants to promote their CD on the Internet, then Peak is the tool for you because it does everything in one program. You can cut your sound files or create fade ins and fade outs, but most of all, you have many tools to enhance the sound quality. To hear audio in real time through the Internet, the sound files needs to be compressed, very much like images, but this then results in a loss of quality. With Peak you can compensate for this, to some extent, with compressors and equalizers that are available as plug-ins.

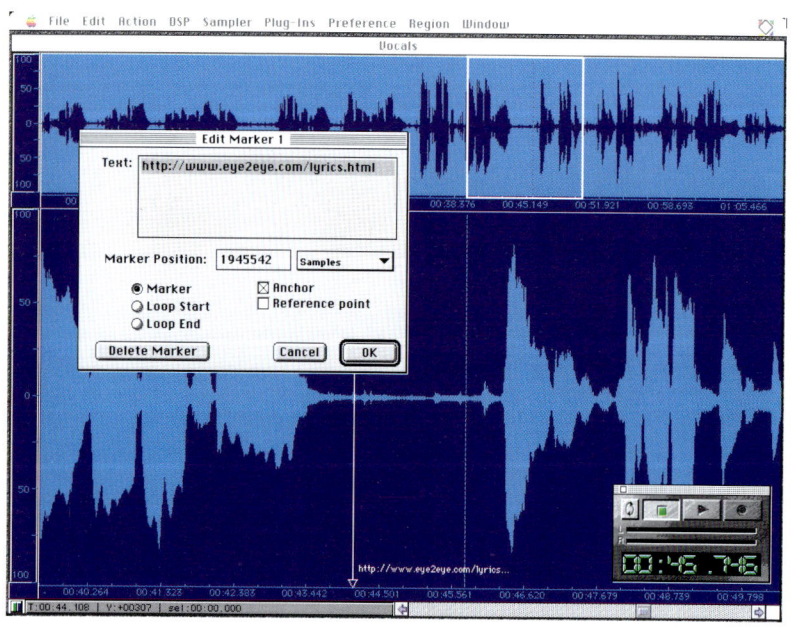

In Bias Peak you can embed an URL in the audio file.

Optimizing CD Tracks for the Web

Being a musician and songwriter myself, creating Web sites for music bands appeals to me. For a website that I created for the band Eye2Eye, I worked together with Hajo Carl, producer and sound-engineer from Berlin, to prepare the CD tracks for the Internet. We used the BIAS PEAK 1.60 Soundeditor and the Waves Native Power Pack plug-in bundle for Macintosh to create a good-sounding RealAudio 28.8 mono/low bandwidth file.

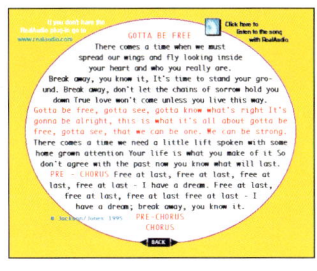

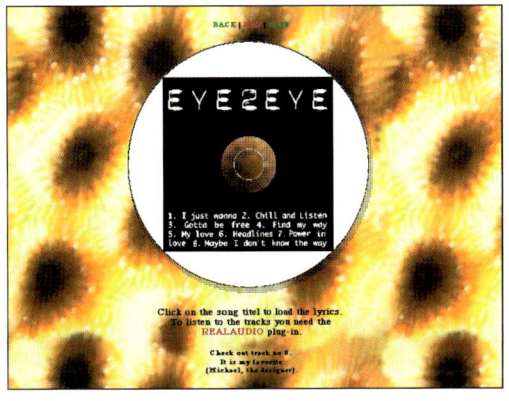

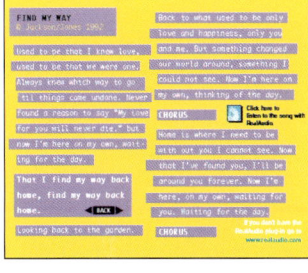

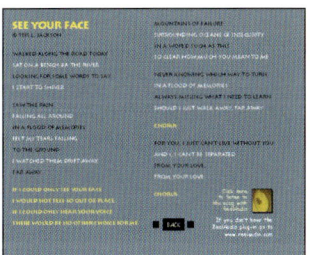

1 The first step was to import a song via Peak's "Import CD Track" function, which creates a 16-bit/44.1 kHz AIFF file on your Macintosh hard drive. Since the chosen RealAudio format will only use a frequency range up to 4 kHz, it's necessary to truncate frequencies to create a sonic balance that works with the constrained format. It is important to do this before the conversion, because after the conversion process it is much more difficult to optimize the sound. We used Waves' Q6 graphic equalizer to cut off the high frequencies that can't be transmitted in the RealAudio file.

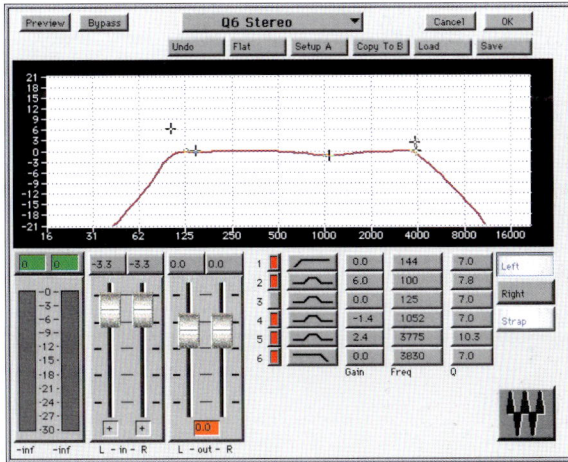

2 To create a sonic balance we cut off the lower frequency spectrum to leave more space for the singer's voice and other higher frequencies. To further increase the intelligibility of the singer we also lowered a frequency in the mid-range.

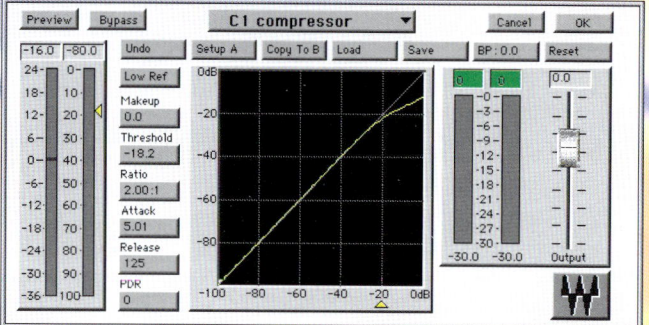

3 RealAudio compression also creates a lower dynamic bandwidth, which is why we set up *Waves' C1* compressor to raise lower level signals in the music material. Suitable settings are very dependent on the source material. Extreme settings may create unwanted effects. To avoid pumping or unnatural peak cutting (most noticeable in percussive sounds), use a working setting twice on the file instead.

4 Before actually converting the soundfile to RealAudio format we increased the general loudness of the song with *Waves' L1 Maximizer*. This process raises the loudness of audio material beyond the effect of normalizing, thus providing extra punch. Since this stereo file will be converted to mono for RealAudio we set the final output of L1 to – 3 dB. This avoids distortion that otherwise could occur by mixing together two high energy 0 dB channels into one.

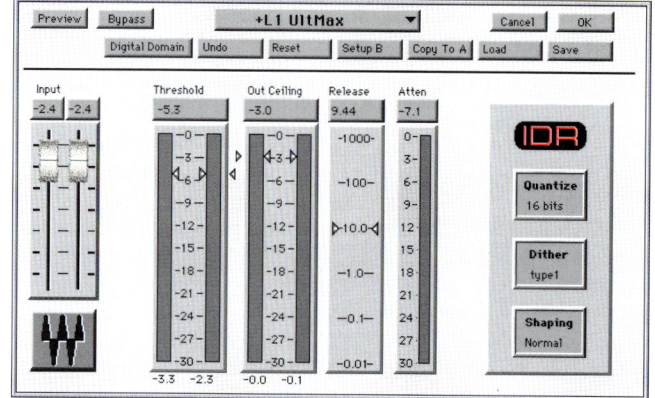

5 We created all the RealAudio files directly from PEAK and chose the RealAudio 28.8 format. Because PEAK produces smoother results we use its sample rate converter for the conversion to RealAudio. The last step is always to check the file with the RealAudio player. If the result isn't satisfactory the whole process needs to be repeated, which is why we usually create different versions at once and then pick the RealAudio file that sounds the best.

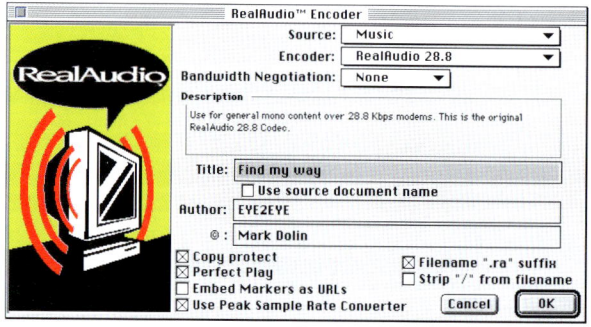

David Bowie Site • N2K, Inc.

**Interview with Marlene Stoffers and Ben Clemens, N2K, Inc.
Designer of the David Bowie home page**

When MTV Online made a survey among their viewers about the best music Web site, they nominated – among four other sites – David Bowie's site, designed by Marlene Stoffers and Ben Clemens from N2K, Inc. This nomination was just another acknowledgement of the extraordinary work that both have done.

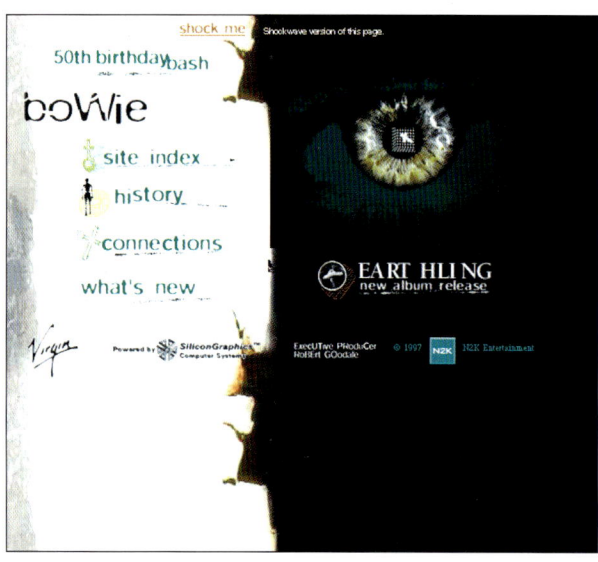

Since the release of David Bowie's CD "Earthling", the Web site has received many awards from all over the world. I spoke to them at the Manhattan waterfront in the Wall Street district, a few blocks away from 55 Broadway – where besides N2K, Inc., many other Web design agencies have their office.

How did you get involved in the redesign of David Bowie's new home page?

Marlene Stoffers: The site was designed before by a few different companies with different artists and what happened was that with Bowie's release of his new album in January and his 50th birthday on January 8th, the record company wanted to do something special. N2K, Inc., had a contract with Virgin Records to fix it up and repurpose it, but we ended up doing a complete redesign of the whole site.
Because of the limited budget, we had to create the whole site in four weeks. It was just Ben and I partnering on the project.

Did you have any clearly defined instructions or was it totally up to you how you designed the site?

Marlene Stoffers: Bowie wanted to incorporate artwork from his album into the web site. Because the site already had four or five different designs, it became clear that it needed a complete redesign. Besides this there was no real navigational structure and a huge volume of content. So we reworked and rethought everything, but because of the time constraints we had to put the navigational structure together in about a day.

For that it seems it worked out pretty well, or is there anything that you would change today?

Ben Clemens: Today the site is divided into five categories: Earthling, Connection, History, Site Index, Beginning. We had to deal with an enormous amount of content and had to organize it around more ambiguous areas with a small number of icons. A colleague of mine, Paul Confrancesco, also contributed very much to the organizational structure of the site. If I would do it over again I would make another interface that would allow you to see the depth of the site more, because the whole site is about 120 pages and is organized into so many arbitrary categories that it is difficult to find specific information.

Was it difficult for you to create artwork based on the existing artwork of the CD?

Ben Clemens: The problem was that if you take static images and artwork and then put it into the interactive world, you have to flesh it out. So we had the existing Bowie site to start with and the artwork of the album, but then we started researching the ideas behind "Kirilian photography". Kirilian photography is a technique and philosophy of health and lifestyle and measuring it through your aura, which can be captured by this special camera.

This sounds like you are very familiar with this. Where did you get all this information and how does Kirilian photography and his Web site reflect David Bowie's personality?

Ben Clemens: We were fortunate enough to find a lot of information on Kirilian photography on the Web. The second part of your question is not easy to answer, but I think David Bowie is somebody who is purposely ambiguous about his aesthetics. He just tries to generate as much doubt as he can, I think. He plays with his identity, he plays with his approach to music all the time and works against a straightforward way of explaining him or his music. So what you could say is that we fleshed out his vague visual ideas to create his web site.

Marlene Stoffers: What Ben was saying is very important. David Bowie is just such an ambiguous character and the site is just an element of his character that we were representing at that time. But at the same time we are also dealing with the whole history of David Bowie, because it was his 50th birthday. So it was kind of a juggle between both of those things. We had to deal with five decades of David Bowie's chameleon-like career. It is really difficult to represent an artist who changes all the time, so we had to decide on a couple of elements and hope that they work.

Ben Clemens: We played with David Bowie's identity as much as he does and the good thing about him is that he allows his identity to be reinterpreted, because he is so ambiguous.

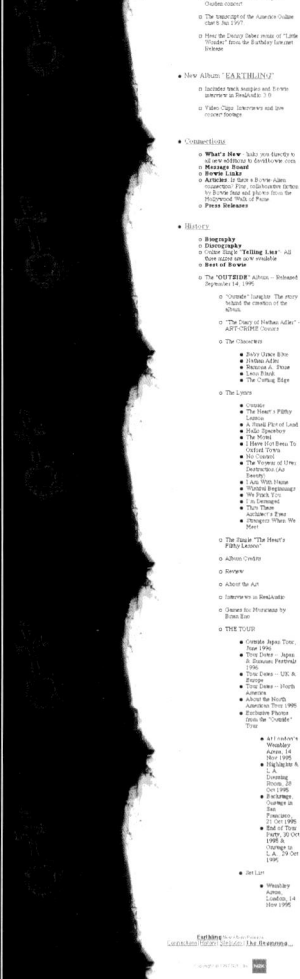

The Site Index reveals the content behind each section.

Did you get any comment from him?

Ben Clemens: We haven't talked to David Bowie directly, but we have been told from Ted Mico that he liked it a lot.

One striking thing about the site is the background that you used. How did you create it and how did you create the other elements?

Marlene Stoffers: A lot of the elements, like the wire frames behind the navigational icons, had been created in the 3D program Infini-D. The background was made of some fluids pressed under glass that I scanned. Ben added some color to it in Photoshop and this obscure background pattern that we sort of re-warped became our main design element. We liked a lot of the artwork from the album and we started using those as navigational items throughout the entire site, but avoided text. You see the text only once you roll over the icons.

Another important factor in the David Bowie site is the use of Shockwave. Was this your first time using it?

Ben Clemens: I have worked with Shockwave before. For the David Bowie site we used Streaming Shockwave, a new concept that allows you to stream the data instead of downloading everything first. The only problem we had was to get the various images and their palettes to run well on a 256-color machine. We did this eight times before it worked out.

Working with colors is one of the main issues in designing with the Web. What do you think is the main mistake that many designers make?

Happy Birthday, Mr. Bowie. One page in the site is dedicated to this event.

Ben Clemens: A lot of designers look at the websites on a monitor with much more colors than 256, where all their images look good. If you look at the same images at 256 colors they can look really wacky. It took many many many tries to get the David Bowie site looking good in 256 colors. We did work with DeBabelizer, but the result was chubby and chunky. So I worked through all the images manually in Photoshop by stripping out all unneeded colors and converting it back and forth from Indexed to RGB.

How did you get into design anyhow?

Ben Clemens: I went to art school but then became obsessed with doing design. To me design has a much more social aspect to it than making art. For a while I worked as an illustrator and I came to New York, because I always wanted to live here. I ran into Nicholas Butterworth, who was starting to do Web sites, and I worked with him for a year and a half on Sonic Net, when there was no music on the web at all. Sonic Net is an alternative music site and it came through Tim Knife, who wanted to originally create a global network of cyberstudios, where bands all over the world could get together on the Internet and play music to each other via MIDI. But then the bottom fell out of financing for that. The American Internet Service Provider Prodigy paid Sonic Net to turn it into an alternative music site and it is trying to compete now with MTV Online.

Marlene Stoffers: I went to Parsons School of Design in New York for four years and during that time I studied painting, photography, and design. I was considering pursuing a teaching career but then I ended up doing some production work at Ziff – Davis Publishing. The last company I worked for was a marketing company, and I was their in-house art department. We dealt with record labels a lot, marketing bands and we also designed our own Web site,

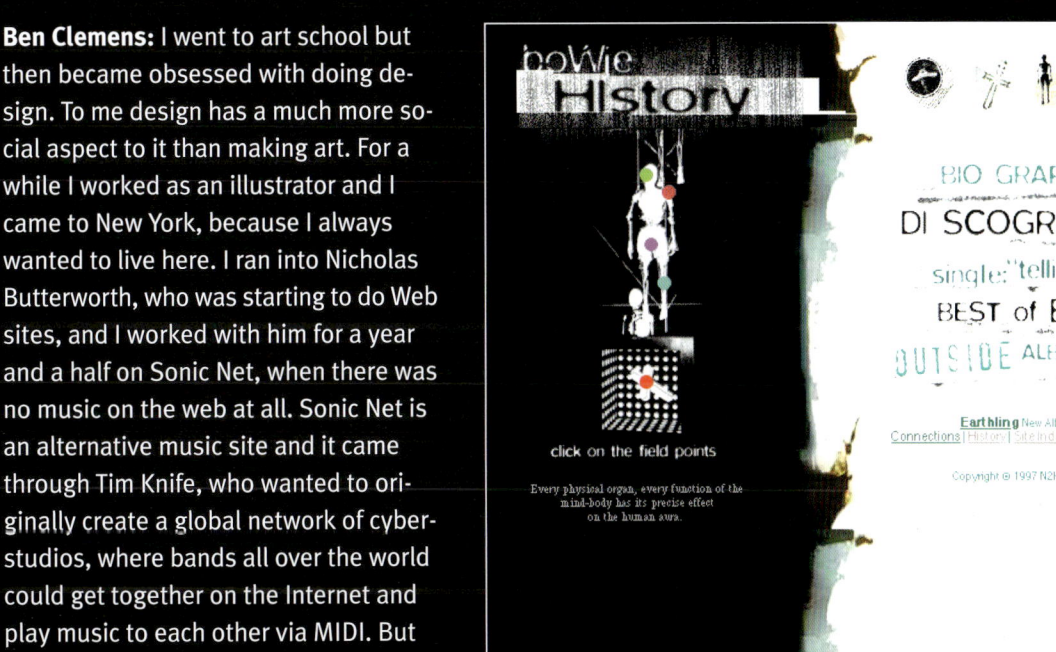

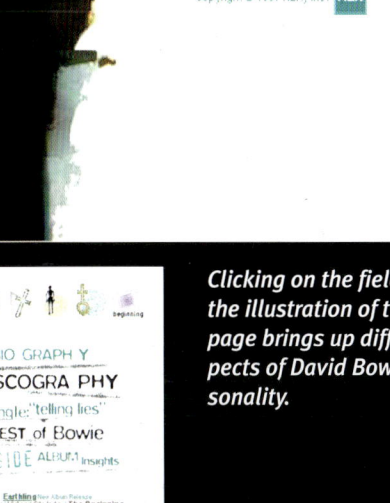

Clicking on the field points in the illustration of the History page brings up different aspects of David Bowie's personality.

eventually started getting clients from this website and Mercury Records in Nashville had me create a Shania Twain Web site, a Terry Clark site, and we kept getting more and more clients. I realized that this was a medium that I was very interested in, because it always was changing and it kept my attention. Sometimes I miss print because there aren't as many limitations, but the great thing about the Web is that anyone can view your work.

So what are the limitations of the web that bother you the most and what is it that you like?

Marlene Stoffers: Keeping the graphics down to a minimum; the color palettes; the fact that you can't bring a font size to lower than 12 points is something that bothers me. But at the same time, to work around that design challenge is what I like about it.

Ben Clemens: What I like about the Web is that it allows me to think of information in a way that I would never have thought about it before. There are a lot of people who spend their time doing information design, thinking about how people experience things. Nobody has any problems with a brochure because everybody knows how to create and use one, but I have really spent a lot of time thinking about the interaction of a site. To me that is a huge design challenge and it is the most interesting part of it. The images are certainly important, but the interaction is where the design challenge is.

So what are the big mistakes that some Web designers make and what do you think is a good interface design?

Ben Clemens: Right now many sites are treated as reference work. It is like going to the library: you pull out the card and then you go to the shelves and pull out the book. There need to be as many approaches to interface design as there are things to talk about. I think the reference model, the top-down tree design like on the Bowie site, is good for some things, but not for everything.

Marlene Stoffers: I think that designers should do more research on the viewers who look at the site. A lot of designers just design sites around what they think would be cool, but user testing is very important, because otherwise we are just guessing, trying to figure out what would be usable.

Simplicity is the key to good interface design in most cases and designing something that is usable by a few different audiences is also important. One idea that I thought of would be coding three different sites with the same content for a few different viewing audiences.

What would be the three viewing models?

Marlene Stoffers: Maybe one audience who likes to browse more, who is not too concerned about text, but likes to click on obscure looking images. Another audience likes it all straightforward and very obvious.

Each person wants to view a site differently, so it is really difficult to pinpoint one exact way of doing it.

Is there any alternative to the current way of Web design and how do you think that Web design will change?

Ben Clemens: The reason why everybody is interested these days in push technology is, that it is the only alternative that people have come up with so far. I think rather than having it all push or all traditional Web design, that the future will be sort of a sliding scale between those two, depending on the needs of the site. Some things I push to you, some things you have to go out and find. This will result in totally different Web sites.

Besides the design, what do you think is going to change?

Marlene Stoffers: User testing will become much more important in the future, like beta testing for software. A site that N2K, Inc., is working on is "www.rocktropolis.com" and we did user testing on 10 different people. As far as I am concerned that is not nearly enough, because the age range of the audience is between 18 to 29, so testing it only with 10 people can't give you sufficient feedback. To know what the audience wants is the foundation to begin a project.

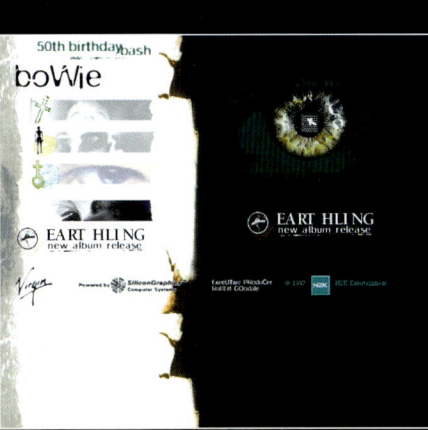

The Shockwave version of the site features RealAudio sound

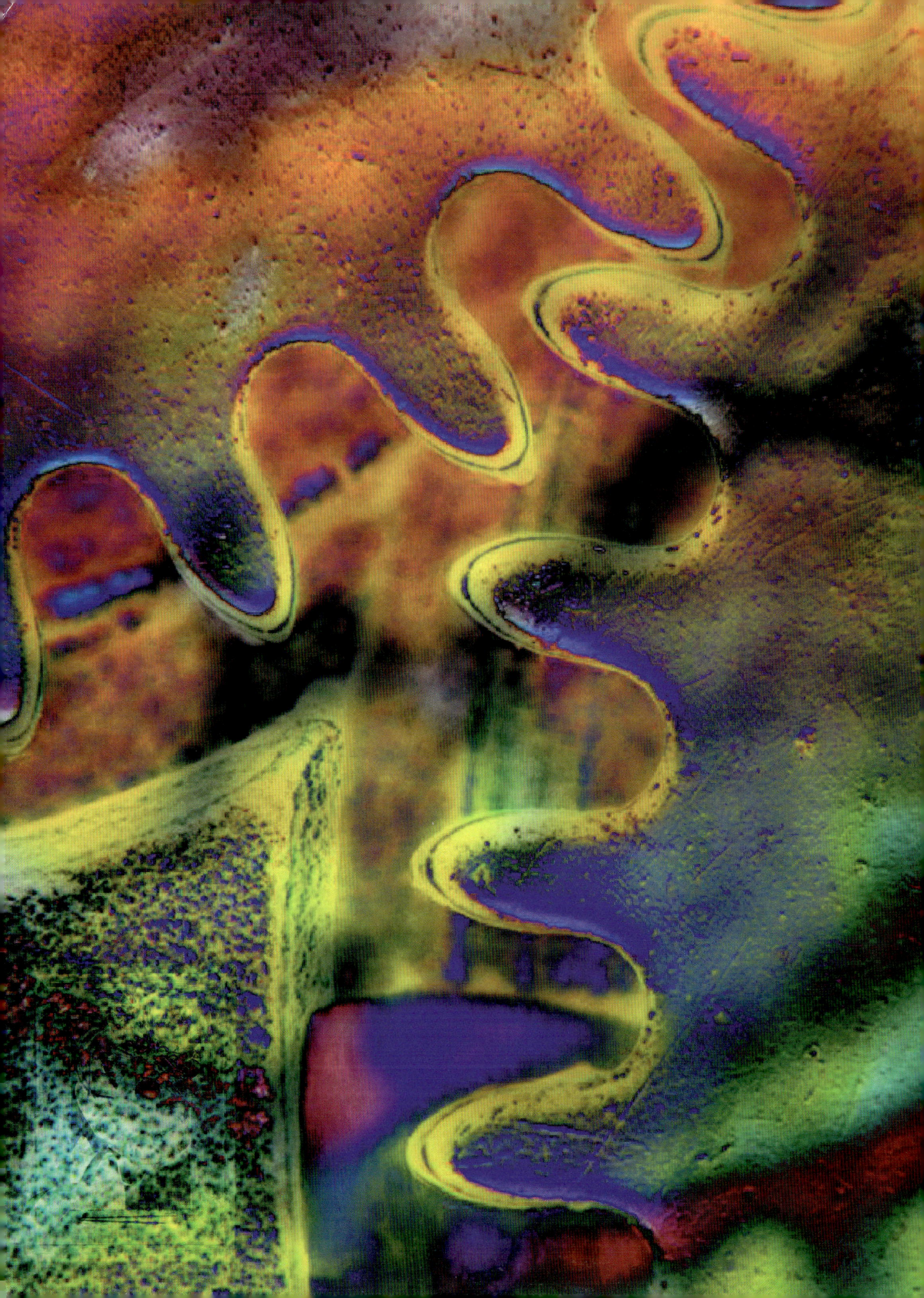

CHAPTER 11

Uploading & Registering

The final step in creating a Web site is registering it with the search engines. These search engines are sometimes called robots or spiders, because they "crawl" from one URL to the next URL, as they register the full text of every home page and sub-page. Eventually they arrive at your site and register it. But instead of waiting for that unknown day you should submit your URL to be registered which then puts you on a waiting list for the agent to visit and index your site. These robots then periodically update the information and in case of a dead link (because you moved your site or took it off the Web) they erase your URL from their records.

One of the popular places to register your URL is Yahoo. Yahoo is not a search engine but a directory. All the listings are divided into directories and subdirectories and you need to find the appropriate heading first and then submit your URL under that heading. Because directories are hierarchical databases divided in categories and subdirectories it is crucial that you find the right category. That is easier said then done: everybody has a different understanding of how to organize directories. So finding the right location for your Web site can take some time, because you need to understand the logic of that directory. You'll know that you've found your place when you find yourself in a directory where similar organizations are listed. If there is no appropriate subdirectory, send an e-mail to the webmaster of that directory requesting a sub-directory be created for you.

Another variation of a directory is an Announcement Site. These specialize in listing the new sites that have been released on the Internet. This is very helpful for people who want to keep track of what's happening on the WWW and it gives you the opportunity to attract many visitors to your site, especially in the beginning. If you get your URL registered with one of the "Guides & Cool Sites" your site will attract many visitors, at least for a period of time, because these guides review only a small percentage of the submitted sites. To get on one of these guides your website needs to be special, so you want to check out these guides to see what they usually consider noteworthy.

How to Be Top in the Search List

A search with "Infoseek" produces a list of sites that contain your keywords together with a percentage for the likelihood of finding the information on that site. Some of the titles have a summary that says more about the site while others don't. Did you know that you can actively influence the search engine result? It is possible and, it makes a huge difference in the number of visitors to your site.

The most important trick is to use the META tag. This is a tag in the head of an HTML document that contains a description of the content of this page. Many search engines use those tags, so make sure your summary is descriptive enough to clearly state what to expect on your site. Place the META tag within the HEAD tags of the first page of your site [11-01].

```
<HEAD>
    <META NAME="description" CON-
    TENT="international design com-
    pany in New York ...">
</HEAD>
```
The META tag 11-01

```
<META NAME="keywords"
CONTENT="design company, desi-
gner, New York, NY, desktop publis-
hing, dtp, world wide web design,
multimedia, ads, advertising, logo,
logos, ...">
```
Using keywords 11-02

```
<HEAD>
<TITLE>Multimedia and Web design
company</TITLE>
    <META NAME="description" CON-
    TENT="design company based in
    New York ...">
    <META NAME="keywords" CON-
    TENT="design company, desi-
    gner, New York, NY, desktop
    publishing, dtp, world wide web
    design, multimedia, ads, adverti-
    sing, logo, logos, ...">
</HEAD>
```
A complete META tag 11-03

You can also use the META tag to provide keywords for the search engine and because the META tag is invisible to the visitor, it helps you particularly if your page doesn't contain these words in the body text. Also include in the META tag singular and plural words as well as active and passive verbs; the result could look like in [11-02].

In the past it was possible to cheat with the <META> tag and put in the same keyword several times to achieve a higher percentage in the search engine, but now search engines are smarter. Infoseek and Lycos check if there is extensive use of a keyword in the META tag and, if so, disregard the META tag and extract keywords only from the content of your page. To use both variants, put both META tags in the head [11-03].

The META tag is particularly important if you are using frames, because the FRAMESET file does not contain any information about your site so the search engine will not find any keywords. Additionally, if you are using a long JavaScript program in your site, <META> tags are very useful, because some search engines extract their keywords from the HTML file and put an emphasis on the text at the top of your site where the JavaScript is usually placed.

Even though not all search engines make use of the META tag, it is very helpful with those who do. Because there are search engines that do not use the META tag, but, instead, use the first line of text on your site to extract their keywords, it is very important to have a clear statement on the first page about the content of the site.

USING MANY IMAGES ON YOUR WEB SITE

You should always use the ALT attribute for your images. So even if the user has

FAO

Peter Seidler, Avalanche, New York

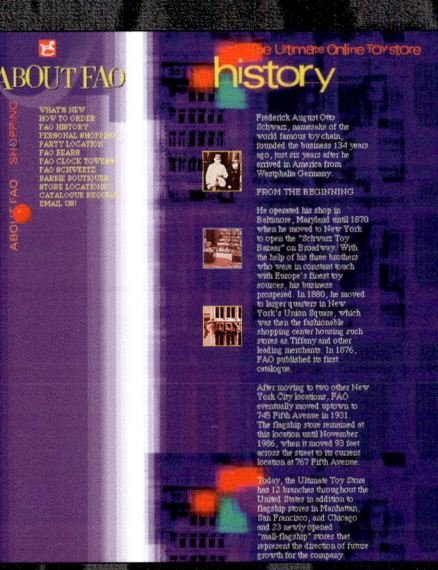

How do you create a Web site for such a well known toy shop as FAO? Peter Seidler, co-founder of Avalanche in New York, likes to get his inspiration directly from the location and he did something similar to the Carnegie Hall project: "We just hung out there for a couple of days, drew pictures of things and suddenly it dawned on me that the toy store is arranged like many distinct little worlds for kids. We would have never gotten that if we hadn't been there. I think that it's very important to spend time at the location, it makes the difference between having a site that is only at the surface and having a site with a strong concept behind it."

turned off images in the browser, at least the text that you have specified in the ALT attribute will be seen. But this ALT attribute is also important for the search engines because some search engines also check the text within the ALT attributes for the creation of the keywords. The ALT tag is placed inside the IMG tag: <IMG SRC="products.gif" ALT="Products: see our special offer on VCRs and CD-Player!">.

USE A STRONG TITLE

Last but not least, the TITLE tag in HTML is used to define the name of the page and occurs at the top of your window. It should sum up the contents of your page in a few words, because the TITLE tag is also used when the search engine displays a search result. You don't want your document to be listed as "untitled", which, unfortunately, can be seen on many web pages. A clear title also makes it easier for visitors to remember your site, because if they bookmark your page, the title of this page gets added to the bookmark list. So take the time to make it more descriptive (for example, use "Studio XYZ: Web and Multimedia Design Company" instead of just your company name).

THE INTRO PAGE

To sum up, in order to get the best search engine results, you need to use the META tag, have a strong title, set the ALT attribute for your images, use text at the top of your first page that gives a clear idea of what to expect in your site, and avoid starting with a framebased page.

All this might conflict with your concept. So to solve that problem, consider using an intro page. This page is basically optimized to be found by the search engines and is linked to your main page.

An intro page can also be used to pre-load some images by placing all the of page images on the intro page and scaling them down to 1 pixel height and width. These images are almost invisible to your visitors so while they are busy reading the text, the images are being loaded into the cache.

SUBMIT-IT

Now that you know all this information you can register you URL with all the search engines and directories on the Web. This can be a painstaking process because you have to click yourself through all home pages of the search engines and directories to find the submitting area, then type in all the required information and submit your URL individually with all of them. A very convenient way of doing this is to use Submit-it (www.submit-it.com), a company based in Massachusetts, USA. On their home page you can register your URL with up to 30 engines for free. Submit-it offers also a Gold and a Pro package, which allows to register your URL with up to 300 search engines, but they charge for this service.

UPDATING YOUR WEB PAGE

In most cases it is not necessary to re-submit your URL to search engines if you update the contents of your page, because the indexing agent automatically visits your site periodically. On the other hand resubmitting will speed up the process and that can be particularly important if your site has changed substantially. In the case of a new URL address you can fill out a dead link form with some of the search engines. For directories like Yahoo, you need to resubmit your URL only if the category classification has changed.

Uploading your Pages to the Server via Fetch

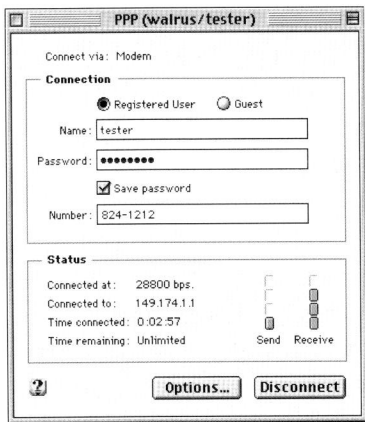

After all the links have been created and tested, it's time to move the data to the server and make it accessible to the world. For this job you need software that understands and manages the FTP (File Transfer Protocol). There are a couple of free and shareware programs that do this, but it is also possible through the Netscape browser.

1 *The most popular FTP program for the Macintosh is Fetch from the University of Dartmouth, and it is pretty easy to use once you have grasped the concept.*
To transfer your data from your Macintosh to the FTP server: first open a connection to a local server through the PPP control panel.

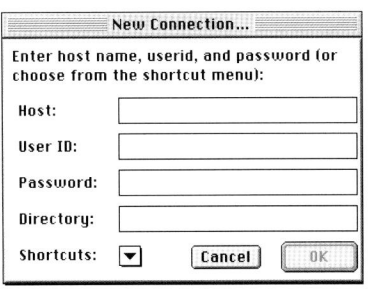

2 *Then start Fetch and enter Servername, Username, Password, and Directory. Keep in mind that the servername is different from the WWW server address (e.g., the name of the server might be "ppp.name.com", even though the URL later uses "www.domain_name.com"). For future use you can create a shortcut, by selecting "Customize: New Shortcut".*

3 *If you don't want to create a subdirectory, which you could by using "Directories: Create New Directory," you put all your files on the server at once by selecting "Remote: Put Folders and Files." Add all the files of your mirror site to the list and click "Done".*

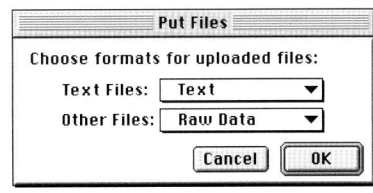

4 *Fetch then asks you how to transfer the files. For "Text Files" choose "Text" and for "Other Files" select "Raw Data". If you upload files using a different format, links will not work as expected, and images will not display.*

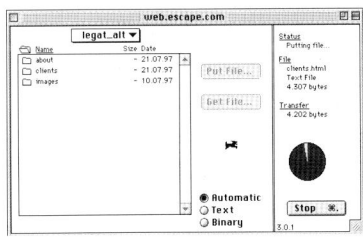

5 *After you click "OK", Fetch gets busy and you see a little animated dog fetching for your data and transferring it to the server. To check after the upload if your site works correctly, you can simultaneously launch your browser and type in the URL. If you get the error "Access denied" or something similar, you might need to set the read permission for the folder where your site is located. In "Remote: Set Permissions" select who you want to give which permissions.*

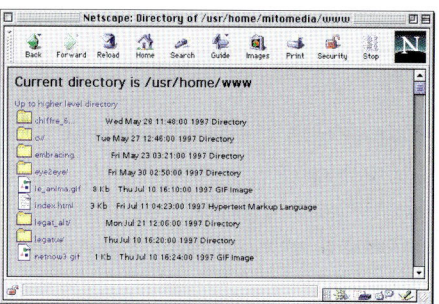

Uploading via Netscape

To upload a document to an FTP site with Netscape, type in the address as "ftp://username:password@name.site.com/path" where username is the name under which the user is registered at this site (for example "steve"). This URL can be stored – like any other URL – as a bookmark. To upload a file just select "Upload" from the File menu in Netscape Navigator 3.0, or "Upload File" in Navigator 4.0. To prevent misuse, if the computer is shared by several people, it is also possible to enter the password on access to the site by simply typing "ftp://username@name.site.com/path". The server then asks for a password before you can connect.

This method has the limitation that you can't set the access permission for the files. Like in your local network, you can restrict who can read and write to your folder and you have to set these permissions, otherwise people will get "Access denied" when they enter the URL. If this hasn't been done by your Internet Service Provider, you still need to go through an FTP program.

Here now some special details on some of the search engines.

Excite

To date, Excite does not use the META tag to create its summaries. They are all generated by the search engine. The search engine is programmed to look for common words in a sentence and, if it finds one, selects this sentence for the summary. Make sure that you describe the contents of your page at the beginning of the page. It is like writing an article for a magazine, where you want an intro that gives a good idea what the article is all about and arouses readers' curiosity. Research about people's reading habits has found that most people decide after only reading the first ten lines if they want to continue reading (don't just assume they are going to read through your whole Web page to find out if it contains something of interest to them).

Infoseek

Infoseek offers you the best control of the summary and the keywords used. InfoSeek's search engine reads the META tag for keywords and description and indexes keywords in the ALT attribute of the IMG tag. The META keywords tag can have as many as 1000 characters of text and the content attribute can have as many as 200 characters of text.

If there is no META tag (or if you have used a keyword more than seven times, in which case Infoseeks disregards the entire keyword list), Infoseek uses the first 200 words after the BODY tag as the Web page summary.

Lycos

The search agent of Lycos selects a portion of the text of your site to create a summary and the title. Although you don't have much control over the selected keywords, nevertheless keep in mind that if your main page contains mainly images, you lessen the chance of coming up in a search.

1. Make sure you use common-sense words to describe your site; if it's about cars, don't title it "Vroom". Use the appropriate words you think your site should be associated with.

2. The more text there is early in your site, the more likely it will be to be listed appropriately.

3. Avoid image maps or other graphics at the beginning of your site; Lycos deals better with text.

4. Don't try to stuff your site with keywords, repeating the same words or phrases again and again. The spider looks for these patterns and penalizes sites that use these tricks.

5. Lycos will use meta tags, but not exclusively. They are treated any other text on your page, and therefore taken into account, but aren't really used any differently than the title or the head, etc.

WebCrawler

WebCrawler uses the TITLE tag in its listings; if there is none, it uses the URL as the title.

Yahoo

Yahoo is a directory, but, unlike other directories, you don't need to submit your URL to get listed eventually. They use a robot to search for new sites and then derive their own keywords. Nevertheless is it helpful to submit your URL to them because it speeds up the process. Keep in mind that you cannot add your site to the first level categories (and even some second level categories). All business links must be placed in a business and economy category and you won't be allowed to put your link in more than two categories. All personal home pages need to be placed into Entertainment/People.

Famous Last Words

I hope that you had fun reading this book and that it was a help to you. Any comments or suggestions are very welcome. You can email me at: MBaumgardt@Compuserve.com

Michael Simross

HTML and Internet Artist

"Communication" combines several GIF animations to generate different strings of characters. If you look long enough, you might even see the word "Communication" appear.

Michael Simross is an artist whose artwork can't be seen in galleries. The only place it can be viewed is on the Internet. This in itself isn't so special, because more and more traditional artists have an online presence, but while others have merely put out a copy of their traditionally created paintings, Michael Simross' artwork is created with HTML. He plays with text, animations, simple images, and JavaScript to create his conceptual art.

Mr. Simross, you are the first artist I know of who creates his artwork with HTML. What fascinates you about this and why did you choose this rather unusual media?

Michael Simross: HTML wasn't intended to create art, the inventors of HTML focused on communication and transmission of information. I like the challenge of taking something out of its context and playing with it to create something totally new. You usually don't think of a programming language as a tool for the creation of art, but it is only logical and appropriate for our time to have computer artists that program their artwork. And there are many artists that alrealdy do this, I am simply one of the first to do this with HTML.

But some of your pieces could also be created as multimedia applications with software like Macromedia Director. What is it in particular about HTML that fascinates you?

Michael Simross: There are a couple of factors. One is that the Internet allows me to make my art available to everyone. In the past I have created many experimental animations with Director, but there is little chance that people can see them. As with any other artist, I want my work to be seen and the Internet is a cheap platform to distribute it worldwide.

Your main reason, then, of using HTML is the cheap distribution?

Michael Simross: No, but it is important to me that as many people as possible can see my work , and, that everybody can afford to see it. If I put my work on CD-ROMs, it will be so expensive that only relatively few people will see it. But again, the distribution is only one reason. More important is that the Internet and HTML is all about communication and connection. This allows me to create what I call Interart. Artwork where the viewer can become part of the artwork, where he interacts with it, even creates it, and all this on a global scale.

"Animation No 5" is a piece where several GIF animations are combined to create a large illustration to give the visitor the impression of an animation that seems to be endless without repetition. Even the background pattern is an animation and clicking on some of the foreground animations will jump to different locations of the image.

I am working currently on an idea in which I want to use the names of the visitors to the site in the artwork. The Internet is so virtual and while we surf on it, we are not aware that we are at the same place with others, except we are not in a chat room. Somehow I want to track down that people are at the same place at different times. Have you seen the movie "Six degrees of separation"?

Ah, yes, years ago.

Michael Simross: I didn't like the movie too much, but what stuck in my mind was a conversation this woman has with her friend about an article that she has read. The article was about the close relationship that all humans on this planet have and that we all are separated from each other by only six degrees. That means that between you and, for example, Bill Clinton are at the very maximum six people in between. After the movie I tried to figure out, why this number six. Finally I realized that the author simply multiplied 40 to the power of 6 which is a little bit over four billion, a number that equals, at least at that time, the world population. This close relationship between humans is one thing that has fascinated me my whole life and with the Internet I can create artwork that incorporates this close relationship. This is something that I couldn't do any other way. Working with HTML is the only logical way then.

In my search on art and Internet I haven't found anything similar to your work. Are there other online and HTML artists?

Michael Simross: There are many designers that create websites that are very artistic, but those sites are all created for a marketing purpose. My Web pages have no other purpose than to just be there. So far I have only seen one Website where I have seen something close. It is a Website that uses many invisible frames and client-pulls to create an always changing image. The artist has a different approach to Web art than I have, because it is more about viewing the artwork than interacting with it. But interaction is my main interest and besides this it was too per-

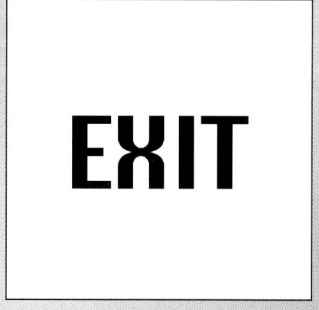

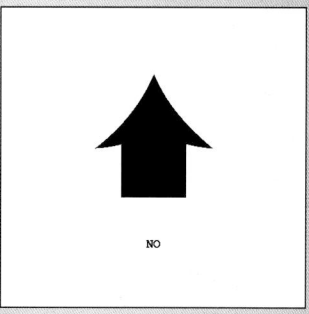

In "Exit" several arrows are linked in a row. Clicking on them will always bring the visitor to the word Exit, which itself is then linked again to an arrow: the visitor is in an endless circle.

fect for me, I like to play with the limitations of HTML and the Web.

Can you give an example how you use the limits of the Web to create artwork?

Michael Simross: One of my first artworks was a piece called "Communication". This is a piece were I created several animations with letters and put those in a row to create the word "Communication". Once the page is loaded the letters start changing and create rows of senseless words, but if you wait long enough, you might see a word be created by accident and eventually, you should see also the word "Communication" again. But seeing it depends also on the width of your browser window. I intentionally didn't place the GIF animation files in a table, because I wanted to leave room for surprises and randomness. If the browser window doesn't have the original size, the individual animations get rearranged and you see something completely different. Those are the kind of things that fascinate me.

But there is no interaction in this artwork, other than resizing the browser window. You said that the interaction is the important thing to you?

Michael Simross: That is correct, in that particular piece I didn't use much interaction in that piece, because it was not necessary for the message. My pieces are not limited to interaction, if I felt one day that I wanted to create a totally static piece, I would do it. And it might very easily be that some of my pieces will not be visual anymore, maybe they will work with audio.

What are your plans for the future?

Michael Simross: Besides audio I am working also on several installations that allow me to integrate the viewer in the creation process. This requires much more programming. While I was able, in the past, to do most of my pieces with HTML and some simple JavaScript, my pieces have gotten much more complex now and take longer to create. I also have a couple of ideas for big installations that I am currently working on.

Thanks and Acknowledgement

This book would have not been possible without the help of the software companies and the people at the Web design agencies. I want to here thank all people who have supported me with this book (in alphabetical order of the companies):

Lynn Rocha (Adobe)
Michael Pilmer (Alien Skin Software)
D'este Hanson (Avalanche; New York)
Carry Walker (Apple Computer, Inc.)
Christopher Stashuk (Aristotle; Little Rock)
Sandy Schneible (Bare Bone Software)
Andrew Calco (Bias; Los Angeles)
David Cherry (Blender Magazine; New York)
Greg Knoll (Blender Magazine; New York)
Dave Pola (Equilibrium)
Leona Lapez (Macromedia)
Marlene Stoffers & Ben Clemens (N2K Inc.; New York)
Mark Patton (NetObjects Fusion)
Robert Gagnon (Rocket Science Games, Inc., San Francisco)
Gregor Reichle and the staff at Springer-Verlag in Heidelberg
Marco Ramm (Steinberg; Hamburg, Germany)
Stephanie Shoemaker (Studio Archetype; San Francisco)
Marsha Vdovin (Waves; Knoxville)

My very special thanks to the people at the Agencies who helped me a lot. It was a pleasure working with you!

I want to also thank my friends and family for their help and support (in alphabetical order):
Michael Adolphs, thank you for all the fun we have together; Christopher Bach; my cousin Friedericke Baumgardt; my sister Heike, my mother Renate and my father Hermann; Nina & Carl Bergengruen, you are truly important to me; Marion & Reimund Bienefeld-Zimanovsky, I love you; Tim & Jennifer Bruhns; Hajo Carl; Angela Carpenter, you did a terrific job with this book and I thank you so much; Christine Cheong; Mark Dulin; Albert Dommer; Ronan Dunlop, you are a great guy; Paul Ehrenreich, thank you for your friendship and I know that I can always count on you; Cordula Fischer; Johannes & Susanne Flörsch; Sabine Frischmuth & Udo Weyers; George Geyer, for being such a fatherly friend; Isabelle Girard & Allonzo in Montreal, I wish you the very best for your future; Alejandro Guiterrez, hasta la vista, baby; Tammi Haas, for the sunshine that you bring to everybody around you; Sabine Hader, the mother of my godchild Felix – thank you for your trust; Mirko & Agniescka Hauck; Ernst & Kathie Hofacker; Cire Jones, you have the right spirit and I wish you all the success you deserve; Larry Jackson, it is always a pleasure to work with you; Erdal Kemal in London who helped me with my project without knowing me – you are a great person and I hope we meet again one day; Christopher LaRiche; Alain Laucon; Theresa Lee; Katja Lerch, congratulations on your marriage; Rachael Lewis; Rich (ard) McCarthy; my cousin Anja Maurus-Lang, hopefully we see each other more often in the future; Meagan Murphy, I love you, you are a great person, a wonderful woman; Tom Nakat, for his everlasting friendship; Lisa Rosenbaum; Manfred Rürup, for being such a great person; Stephen Salters in Paris, the greatest singer on this planet, for his help; Andreas Schaetzl; Anja Schneider & Stefan Beck, you both are a great couple and your generousity is amazing; Michael Seipel, I like you more than I can tell you; Gia Stemmer; Lisa Tran, I wish we could spent more time together; Lars Wagner, you know you can always count on me; Vera Waldmann, for being my best friend; Corinne Werner; Klaus Wittig , where are you?; Karen & Kim Young; Steve Zierer, thank you for your generosity, I really appreciate it.

URLs

Title of Site: Rocket Science Games
URL: www.rocketsci.com
Designer: Robert Gagnon

Title of Site: David Bowie
URL: www.davidbowie.com
Designer: Marlene Stoffers, Ben Clemens
Creative Director: Mary Kay Fletcher
Web Design Agency: N2K

Title of Site: Avalanche Systems
URL: www.avsi.com
Creative Director: Peter Seidler
Web Design Agency: Matthew Pacepti

Title of Site: BMG Entertainment
URL: www.bmg.com
Creative Director: Peter Seidler
Web Design Agency: Avalanche

Title of Site: Lee Jeans
URL: www.leejeans.com
Creative Director: Peter Seidler
Web Design Agency: Avalanche

Title of Site: Carnegie Hall
URL: www.carnegiehall.com
Creative Director: Peter Seidler
Web Design Agency: Avalanche

Title of Site: Polygram Filmed Entertainment
URL: www.reellife.com/PFE
Creative Director: Peter Seidler
Web Design Agency: Avalanche

Title of Site: FAO Schwarz
URL: www.faoschwarz.com
Creative Director: Peter Seidler
Web Design Agency: Avalanche

Title of Site: Warner Music Latin
URL: www.warnermusiclatin.com
Creative Director: Peter Seidler
Web Design Agency: Avalanche

Title of Site: Carnegie Hall
URL: www.carnegiehall.com
Creative Director: Peter Seidler
Web Design Agency: Avalanche

Title of Site: Studio Archetype
URL: www.studioarchetype.com
Web Design Agency: Studio Archetype

Title of Site: 24 Hours in Cyberspace
URL: www.cyber24.com
Web Design Agency: Studio Archetype

Title of Site: Blender
URL: www.blender.com
Art Director: Greg Knoll
Creative Director: Jason Pearson
Design Agency: Dennis Interactive
Client: Blender

Title of Site: Aristotle Web Design
URL: www.aristotle.net/design
Art Director: Christopher Stashuk
HTML Author: Elton Pruitt
Design Agency: Aristotle Web Design

Title of Site: Oaklawn Jockey Club
URL: www.oaklawn.com
Art Director: Christopher Stashuk
HTML Author: Nancy Mitchell
Design Agency: Aristotle Web Design

Title of Site: Persistence of the Spirit
URL: www.aristotle.net/persistence
Art Director:
Christopher Stashuk, Ken Hubbell
HTML Author: James Norris
Design Agency: Aristotle Web Design
Client: Arkansas Humanities Resource Center

Title of Site: KATV-Little Rock
URL: www.katv.com
Art Director: Christopher Stashuk
HTML Author: Dina Crane, Elton Pruitt
Design Agency: Aristotle Web Design
Client: KATV

Title of Site: B-98.5 KURB
URL: www.b98.com
Art Director: Christopher Stashuk
HTML Author: Nancy Mitchell
Design Agency: Aristotle Web Design
Client: KURB 98.5

Title of Site: Pixelpark
URL: www.pixelpark.com
Art Director: Rikus Hillmann
Creative Director: Tanja Diezmann
Design Agency:
Pixelpark Multimedia-Agentur GmbH

Title of Site: Wildpark
URL: www.wildpark.com
Art Director: Rikus Hillmann
Creative Director: Tanja Diezmann
Design Agency:
Pixelpark Multimedia-Agentur GmbH
Client: Pixelpark Multimedia-Agentur GmbH

Title of Site: Rotring
URL: www.rotring.de
Art Director: Frank Krugmann, Martina Pohl
Creative Director: Claudius Lazzeroni
Design Agency:
Pixelpark Multimedia-Agentur GmbH
Client: Rotring GmbH

Title of Site:
Deutsches Jugendherbergswerk Online
URL: www.djh.de
Art Director: Rikus Hillmann
Design Agency:
Pixelpark Multimedia-Agentur GmbH
Client: Deutsches Jugendherbergswerk

Title of Site: Sapphire
URL: www.walrus.com/~sapphire
Designer: Michael Baumgardt
Web Design Agency: MitoMedia

Title of Site: Legatus
URL: www.legatus.com
Designer: Michael Baumgardt
Web Design Agency: MitoMedia

Title of Site: Eye2Eye
URL: www.jaxmanmusic.com
Designer: Michael Baumgardt
Web Design Agency: MitoMedia

Title of Site: VUW
URL: www.vuw.de
Designer: Michael Baumgardt
Web Design Agency: Legatus/MitoMedia

Title of Site: MitoMedia
URL: www.mitomedia.com
Designer: Michael Baumgardt
This Web site will contain *the* updates to this book.

All images and Web sites were reprinted with kind permissions of the Web design agencies and their clients.

INDEX

256 colors 49, 50

A

Adobe acrobat 34
AIFF (.aiff) 133
Alien skin - Eye candy 131
ALIGN 51
ALINK 33
ALT 51
Anchor 30, 36
Animation
- director 96
- disposal methods 95
- looping 96
- META tag 96
- optimizing 95

APPLET 125
AU (.au) 133
Audio 133
- compressor 138
- equalizer 138
- normalize 138
- optimizing 135, 141
- recording 134

Audioformats
- MPEG layer 3 135
- RealAudio 138

AUTOSTART 133

B

BACKGROUND 33
Background
- special effects 59
- tiles 57, 59

BASEFONT 30, 35
BGCOLOR 33
BGSOUND 133, 134

BIAS peak 140
BLINK 35
BODY 31
BORDER 51
Browser
- offset 60
- procedural tags 15
- structural tags 15

Buttons - creating 131

C

CAPTION 66
Cascading style sheet 16, 34, 09
- background color 111
- background image 111
- background repeat: 111
- condensed guide 110
- font size 111
- font style 111
- font variant 111
- font weight 111
- installing 112
- text align 114
- text color 33
- text transform 114

CELLSPACING 66
CIRCLE 56
Client side image map 56
Color 32
- depth 48
- table 49
- text 33

COLSPAN 65
Compressor 138
Cubase VST 139

D

Diffusion dither 49

E

Embed 133
Equalizer 138
Equilibrium DeBabelizer 53
Excite 156

F

FACE 35
Fetch 155
FONT 35
FONT - SIZE 35
Font 111
- backward compatibility 114
- changing 34
- face 35
- size 35

Frames 83
- controlling two frames 88
- disabling resizing 85
- document 83
- invisible borders 85
- margin 84
- mistakes 85
- naming 86
- nesting 86
- positioning 34
- resizing 85
- scrollbars 85
- sizes 84
- target names 87
- targeting 86

FRAMESET 83, 85
FTP 154

G

GIF 45
- animation 93
- history 93
- invisible trick 33
- preparing 52
- programs 93
- transparency 54

GIFBuilder 94

H

HEAD 31, 32
HEIGHT 51
Horizontal rule 37
How to be top in the seach list 151
HSPACE 51, 53
HTML - Basic 15, 31
Hypertext link 35

I

Image
- color depth 48
- color table 49
- differences 45
- diffusion dither 49
- GIF 45, 46
- imagemaps 55
- JPEG 45, 46
- optimizing 50
- placing 51
- PNG 47
- preloading 60
- raster 48
- vector 48

Imagemap 55
- client side 56
- server side 59

Imagetable 69
- pitfall 72

Infoseek 151, 156
Interactive buttons 127
Interface
- content surfacing 18
- design 17
- global navigation 17
- local navigation 17
- parallel navigation 17
Internet service provider
- america online 14
- basic information 14
- compuserve 14
- getting an 13
Intro page 154
ISMAP 51

J

Java 125
JavaScript 125
JPEG 45

L

LANGUAGE 126
LINK 33
LOOP - sound 133
LOWSRC 51, 53
Lycos 156

M

Macromedia - Shockwave 117
MARGINHEIGHT 85
MARGINWIDTH 85
META 152
- description 152
- keywords 152
Metatools painter 55
MIDI (.mid) 133, 139
Mirror Site - setting up 19
Musik 133

N

NAME 51
NOBR 72
Normalize 138
NOSHADE 37

P

Page
- change color 130
- loading several pages 129
Pantone internet color guide 50
Paths - how to work with 37
PNG 47
POLY 56
preloading images 60
procedural tag 15

R

Raster images 48
RealAudio 138
RECT 56
Registering 151
Resolution 48
Rotating banner 127
ROWSPAN 65

S

Scrolling status bar 128
Server side image map 59
Shockwave 117
- audio 118
- behavior palette 118
- flash 48
SPAN 110
SPACER 30, 33
SRC 51
Steinberg Cubase VST 139

Streaming audio 133
Streaming shockwave
   - how to prepare 117
structural tag 15
STYLE 110
Style sheets - combining 110
Submit-It 154

T

TABLE 30, 65
   - background color 68
   - background images 68
   - imagetable 69
TARGET 36
TD 65
TEXT 33
TR 65

U

Updating your web page 154
Uploading 151
Uploading pages 154, 156
USEMAP 51
Using a strong title 154

V

Vector images 48
Vertical-align 114
VLINK 33
VSPACE 51, 53

W Y

WAV(.wav) 133
Web crawler 157
Web design - programs 16
   - Adobe PageMill 27
   - Adobe ScreenReady 27
   - Barebone BBEdit 112
   - Bias Peak 140
   - Equilibrium DeBabelizer 53
   - Metatools Painter 55
   - NetObjects Fusion 25
   - Steinberg Cubase VST 139
   - Adobe Acrobat 34
WIDTH 51
Window - opening a new 129
World Wide Web Consortium 20

Yahoo 157

About the Author

Michael Baumgardt, designer and author, has lived and worked since 1992 in the United States. He is well known in Germany for his books on Adobe Illustrator, Macromedia FreeHand and MetaCreation Painter, and also through his work as US correspondent for the German DTP Magazine PAGE. With *Creative Web Design* he presents the second book of his *Creative* series, published by Springer. This series is unique in the field of computer books because it combines interviews, step-by-step-stories and technical background information. His years of experience as editor-in-chief of KEYS, a keyboard and computer magazine, as well as his experience as designer went into this book: "I always try to make my books as visual as possible. On one hand because I am a designer, but on the other hand, because they are intended for designers, who naturally perceive visual information more easily. What makes this book so special to me is that the borders of magazines and books vanish. My idea behind *Creative Web Design* was to create a magazine in bookform."
Since 1996 he has worked more and more in the Web design field: "The Web and HTML bring together for me two of my interests – designing and programming – and I find it very exciting to follow the developments of the Internet.

Like for many DTP designers it was quite a change to design for the Web and I wanted to write a book that gathers all the important informations." *Creative Web Design* is the first book of the Creative series, to be written both in English and in German and to be released in America and Europe simultanously. His Web Site features many tips and tricks (www.mitomedia.com) which came too late for the book and will also present updates to the chapters of this book.

Gregor Reichle
Editor, Springer-Verlag
Berlin Heidelberg New York

The CD-ROM

On the CD-ROM accompanying this book, you will find most of the Web sites featured in the book. The CD-ROM is compatible with Windows 95 and Macintosh and you can view the sites with Netscape Navigator or Microsoft Internet Explorer.

Rocket Science Games

David Bowie

BMG Entertainment

Lee Jeans

Carnegie Hall

Polygram Filmed Entertainment

FAO Schwarz

Warner Music Latin

Blender

Aristotle Web Design

Oaklawn Jockey Club

Persistence of the Spirit

KATV-Little Rock

B-98.5 KURB